Mental Health Consultation in the Schools

◙ ◙ ◙ ◙ ◙ ◙ ◙ ◙ ◙ ◙ ◙

A Comprehensive Guide
for Psychologists, Social Workers,
Psychiatrists, Counselors,
Educators, and Other
Human Service Professionals

Joel Meyers
Richard D. Parsons
& Roy Martin

Mental Health Consultation in the Schools

Jossey-Bass Publishers

San Francisco • Washington • London • 1979

MENTAL HEALTH CONSULTATION IN THE SCHOOLS
*A Comprehensive Guide for Psychologists, Social Workers, Psychiatrists,
Counselors, Educators, and Other Human Service Professionals*
by Joel Meyers, Richard D. Parsons, and Roy Martin

Copyright © 1979 by: Jossey-Bass, Inc., Publishers
433 California Street
San Francisco, California 94104
&
Jossey-Bass Limited
28 Banner Street
London EC1Y 8QE

Library of Congress Catalogue Card Number LC 79-83567

International Standard Book Number ISBN 0-87589-400-3

Manufactured in the United States of America

JACKET DESIGN BY WILLI BAUM

FIRST EDITION

Code 7903

The Jossey-Bass
Social and Behavioral Science Series

Preface

□ □ □ □ □ □ □ □ □ □ □

During the past thirty years mental health professionals have increasingly focused on mental health consultation as a useful professional technique and, as a result, several major works in this field were published in the late 1960s (for example, Sarason and others, 1966; Newman, 1967; Caplan, 1970). This literature, as well as the attention given to preventive mental health and indirect service techniques, has been followed by exponential increases in the writing, research, training, and practice of mental health consultation.

Schools have become recognized as the place where mental health specialists can affect *all* children, and this setting may be the most important one for mental health consultation. Indeed, in recent years, mental health consultation techniques have been observed particularly in schools, and now a number of related professions—for example, clinical psychology, community psychology, counseling psychology, psychiatry, school psychology, and social work—also consider mental health consultation as part of their roles in the schools.

This book has been written to fill the need for a comprehensive volume reflecting the important developments that have occurred in the past ten years. Further, it has been designed to examine in detail the problems inherent in *school* mental health consultation.

The beginning of the book provides a working definition of consultation, outlines those social factors that have fostered the recent interest in consultation as a mental health tool (Chapter One), and discusses the history of consultation (Chapter Two). The next two chapters discuss how consultation is done by considering two aspects of the *process* of consultation—the interpersonal factors that provide the conditions under which successful consultation can take place (Chapter Three), and those stages involved in the development of the consultation experience (Chapter Four).

The subsequent four chapters consider the *content* of consultation by looking at four broad types of consultation that are organized according to how directly the consultant's services are provided to the child. The first type, "Direct Service to the Child" (Chapter Five), is when the consultant focuses primarily on the child and is directly involved in diagnosis, treatment, or referral. In addition to direct service provided by traditional psychodiagnostic or treatment models, this type of consultation also emphasizes indirect treatment by a consultee, usually the teacher. With the second type, "Indirect Service to the Child" (Chapter Six), the consultant's major aim is to help the teacher change behavior in the classroom; extrapersonal factors such as curriculum, teaching techniques, and teacher-student interaction are stressed. The third type, "Direct Service to the Teacher" (Chapter Seven), is when the consultant attempts to increase the teacher's understanding and objectivity in dealing with his or her students. With the last type, "Service to the School System" (Chapter Eight), the consultant develops inservice training workshops, helps to change behaviors of various subgroups in the school organization, and works to improve the general quality of communication and problem solving.

The last two chapters summarize trends and research in consultation, giving particular emphasis to research methodology (Chapter Nine) and to the future of consultation practice (Chapter Ten).

The view of mental health consultation presented in these chapters is not tied to a specific theoretical conceptualization of behavior. Even though the book relies heavily on the concepts that underlie the preventive mental health movement, the major focus is a pragmatic one—it explores what consultation is and how it can be implemented effectively. It is specifically guided by the idea that, in the long run, techniques aimed at prevention of mental health problems will be more effective than the crisis-oriented approaches prevalent in practice today.

Several teachers and former students from the University of Texas, Austin, had an impact on the approach to consultation and preventive mental health presented in this book. Among these are June Gallessich, Ira Iscoe, Phillip Mann, Beeman Phillips, Mary Berk, Robert Dain, James Paavala, Matthew Snapp, Donald Williams, and Sidney Winicki. A special thank you is extended to Beeman Phillips, since he provided the initial impetus for the development of these ideas.

The approach to consultation that emerged at Texas has been developed, changed, implemented, and elaborated during the past eight years at Temple University. Our colleague Irwin Hyman has provided a continuous stimulus, and his thinking is reflected in some sections of this book. Several students from Temple University's Department of School Psychology also have contributed. Although they are too numerous to mention here, significant contributions were made by Michael Friedman, Norman Pitt, Edward Gaughan, Judy Goldberg, and Mark Fedner.

Whenever we have read prefaces in other books, it has been our impression that wives and family are always thanked in a perfunctory manner because that is what is expected. Before undertaking this task we had no idea how much sacrifice and stress writing a book can place on a family. In the future we will have a different perspective on the meaning underlying these expressions of gratitude, for in a very real sense this book could not have been completed without the patience and support of Barbara, Adena, and Raina Meyers; Karen, Kristian, and Drew Parsons; and Janet Martin.

February 1979

JOEL MEYERS
Philadelphia, Pennsylvania
RICHARD D. PARSONS
Aston, Pennsylvania
ROY MARTIN
Philadelphia, Pennsylvania

Contents

◙ ◙ ◙ ◙ ◙ ◙ ◙ ◙ ◙ ◙ ◙

The Authors

◙ ◙ ◙ ◙ ◙ ◙ ◙ ◙ ◙ ◙ ◙

JOEL MEYERS is associate professor of school psychology in the Department of School Psychology, Temple University, where he has taught since 1970. He also serves as a consultant to many schools in the Philadelphia area.

Meyers was awarded the B.A. degree in psychology from Western Reserve University (1966) and the Ph.D. degree in educational psychology, with specialization in school psychology, from the University of Texas, Austin (1971).

Meyers co-edited *School Consultation: Readings About Preventive Techniques for Pupil Personnel Workers* (with R. Martin and I. Hyman, 1977) and has written many articles related to practice and research in mental health consultation. His professional interests also include school psychology and preschool education.

Meyers and his wife, Barbara, live with their daughters, Adena and Raina, in Philadelphia. He enjoys playing the guitar and bass with friends as well as writing an occasional song.

RICHARD D. PARSONS is an assistant professor of psychology at Our Lady of Angels College, Aston, Pennsylvania, where he is coordinator of the psychology program. He also serves as psychoeducational consultant to several inner-city schools and has a part-time private practice in Aston.

Parsons was awarded the B.A. degree in psychology from Villanova University (1968) and the M.A. degree in psychology and the Ph.D. degree in school psychology from Temple University (1971 and 1976, respectively). Prior to receiving his doctorate, he taught in an inner-city high school for eight years. His teaching experience, along with four years working as a counselor and director of pupil services for high school students, provided him with the opportunity to view the problem learner from the perspective of the teacher as well as of the psychologist.

Parsons is active in Division 16 of the American Psychological Association and continues to do research in the areas of consultation and consultation process. His most recent publications have focused on the utilization of behavior modification, teacher inservice, and para-professionals as part of an overall preventive consultation service delivery model. His present research interests lie in the areas of social acceptance among preschoolers and the identification of factors facilitating or impeding such acceptance.

Parsons and his wife, Karen, live with their children, Kristian and Drew, in Chester County, Pennsylvania.

ROY MARTIN is associate professor of psychology and education in the Department of School Psychology, Temple University, where he has taught since 1970.

Martin was awarded the B.A. degree in psychology and the M.A. degree in guidance and counseling from the University of New Mexico (1966 and 1967, respectively) and the Ph.D. degree in educational psychology, with specialization in school psychology, from the University of Texas, Austin (1970).

Martin has co-edited *School Consultation: Readings About Preventive Techniques for Pupil Personnel Workers* (with J. Meyers and I. Hyman, 1977) and has contributed chapters to C. D. Spielberger (Ed.), *Anxiety: Current Trends in Theory and Research* (1972, with B. Phillips and J. Meyers); and to G. R. Gredler (Ed.), *Ethical and Legal Problems in School Psychology* (1974). He has also published several articles in such periodicals as the *Journal of School Psychology*. He is currently doing research in the areas of social power considerations in consultation and the educational effects of malnutrition.

Martin and his wife, Janet, live in suburban Philadelphia. His chief hobbies are distance running and music.

Mental Health Consultation in the Schools

▣ ▣ ▣ ▣ ▣ ▣ ▣ ▣ ▣ ▣ ▣

*A Comprehensive Guide
for Psychologists, Social Workers,
Psychiatrists, Counselors,
Educators, and Other
Human Service Professionals*

CHAPTER ONE

Primary Prevention of Mental Health Problems

◙ ◙ ◙ ◙ ◙ ◙ ◙ ◙ ◙ ◙ ◙

Since World War II, psychologists and other mental health specialists have played an increasingly important role in education. Virtually all aspects of school life have been studied by psychologists, and the personal intervention skills of mental health specialists have been used to solve such diverse problems as assessing the intrapsychic conflicts of the elementary school child and fostering better interpersonal relationships between members of the board of education. The variety and complexity of the problems encountered in educational settings have brought forth a response from professionals working in a number of specialized disciplines, including community psychiatrists, community psychologists, counseling psychologists, educational psychologists, human relations experts, organization development experts, school psychologists, and social workers.

1

Despite the increase in the number and types of mental health specialists in education, many of these professionals feel that their knowledge and skills have had little impact on the day-to-day life of students in classrooms. Many children still do not meet minimum standards of literacy; many exceptional children still are not receiving skilled individualized instruction; large numbers of students are discouraged by failure in school; and the creativity and joy of learning of most students seem blunted by their school experience. Mental health professionals feel that their concepts and skills could greatly improve the present educational situation, but they feel that their ideas and innovations have been overlooked, resisted, feared, and distorted by educators.

Educators, however, often feel that mental health professionals have oversold the public and some members of the educational establishment on the value of their contributions. Many educators believe that these specialists have been trained only in general theories, which are too broadly conceived to be of practical value, and about which there is no general agreement even within the psychological community. Others feel that mental health professionals foster values that are not congruent with the values of the school, that these professionals fail to understand the goals and values of the school, and that they are disrespectful of the power structure of the school.

Consultation, whether perceived as a technique, a professional role, or a service delivery system, is a process that seems uniquely appropriate for bridging the gap between the mental health professional and the educator. The goal of consultation is increased communication in the broadest sense of the word. Consultation is a process that takes into account the intrapersonal and the interpersonal processes in communication as well as possible differences in attitude, language, and skill of the communicating parties. Consultation emphasizes the two-way nature of communication.

Recently, consultation has become one of the most widely discussed techniques in the mental health profession. It has become fashionable for the mental health professional to call himself* a "consultant," much as it was previously fashionable to refer to one-

*The traditional use of the masculine pronoun has not yet been superseded by a convenient, generally accepted pronoun meaning either

self as a "therapist." As the mental health community has shifted the focus of attention from remediation to prevention, consultation has begun to rival therapy as the predominant mode of intervention in the lives of children, adults, families, and institutions.

The Purpose of this Book

The relatively recent emergence of consultation as an important mental health tool has created a number of problems for the serious student of the process. First, the sudden popularity of the concept has generated a great deal of writing in the professional literature, much of which is superficial. Few thoughtful theoretical analyses, carefully described case studies, or rigorous empirical investigations exist. This situation makes it difficult to separate the essential characteristics of consultation from those that are faddish (Reschly, 1976). Second, the few examples and descriptions that are of high quality tend to focus on a variety of consultation settings and circumstances, and the generalizability of these processes is unknown. Third, the consultation process is discussed from a variety of theoretical viewpoints, each of which focuses on different aspects of the process. Finally, the ideology and rationale of these viewpoints are sometimes contradictory.

The purpose of this book is to discuss that part of the consultation literature which, in the authors' opinion, is most essential for the training of mental health professionals who will serve as consultants in the schools. This discussion is purposely limited to school-related consultation because of its unique characteristics. To mention only one example, school personnel may expect counselors to spend their time with individual students, because this is the role that has traditionally been implemented, and this "set" may create resistance for counselors who wish to consult with teachers. These sorts of expectations, which are characteristic of counseling in schools, must be understood and responded to for consultation to be effective.

Our discussion is limited in two other important ways. First, we make no attempt to discuss in detail the variety of theoretical orientations (behaviorist, ego psychology, self-actualization, and so

_he_ or _she_. Therefore, the authors will continue to use the masculine pronoun while acknowledging the inherent inequity of its traditional preference.

forth) that consultants may use to conceptualize the services provided in the school. Instead, this book takes a pragmatic orientation
and focuses on what consultants do and how they do it. This does
not imply that such theoretical questions are unimportant; they
simply are outside the scope of the present discussion. Second, our
presentation is limited to a discussion of one schema for classifying
consultation service, namely the schema outlined previously by
Meyers (1973b). Although this classification has much in common
with some other systems, particularly the system set forth by Caplan
(1963, 1970), we make no attempt to discuss the variety of classification systems that have been presented in the literature. Numerous assumptions, commitments, and values are involved in the
choice of a classification system, and the authors realize that aspects
of any phenomenon are omitted when that phenomenon is classified in one way rather than another.

Definition of Consultation

Consultation is often defined as any service provided by a
professional or specialist. Webster's (eighth edition), for example,
defines a consultant as "one who gives professional advice or services." In this book the term is used more specifically by delineating
one type of professional service.

To arrive at some consensus regarding the current meaning
of this term, we present common aspects of the definitions presented by four writers on the subject. This composite definition is
derived from those of Bergan (1977), Caplan (1970), Dinkmeyer
and Carlson (1973), and Lippitt (1959), each of whom discusses
consultation from a different theoretical viewpoint (behaviorism,
ego psychology, Adlerian psychology, and organization development, respectively). Consultation is a technique that, at a minimum,
always has the following six characteristics: (1) it is a helping or
problem-solving process; (2) it occurs between a professional
help-giver and a help-seeker who has responsibility for the welfare
of another person; (3) it is a voluntary relationship; (4) the help-
giver and help-seeker share in solving the problem; (5) the goal is
to help solve a current work problem of the help-seeker; and (6)
the help-seeker profits from the relationship in such a way that
future problems may be handled more sensitively and skillfully.

Throughout this book the help-giver will be referred to as

the *consultant,* the help-seeker as the *consultee,* and the person for whom the consultee has responsibility will be referred to as the *client.* The consultant typically includes such mental health professionals as community psychologists, counselors, psychiatrists, school psychologists, and social workers. The consultee includes classroom teachers and school administrators (although a consultee could be any school professional), and the client typically is the student. Thus, school consultation is defined as a process characterized by shared expertise between a mental health professional and an educational professional. The goal of consultation is to help solve a current problem involving students and to help the educational professional to deal more effectively with similar problems in the future.

Although there is substantial agreement within the literature regarding the six characteristics of consultation in our definition, authorities disagree regarding other aspects of the process. For example, Lippitt (1959) sees the relationship between a single consultee and a consultant as being equivalent to a therapy or counseling relationship; only if the consultant works with an institution or social system does he apply the term *consultation.* Dinkmeyer and Carlson (1973) and Bergan (1977) see consultation and therapy as essentially the same process; they do not make the distinction between consultation to a system and to an individual that Lippitt makes. Caplan (1970), however, goes to some length to point out the differences between consultation and therapy. In particular, he believes that therapists have more influence over their clients than consultants have over their consultees. Because he does not see therapy as a sharing, coordinate relationship, he distinguishes it from consultation. Further, he defines therapy as a relationship in which intrapsychic conflicts and personal problems are the primary focus, whereas in consultation, work-related problems are the primary focus. To complicate the definition even more, Martin (1977) has discussed consultation as an influence process in which the consultant has more power than the consultee during some periods of the process. The consultant produces change in the consultee by the skillful use of this power. In some respects, this point of view contradicts Caplan's notion of consultation as a coordinate process.

This type of definitional disagreement is usually related to

theoretical considerations about the manner in which change occurs in interpersonal processes. Although such theoretical discussions are important, they are outside the focus of the present discussion. However, some of these issues, including the differing
orientations toward consultation as a coordinate process offered by
Caplan and Martin, will be discussed in more detail in later sections
of this book because of their pragmatic implications for consultation practice. Our general position is that in some circumstances,
consultation has much in common with therapy, while in other
circumstances it has much in common with other professional activities, such as teaching. Further, we consider the complex processes that produce change in consultation to include cognitive
problem-solving components, social-influence components, and
self-actualization components.

The Emergence of Consultation

The growing professional interest in consultation is part of a
broader professional trend emphasizing preventive mental health,
indirect service delivery, community interventions, and new
sources of mental health manpower. The origins of this trend in
mental health, and particularly in school consultation, cannot be
understood without considering what preceded it, for in large part
this trend is a reaction against an earlier conception of professional
practice.

Psychological Services in the Schools. In the years just prior to
the turn of the twentieth century, two social forces greatly increased
the difficulties faced by public schools. First, the industrial revolu-
tion had a major impact on schools, because it fostered the growth
of cities and massive rural-to-urban migration. This population
shift brought together in schools children from different
backgrounds. The stresses faced by children and families who had
been uprooted from one social system (rural-agrarian) and placed
in another, more complex and rapidly evolving system (urban-
industrial) were thus brought into the schools. The strain on the
schools was further aggravated by two other population shifts that
were taking place at the same time. Large numbers of black
families, freed from slavery only forty years earlier, migrated to
the cities. Also, immigration from Europe was at its peak at the turn

of the century. In the years between 1900 and 1920, 14.5 million immigrants arrived in the United States (Cooke, 1973), and in New York City in 1900, four out of five persons were foreign-born (Edwards and Richey, 1963).

The second social force that increased individual differences in school populations was the growing sentiment for universal education. From 1870 to 1890, for example, enrollments in elementary schools doubled, and enrollments in high schools increased four times (Edwards and Richey, 1963).

In response to the difficulties experienced by children, their families, and the school during this period, a small number of people began to see the importance of social and psychological factors in the life adjustment of the child, particularly in school. In 1893, Lightner Witmer established a psychological clinic that focused on educational problems at the University of Pennsylvania. Most authorities credit Witmer for being the first to implement psychological services to the schools (Wallin and Ferguson, 1967).

The beginnings of the counseling and guidance movements can be traced to the same period. These movements resulted from the same stresses and attempted to meet similar needs to those addressed by Witmer. In 1908, Frank Parsons began the Boston Vocational Bureau in an attempt to match rural people with industrial jobs. The process involved assessment of the abilities and temperament of the applicant and an attempt to match the applicant with jobs that required similar abilities and temperament. The same process was applied to the Boston schools in 1909, one year after the founding of the Bureau, in an attempt to match high school students with prospective careers (Miller, 1961).

The beginnings of professional social work, particularly case work, have also been traced to this period (Lubove, 1965). In 1895, a physician named Cabot used social workers to bring together information from families and the school to plan medical treatment for children. A short time later, social workers began to serve a similar function in the schools — that is, to bring to the school information regarding the social circumstances of children who were having difficulties, to better plan their educational experiences. Such social workers, called *visiting teachers,* also communicated information from the school to the parent.

By the early part of the century, then, psychologists, counselors, and social workers had begun to establish professional identities and to focus on the school as a major area of professional activity. These groups were small in number, were located primarily in the major cities of the eastern seaboard, were perceived by educators as low in status, and had limited impact on education. However, about this time a new technology was developing, which ensured a place for psychologists (and to a lesser extent guidance personnel and social workers) in the schools.

In Europe, universal education was coming to fruition and facing problems similar to those experienced in the United States. In response to initiatives made by the French government, Alfred Binet began to develop a test of complex intellectual functioning to help assess to what extent a child could profit from public schooling. This instrument, the Binet-Simon scale (published in 1905), was not the first attempt to measure individual differences of an intellectual nature, but it was unique in its concentration on complex intellectual functioning, the number of tasks studied, and the sophistication of its norms. This instrument required specialized training to administer and interpret its findings appropriately. Thus, not long after the introduction of the instrument in the United States by Goddard in 1911 and its revision by Terman in 1916, the psychometrist became one of the helping professionals in the school (Mullen, 1967; Wallin and Ferguson, 1967). The first person to have the title *school psychologist* was Arnold Gesell, who, in 1915, began to work for the State of Connecticut. His role was to go to rural areas and small towns, to examine children suspected of being retarded, and to aid schools in making arrangements for such children (Tindall, 1964).

The Binet scale gave the primary impetus to the testing movement, which has produced an extensive array of intellectual, academic achievement, and personality measures. This technology was used by psychologists and guidance personnel for purposes of special class placement, to better understand the behavior of children who were having difficulties in school, and in career planning for students.

As important as the testing movement was in establishing a place for the mental health professional, the role of these professions in the schools received an even greater boost from the impact of Freudian thought. The writings of Freud had an enormous impact on the thought of Americans during the early part of this century, with a resultant major influence on school policy. The Freudian ideology was not only a major factor in the Progressive Education Movement, but it also opened the minds of educators and the public to the influence of the emotional, intrapsychic life of the child (Cremin, 1961). In the therapeutic techniques used by psychoanalysts, mental health professionals found procedures that could be used with school children to remediate their problems. Public awareness of analytic concepts, and their modifications by followers of Freud during the first forty years of this century, established a climate in which it was possible to offer therapeutic interventions as an adjunct to or as a part of the regular school experience. Thus, social workers began to take a more analytic, clinical approach, and many psychiatric social workers found a place in the school (Lubove, 1965). To an even greater extent, guidance personnel augmented their vocational counseling activities with personal counseling. Psychologists working in schools continued to emphasize diagnostic activities, but now the diagnostic process placed much more emphasis on the emotional life of the student, using self-report personality measures as well as projective techniques.

The period just prior to World War II found mental health professionals who practiced in the schools focusing more on the individual child's abilities, achievements, and intrapsychic conflicts. School psychologists, counselors, and social workers were emulating clinical psychologists in their emphasis on abnormality, a reliance on one-to-one therapeutic interventions, and a disease model for psychological problems. This trend was strengthened even further by World War II. Under the auspices of the Veterans Administration, clinical psychology played a major role in the diagnosis and treatment of the casualties of the war. Through this experience, clinical techniques were refined and formalized, and, as a result, clinical psychology became the leader in applied psychology. Thus, the practice of mental health professionals in the schools took an increasingly clinical flavor and became thoroughly committed to the medical model in all its manifestations. This clinical period probably reached its zenith in the 1950s.

The Decline of the Clinical Model. A number of trends have resulted in the decline of the clinical or medical model of mental health practice in the schools. Since these factors have been outlined extensively elsewhere (Bloom, 1973; Cowen, Gardner, and Zax, 1967; Krasner and Ullman, 1965; Szasz, 1961; Ullmann and Krasner, 1969; Zax and Spector, 1974), they will be briefly outlined here. We will summarize these trends under three topics: questions raised about the analogy between physical and mental illness, questions raised about the efficacy of traditional psychotherapy, and questions raised about the service delivery system implied by the clinical model.

The clinical model held as one of its major tenets that an inappropriate or abnormal behavior was the symptom of an underlying cause, such as psychic conflict, which generated anxiety and brought "to the surface" the behavior observed. In the late fifties and early sixties, this notion was criticized by psychotherapists using conceptual models based on learning theory (Krasner and Ullman, 1965; Wolpe, 1958). One clearly testable hypothesis of the clinical model of mental illness is the notion of symptom substitution. This hypothesis assures that if the manifest abnormal behavior is treated directly instead of attacking the cause of this symptom, a new abnormal behavior will appear. Learning theorists hold that direct treatment of the problem behavior is both necessary and sufficient treatment. They argue that there is no need to speculate about or even to treat the underlying cause. Although the position that symptom substitution does not exist is difficult to prove (the null hypothesis cannot be proved), an accumulation of case studies suggests that "symptom substitution rarely if ever occurs" (Ullmann and Krasner, 1969, p. 158).

For mental health practitioners in the school, the clinical model of abnormality always presented problems, because the intervention was not education and it did not involve the school. The child's problem was usually conceptualized as being of parental origin, and it had to be treated by highly specialized, medically oriented methods, such as psychotherapy at a clinic away from the school. Counselors, social workers, psychiatrists, and psychologists working in the school were limited by this conception, since the important problems were typically referred to outside, medically oriented professionals, rather than being dealt with in the school.

When learning theorists and other therapists with nonmedical orientations began to conceptualize the abnormal behavior of children as the result of faulty learning, and therapy as a learning-teaching process, the process of treatment became much more compatible with the mission of the school. Given this theoretical stance, the mental health specialists who worked in schools with educators could take greater responsibility for remedial activities in the school.

Besides the failure to find support for the medical model's notion of symptom substitution, another trend in psychology has tended to redefine the concept of abnormality. Abnormal or inappropriate behavior has come to be defined more in terms of social-role behavior on the part of the person defined as abnormal and the person or group doing the defining. The process of labeling a person as abnormal is now seen as a social act, the purpose of which is to protect the group from those who make the group uncomfortable (Szasz, 1961). In this conceptualization, abnormality is relative to group standards or "culturally particular normative networks" (Scheff, 1966); abnormality is not defined relative to absolute standards of psychological health, as was the case with the medical model.

As this concept of abnormality began to have an impact on the public and educational policy makers, the function of the school as a labeler and thus as a manufacturer of abnormality began to be better understood. Is the school intolerant of individual differences? Does the society expect children to adapt to the school, or should the school adapt to the needs of children? Is the school having lasting detrimental effect on those children who are labeled as abnormal? Such questions refocused some of the attention that the medical model had previously focused on the child and his family back onto the school, and they diminished the hold of the medical model on school psychological services.

The basic therapeutic tool of the medical model—traditional evocative psychotherapy—also began to come under attack in the decade of the fifties. Eysenck (1952) compared the rate of improvement or recovery in patients receiving therapy with the rate of improvement generally occurring when no treatment was given, and he found no significant differences. Levitt (1957, 1963) extended Eysenck's studies into the area of psychotherapy with children. He estimated the base rate of improvement (improvement occurring without formal therapy) to be 72 percent, based on two empirical studies of children evaluated at children's clinics but not seen for therapy. In reviewing thirty of the best-documented studies of therapy outcome encompassing over five thousand children, he determined that the percentage of improvement reported in the studies was 66 percent, which was a rate not significantly different from the predicted base rate. Although the studies of Eysenck and Levitt have been criticized regarding some aspects of their methodology (Heinicke, 1960; Rosenzweig, 1954), their data have raised real questions about the efficacy of traditional therapeutic endeavors.

The medical model made educators feel that somewhere outside the school were agencies and private practitioners who, because of their extraordinary training and access to strong remedies, could resolve the emotional problems of the child that impeded his or her school progress. As these educators, mental health professionals, and the public became more aware of the shortcomings of traditional psychotherapy and began to experience its failures, the place of the school in the prevention of emotional problems began to be understood. The school is the primary socialization agent of the culture; almost all children pass through its doors. If school personnel could be made more sensitive to the origins of emotional problems and to those social factors that seem to foster mental health, they could perhaps prevent small problems from becoming larger ones and generally become a more positive force in the social and emotional growth of children (Allen and others, 1976; Bower, 1969).

Not only were the cause-and-effect aspects of the medical model being questioned along with the efficacy of therapy based on this model, but the service delivery aspects of the model (the clinical or direct service model) were also questioned. Two interrelated problems have been particularly emphasized, although many others have been mentioned: the time-consuming nature of the direct service model and the shortage of trained personnel to meet adequately the mental health needs of the population.

The clinical model mandates a two-stage process—a diagnostic phase and a remedial phase—in which a mental health professional engages in direct service to the client. Each stage of this process makes heavy time-demands on the mental health practitioner and the client. The typical diagnostic process, with its emphasis on a detailed developmental and family history as well as a thorough evaluation of the client's abilities, attitudes, and intrapsychic conflicts, may require from three to twenty hours to complete. At the termination of the initial diagnostic phase, a report is written, typically with recommendations for therapy or special class placement. The therapy may take from six weeks to many years to complete, and it often has no relevance to school. Similarly, there may be a long wait for special class placement, and the procedures used may not be clearly different from those in the regular classroom. Furthermore, because of the time required for the initial diagnostic phase, the mental health professional often has little time to discuss the findings and their implications with those persons involved in the case (the client, the family, the teacher, and the therapist). The professional who is in charge of the remedial phase is often so overwhelmed with referrals that the client must be put on a lengthy waiting list. The result may be children who are thoroughly diagnosed but who receive no meaningful treatment.

All the problems associated with the direct service model have been painfully experienced by the mental health professional working in the school. Children often wait for six months to one year for a psychological evaluation; the school psychologist is often so bogged down with diagnostic work that effective communication with children, parents, teachers, and other mental health professionals is improbable; and there are insufficient educational placements or mental health resources inside or outside the school system to make an appropriate and timely referral. Counselors and social workers (when present in the school at all) are so deluged with referrals that providing sufficient time to any one student is seldom possible. Dissatisfaction with these aspects of the medical model have led to extensive criticism by mental health professionals and a call for a change in the focus of professional services (Albee, 1967; Aubrey, 1969; Eckerson, 1971; Engelmann, 1967; Goodman,

1964; Henry, 1965; Jackson, 1968; Kennedy, 1971; Kozol, 1967; Kuriloff, 1973; Lighthall, 1969; Lundquist and Chamley, 1971; Morice, 1968; Palmo and Kuznian, 1972; Reger, 1971; Roberts, 1970; Sarason and others, 1966; Singer, Whiton, and Fried, 1970; Smith and Eckerson, 1966; Tindall, 1964; Valett, 1968).

A problem related to the time-demands of the direct service model is the shortage of mental health workers. Popular literature, familiarization via mass media, formal education, and legislative action have all helped to make the public much more aware of the tools and services available through various mental health professions. Although this increased awareness has contributed to the advancement of applied psychology, it has also created increased demand for services. A manpower shortage in the mental health professions was predicted by Albee (1967), who surveyed these needs for the Joint Commission on Mental Illness in the late 1950s. Albee (p. 63) stated: "The manpower demands projected over the next twenty years in the fields concerned with professional care of people with emotional disorders are so far beyond probable supply of people available as to constitute a major national crisis."

Although training programs have greatly increased the number of mental health professionals available for employment since Albee's prediction was made, service still lags far behind demand in the late 1970s. The country is unable to hire the help that is available and needed because of the shortage of funds.

Data on the mental health needs of children helps to put this problem in perspective. Glidewell and Swallow (1969), reporting on a study sponsored by the Joint Commission on Mental Health of Children, stated that 2 percent of the population are severely emotionally disturbed, another 8 to 10 percent are disturbed to the point of needing assistance from a mental health worker, and 30 percent have some form of school maladjustment. Thus, between 8 and 30 percent of the school population of the country needs help.

What percentage of these children receive help? Hyde (1975) reported the result of a study in which only 2 percent of the population of one school district were referred to school psychologists. In another report of the use of psychological services for the 1976–77 school year, a major urban school district reported

that 4 percent of its population were referred for psychological evaluations. In this same school district, the ratio of counselors to pupils was 1 to 476, and the ratio of school psychologists to students was 1 to 5,375. The population of this district included 258,003 students, and if 30 percent of this population were in need of help, this would demand a counselor-student ratio of 1 to 143 and a psychologist-student ratio of 1 to 1,613, both of which are far more favorable than the ratios reported by Hyde. Furthermore, Kicklighter (1976) reported that the national median ratio of pupils to school psychologists is 4,800 to 1, and the mean is 8,100 to 1. These figures indicate clearly that only a small percentage of the students needing mental health services can possibly receive them, when service is defined as direct contact between the mental health professional and the client.

Consultation: An Alternative to Direct Service. The obvious problems with the medical model have created great pressures for change within the mental health professions. From these pressures has come a model of service delivery that emphasizes the following: (1) a community rather than a clinical orientation, (2) prevention rather than therapy, (3) a readiness to experiment with innovative, short-term remedial strategies, (4) uses of new sources of manpower, (5) a commitment to client and community control of mental health policy rather than professional control, (6) identification of environmental stresses present in the community that could cause mental health problems, and (7) indirect service rather than direct service (Bloom, 1973).

Perhaps the major change in mental health practice demanded by this movement is the emphasis given to indirect service, including consultation, inservice education, and liaison functions. (All three of these services are referred to as *consultation* in the remainder of this book.) Most of the characteristics of the movement mandated indirect service. For example, if new manpower sources were to be used, they would be given support through short-term, inservice training and frequent follow-up communications with professionals. Enlightened community control of mental health policy demands constant two-way communication between professionals and community groups. The preventive emphasis is based

upon a process of joint community and professional identification of stresses in the community and high-risk populations and joint action to alleviate these stresses and to meet the needs of the populations at risk. Such cooperative activity requires large amounts of skilled consultation activity. For these reasons, even though it is not the only technique derived from this new model of service delivery, consultation "is a major, if not the major, technique and focus of . . . community mental health" (Mannino and Shore, 1971, p. 1).

Mental health professionals working in schools have been significantly affected by the community mental health movement. They have begun to see that they are at a pivotal position in the community mental health system, and that they must broaden their role definitions and augment their job responsibilities to maximize their effectiveness. Primarily, this means that increased emphasis must be given to consultation activities. Although there are differences in the approaches taken by the various mental health professions, important areas of commonality have been suggested by counselors, psychologists, and social workers (counselors include Bernard and Fullmer, 1972; Carlson, 1972; Ciavarella, 1970; Dinkmeyer, 1968; Eckerson, 1971; Faust, 1967; Kuriloff, 1973; Lewis and Lewis, 1977; Smith and Eckerson, 1966; psychologists include Bardon, 1964; Bergan and Caldwell, 1967; Fine and Tyler, 1971; Hyman, 1972a; Kraft, 1970; Lambert, 1974; Meyers, 1973b; Meyers, Martin, and Hyman, 1977; social workers include Alderson, 1972; Costin, 1972; Nieberl, 1972). Each of these professional groups has suggested greater emphasis on teacher consultation, administrative consultation, parent consultation, inservice coordination, and community liaison.

Not only are mental health professionals recognizing their responsibilities to provide consultation, but the consumers of mental health services in the schools are also expressing a need for such services. Recently, when teachers have been asked to indicate the roles and functions they prefer from mental health professionals, they have frequently responded with a preference for a consultation role-model (Gilmore and Chandy, 1973; Gutkin, Singer, and Brown, 1978; Waters, 1973) as well as a general increase in personal contact and communication. Lesiak and Lounsbury (1977) surveyed ninety-eight principals who rated consultation with

teachers as an extremely important activity for school-based mental health professionals. Similarly, Kaplan, Clancy, and Chrin (1977) surveyed five hundred superintendents in Ohio and found that preventive mental health activities, including consultation, were given high priority.

Despite provider and consumer interest in consultation, change is occurring slowly in the day-to-day practice of mental health professionals in the schools. For example, in recent surveys, school psychologists have rated consultation as one of the most important functions they can serve (Barbanel and Hoffenberg-Rutman, 1974; Cook and Patterson, 1977; Giebink and Ringness, 1970). However, the most recent of these surveys (Cook and Patterson, 1977) found that, while school psychologists in Nebraska reported consultation to be their most important function, a significantly greater amount of time was spent in psychological assessment. In the two recent surveys of school administrators' attitudes toward mental health consultation mentioned earlier (Kaplan, Clancy, and Chrin, 1977; Lesiak and Lounsbury, 1977), both samples rated traditional diagnostic functions of the school psychologists to be at least as important as consultation. Costin (1972) reported the results of a survey carried out in 1968, in which it was found that most social workers practicing in the schools still cling to a casework model whereby school problems are viewed as arising primarily from personal characteristics of the child or family. These social workers emphasized helping the student adjust to the school instead of exploring ways in which school operations could be modified to meet student needs. They reported that school consultation and community agency consultation were used exclusively for individual remediation.

The authors of this book do not take the position that individual counseling, diagnosis, or case work are inappropriate professional activities; these activities are now, and will continue to be, some of the major functions of school-based mental health professionals. However, it is clear that the consultation aspects of these functions have been underemphasized in the past. The image of the counselor and social worker whose only remedial tool is individual therapy and who has little time for teachers, or the visiting school psychologist who tests and one week later sends a jargonish, abbreviated report to the school, is only too prevalent. It is also clear that attempts to promote mental health by trying to deal with the consequences of mental illness are doomed to failure. Bower (1969) has suggested that this is analogous to trying to turn back the Mississippi River at New Orleans. Unless preventive consultation is given more emphasis by mental health professionals who work in schools, the needs of society will remain unmet, and society will, with justification, turn to other professional groups for help.

CHAPTER TWO

Consultation in Historical Perspective

▣ ▣ ▣ ▣ ▣ ▣ ▣ ▣ ▣ ▣ ▣

The community mental health movement has done much to create recent interest in consultation as a tool of mental health professionals in the schools. However, the roots of consultation extend far beyond the recent emphasis on community mental health. From the time that the first counselor, psychiatrist, psychologist, or social worker became interested in the problems of children and began to talk with teachers about their students, school consultation has been practiced. Even during the past forty years, while the clinical model has dominated school practice, the best mental health workers have provided consultation services.

It is customary for the proponents of a technique to assert that it is innovative or unique and to imply that it has no history. Most writers on consultation have followed this custom in that they have failed to place current thought about consultation in historical perspective (see, for example, Bergan, 1977; Caplan, 1970; Dinkmeyer and Carlson, 1973). To develop a thorough understanding of this technique, historical factors must not be over-looked. Therefore, the first two chapters of this book provide such a perspective. Chapter One attempted to describe the historical factors that brought about the recent interest in consultation. This chapter outlines the history of consultation practice from its rudimentary beginnings at the turn of the century to the present. Major emphasis will be devoted to those writers on consultation practice who have been most influential in formulating the current theory and practice of consultation.

The Early Years

As described in Chapter One, at the turn of the century, the schools were under tremendous stress from the increased variety of students. Further, more than at any time in the past, society expected the school to be the primary socialization agency of the culture. These social pressures created a climate for school reform in which government officials, journalists, and various intellectuals began to offer the schools advice. Among the intellectual reformers were some of the major figures in academic psychology, including Hall, Thorndike, James, and Dewey (Levine and Levine, 1970). These illuminaries of American psychology did not engage in a great deal of face-to-face problem solving with teachers; at least, there are few historical accounts of such activity. Their contributions were primarily writing and lecturing to teachers on what the psychology of the day had to say about the teaching-learning process. In this way, they established a tradition of involvement with the educational community that laid the groundwork for much current consultation practice.

In the 1880s, for example, G. Stanley Hall gave Saturday morning lectures to teachers in the Boston area on current educational problems. William James delivered a series of "talks to teachers" in Cambridge in 1892, which gained such popularity that he eventually gave them throughout the country (Cremin, 1961). These lectures were published in 1899 as *Talks to Teachers on Psychology and to Students on Some of Life's Ideals*. In 1906, Thorndike's *Principles of Teaching* appeared, which presented those principles of learning and individual differences that had been the focus of his laboratory work.

Although the problems of communicating psychological principles to educators and others was not addressed directly in the writings of these early psychologists, one paragraph in James' ([1899] 1962) *Talks to Teachers* does relate to this issue. James told teachers that the science of psychology had little to offer them in the way of help with daily problems. "I say moreover that you make a great, a very great mistake, if you think that psychology, being the science of the mind's laws, is something from which you can deduce definite programs and schemes and methods of instruction for immediate schoolroom use. Psychology is a science, and teaching is an art; and sciences never generate arts directly out of themselves. An intermediary inventive mind must make the application, by using its originality" (1962, p. 3).

James was apparently referring to the inventive mind of the teacher, but he left the door wide open for the type of consultation where two inventive minds come together, one trained in psychology and one in education, to translate the science into the art.

Not only were academic psychologists writing and lecturing on the relevance of psychology to education, but several also began to work directly with teachers and students having academic problems. Perhaps the most famous example is that of Witmer, who, at the American Psychological Association (APA) meeting in 1896, expressed his interest in working out a relationship between the psychology department of the University of Pennsylvania and the public school system of Philadelphia (Levine and Levine, 1970). Witmer felt that the best approach to a relationship of this kind was through the study and remediation of the exceptional child. Although his interest was clinical in the sense of focusing on the individual, and typically the exceptional, child, Witmer took major steps toward promoting preventive measures through consultation. This was done partly through the instruction he provided for public school teachers in child study. According to Levine and Levine (1970, p. 59), this instruction was particularly noteworthy for its anticipation of the ideals of the modern community mental health orientation, where mental health specialists and teachers work together: "These were more than summer institutes condescendingly offered for teachers. Classes for observation and experimentation were conducted as part of the clinic teaching and therapy program.

They provided a situation in which clinical psychologists and teachers participated completely in the training of each other."

In his APA address of 1896, Witmer also demonstrated his awareness of the need for the two-way, collaborative communication that is an essential component of consultation. In this address, he stated that he sought the development of special classes under the control of the city school authority but in "harmonious and effective relationship" with the University psychology department (Levine and Levine, 1970).

Social workers in the early 1900s, perhaps more than any other professional group, anticipated the current community mental health spirit, particularly its emphasis on consultation. Tracing the beginnings of social work in America, Lubove (1965) points out that the first social workers were medical community workers. Their primary function was to act as an intermediary between the physician and the patient to interpret the physician's recommendations to poor immigrant families, help patients understand the reasons for the recommendations, and help them carry out the recommendations. Further, they helped to educate the poor regarding the causes of health problems, thereby serving a preventive function.

When social workers (known as *visiting teachers*) began to work in schools, they served much the same liaison and preventive functions. Their remedial strategies were primarily aimed at making adjustments in the environment of the child to enhance his mental and physical health and indirectly his education. There was an early realization, for example, of the importance of the teacher in the school adjustment of the child, and considerable emphasis was given to teacher consultation: "The teacher had to realize that if only one factor in a child's maladjustment at school can be changed, the attitude of the teacher will usually be found to be the most important and its alteration most immediately effective in bringing about improvement" (Taft, 1923, cited in Lubove, 1965, pp. 98–99).

In many localities, the visiting teacher served many school consultation functions in place of the psychologist or psychiatrist. For example, Levine and Levine (1970) report that in Hartford, visiting teachers obtained family histories for the school psychologist and helped to implement his recommendations in the home and the school. Witmer used social workers in a similar capacity in his clinic in Philadelphia. Often, psychologists, psychiatrists, and other physicians used social workers as liaisons and consultants, rather than carrying out these functions themselves. Consultation may have been viewed as of secondary importance or as requiring less skill than the diagnostic and remedial functions. Status differences were associated with these tasks, because the primary clinical staff who provided individual diagnostic and remedial work (psychologists and physicians) was more highly trained and predominantly male, whereas the staff that provided consultation was less well trained (in the early years visiting teachers were primarily volunteers) and was predominantly female. Social workers were seen as equivalent in status to nurses; they were serving the second-order mental health functions, including consultation.

Despite the lesser value placed on consultation during this period, consultation was being implemented. Consultation was conceptualized as a process of the transfer of knowledge from one person who was more knowledgeable (the consultant) to another person who was less knowledgeable (the consultee). The process was not viewed as an exercise in problem solving on the part of two persons with different kinds of expertise. Despite this emphasis on expert knowledge, there was also some sensitivity to the dynamics of the relationship between consultant and consultee, as exemplified in the following remark: "The ability to affect attitudes depended upon the social worker's skill in establishing a satisfactory relationship with others through utilization of the 'facts and concepts of psychiatry and social science' along with an 'ingenious and imaginative use of a multitude of minor devices, emphases, suggestions, and so on'" (Lee and Kenworthy, in Lubove, 1965, pp. 98–99).

1930 to 1960—The Clinical Period

In Chapter One, we discussed the social forces that fostered the development of the medical model. The effects of this model on consultation practice can be exemplified in the history of the child guidance clinics. One of the basic concentrations of the early child guidance clinics was indirect service. Indirect service to the schools included training sessions for teachers, open case conferences in which school personnel played an integral part, and consultation with teachers and administrators about individual cases. The expressed purpose of having psychologists on the staff of these clinics was to aid in discussions with school personnel. Psychologists were thought to be helpful in this regard because of their knowledge of tests and because their primary remedial strategy was tutorial (Levine and Levine, 1970). Social-work case reports of the early years of these clinics showed frequent references to school visits, teacher conferences, and conferences with administrators.

For many reasons, the indirect emphasis of the early clinics began to be overshadowed by analytically based remedial strategies toward the end of the 1920s: "by 1930 open case conferences or cooperative treatment relationships were just about extinct" (Levine and Levine, 1970, p. 264). The decrease in indirect services can be attributed to three general causes. First, much mental health consultation during the 1920s and 1930s consisted of communication of diagnostic labels and categories derived from Kraeplin. However, educators soon came to understand these diagnostic categories, thereby reducing the need for psychological and psychiatric consultants. Second, the diagnostic labels did not translate readily into treatment programs. Third, although Freudian thought was a major interest of the intellectual community and the mental health profession during this period, many educators and parents of school children found the interpretative concepts of psychoanalysis repugnant, or at least alien.

It is clear from consideration of these factors why consultation rapidly declined. The mental health professionals who staffed child guidance clinics, and other mental health professionals who worked in schools, were communicating in a language that either was not understood by school personnel or was distasteful to them. Further, the content of the communication seemed irrelevant to the teaching experience.

Foundations of Current Consultation
Theory and Practice

With the development of other therapeutic approaches (Rogerian counseling, behavior modification, group techniques, and so forth) in the 1950s, mental health professionals no longer had to rely on the psychiatric categorization techniques, the labels of Kraeplin, or the conceptualizations of Freud. Mental health professionals now had more to say to teachers that was both concrete and readily understood, and this knowledge could be communicated in ways that were more congruent with the values of the schools.

During the late 1950s and early 1960s, educators again sought increased communication between mental health professionals and the schools. In 1955, for example, The Thayer Conference of leaders in school psychology and educators was held. The purpose of the conference was to discuss the qualifications and training of psychologists who work in the schools. During the conference, school administrators were questioned regarding their greatest concerns about psychologists. They reported that psychologists failed to communicate with school personnel, had poor community skills, had poor human relations skills, and did not understand the practical problems of the classroom (Fein, 1974). These criticisms, in conjunction with psychologists' dissatisfaction with their roles in the schools, led to recommendations that doctoral level school psychologists be trained to serve at the policy-making level of the school to help plan curricula and to help change attitudes of school staff, parents, and the community.

In guidance and counseling, similar trends were beginning to take shape. In 1960, a citizens' White House Conference on Children and Youth made twelve recommendations in the area of guidance. A part of one recommendation stated that "community counseling services be made more widely available to youth and their parents; and that coordination between school and community service be emphasized" (Miller, 1961, p. 42). Although this was not a direct reference to consultation services, it did show increased awareness of the importance of communication with parents and community agencies in guidance services. The trend toward consultation was seen much more strongly in 1966, when the ACES-ASCA committee of the American Personnel and Guidance Association identified consulting as one of the three major areas of service for elementary school counselors. In addition to counseling, the third essential function was coordination, an activity that is highly related to consultation.

Although school mental health personnel were beginning to

see increased possibilities for consultation activities and to understand their importance, little in the way of specialized theory or guidelines for practice existed. Specialized writing on consultation began to appear during this period, although its influence on school practice was limited. In retrospect, two sources of consultation theory seem to have had the most influence on school consultation: community psychiatry, especially the writings of Caplan (1951, 1955, 1963, 1964, 1970, 1974), and organization development (Lippitt, Watson, and Westley, 1958; Schein, 1969; Schmuck and Miles, 1971).

Obviously, other factors have had an impact on the development of school consultation. For example, behavior modification, which has developed dramatically as an educational implementation since 1960, makes specific recommendations available to consultants from an impressive data base. However, this approach has not yet generated a sophisticated technology or adequate data to influence the *process* of consultation. In other words, although the behavior modification literature has made a contribution in developing clear recommendations to teachers, it suggests little about *how* to consult. John Bergan's recent work (1977) constitutes a promising beginning in this area by behaviorists, but there is not yet a historical tradition of the impact of behaviorism on the process of consultation. Nevertheless, this approach will receive considerable attention in Chapter Four because of its contribution to the content of consultation.

The Contributions of Gerald Caplan. While working in Israel in 1948 with a small staff of psychologists and social workers, Caplan was asked to supervise the mental health of approximately sixteen thousand new immigrant children. During the first year, he received over one thousand referrals. The staff, working in the traditional diagnostic-prescription-remediation paradigm, was unable to keep pace and soon was bogged down in report writing at the expense of remedial intervention. At the same time, the staff began to notice patterns in the referrals coming from specific institutions—that is, certain institutions seemed to be having difficulty with specific types of children: "Thus, although the population of immigrant children was fairly randomly distributed among the different institutions and did not appear to vary much in its composition from one another, we began to notice that one institution was continually referring bed-wetters, while another was referring children with learning disabilities and a third was plagued by aggressive children" (Caplan, 1970, p. 9).

This observation, along with the inadequate manpower to cope with the rate of referrals, led Caplan to experiment with preventive techniques, particularly consultation. Staff time in working with individual children was reduced, and staff were deployed to local institutions to see if problems could be handled by the caretakers of the children. The staff spent most of their time counseling caretakers and dealing with the problems of the caretakers as the caretakers saw them. Thus, the consultation was not aimed at changing the caretakers' minds about what they perceived their problems to be, but it simply provided new techniques for coping with the problems as already defined.

In 1952, Caplan began work at the Harvard School of Public Health. During his early years at Harvard, his thinking about consultation was strongly influenced by his colleague Erich Lindemann, who sometime earlier had initiated a preventive psychiatry program at the Wellesley Human Relations Service (Caplan, 1970). In this work, Lindemann had developed methods for observing children in classrooms to screen school populations for emotionally disturbed children. At first, these observations were carried out only for research purposes. Later it was found, however, that teachers wanted to talk about the observations to increase their understanding of children's problems. As the process involved in the talks became more thoroughly understood and systematized, it became known as consultation and was differentiated from the counseling technique of Rogers and traditional psychiatric therapy.

Caplan began his intensive study of the consultation process in 1954, when, as part of his duties at the Harvard School of Public Health, he and his staff provided extensive mental health consultation to public health nurses. Since then, he has provided mental health consultation to school systems, antipoverty agencies, the Job Corps, religious organizations, rehabilitation agencies, army units, and general hospitals.

Caplan's writings in preventive psychiatry and consultation

have been extensive. In "A Public Health Approach to Child Psychiatry" (1951), he reported on his early experimentation in preventive mental health in Israel. These ideas were expanded in 1964 with the publication of *Principles of Preventive Psychiatry*, which contained his first detailed discussion of the consultation process and laid the foundation for his major work on the subject, *The Theory and Practice of Mental Health Consultation* (1970). His latest book, *Support Systems and Community Mental Health* (1974), is a compilation of edited papers on community psychiatry.

Many aspects of Caplan's writing have had impact on school consultation practice, but three contributions seem to stand above the rest: his conceptualization of consultation as a coordinate relationship, his ideas about the confrontation of consultee defenses, and his categorization of the different types of consultation.

The cornerstone of Caplan's theory of consultation is that it is a nonhierarchical, or coordinate, relationship. This kind of consultation is possible, in Caplan's opinion, only between two professionals, the mental health professional and a professional trained in another discipline, such as medicine, religion, or education. The coordinate aspects of consultation separate it from counseling, therapy, or education, in that the mental health professional has varying degrees of direct power over the consultee in these activities. This notion of a coordinate relationship has done much to ensure a place for consultation in schools. Much traditional school consultation has consisted of experts in psychiatry or psychology giving advice to school personnel. Of course, giving such advice strongly implied ignorance or inferiority on the part of the consultee, and it produced resistance. Caplan's approach, conceptualizing consultation as communication between two experts, does much to alleviate this type of resistance.

Caplan's ideas regarding the confrontation of consultee defenses are related to his coordinate relationship concept. Caplan believes that many work problems of teachers and other caretakers are related to a lack of professional objectivity about their clients. That is, caretakers frequently have "emotionally toned cognitive constellations," called *themes*, relating to personal conflicts that have not been resolved. Caplan considers it inappropriate and counterproductive for the consultant to confront these themes or conflicts directly, and he advises consultants to keep the focus of consultation on the client. He discusses indirect techniques for changing consultee attitudes (for example, theme interference reduction) that are designed not to threaten the defenses of the consultee. This stance is contrary to the training of most analytically trained mental health workers, who focus on their patients' intrapsychic conflicts and confront these conflicts as a central part of therapy. As a result, Caplan's work represents a major departure from traditional approaches to helping. This notion will be explored in more depth in Chapter Five.

Caplan has categorized consultation into four different types: client-centered case consultation, program-centered administrative consultation, consultee-centered case consultation, and consultee-centered administrative consultation. Since this categorization schema has laid the foundation for most thinking about the consultation process, each type of consultation will be described briefly.

In client-centered case consultation, the focus is on the consultee's difficulties with a professional case. The primary goal is to help the consultee find the most effective treatment for the client. A secondary goal is to increase the knowledge and techniques of the consultee so that he or she is better prepared to deal with similar types of clients in the future. To achieve these goals, the consultant focuses his attention on the client; therefore, in client-centered case consultation, the consultant is expected to diagnose the client accurately and give the consultee a remedial prescription.

The second type of consultation noted by Caplan is program-centered administrative consultation. In this type of consultation, the consultant is called upon by a consultee or, more often, a group of consultees to help solve current problems in the administration of programs for the prevention, treatment, or rehabilitation of mental disorders. The consultant focuses on a specialized assessment of the current program and recommends a plan to resolve the difficulty. A secondary goal, as in the first type of consultation, is the education of the consultees so that they will be able to deal with similar problems without consultant assistance in the future.

Consultee-centered case consultation, the third type, focuses on the consultee rather than on the particular client with whom the consultee is currently having difficulties. The primary goal is to improve the consultee's functioning, which hopefully would lead to an improvement in the consultee's handling of the client. When the consultant has pinpointed the nature of the consultee's difficulty, he attempts to help the consultee master the significant issues. This can be accomplished through a discussion of the client's problem and the consultee's contribution to the resolution of the problem. The focus may be to improve the consultee's skill, objectivity, knowledge, and self-confidence.

Consultee-centered administrative consultation is the fourth type of consultation presented by Caplan. The primary goal here is to help consultees to master problems in the planning and maintenance of programs for the prevention and control of mental disorders, and to manage the interpersonal aspects of the operations of their agencies. This method can be applied in group situations or with a single administrator.

Organization Development

In addition to Caplan's work, current thinking on methods of consultation has been strongly influenced by a loosely connected set of techniques and theoretical ideas known as *organization development* (O.D.). Organization development is the application of behavioral science knowledge, particularly social psychological principles of group dynamics, to the problems of organizations. A change-agent or consultant is necessary to help the organization apply behavioral science to its problems. The application of this knowledge by the change-agent has as its goal a more adaptive, flexible, and self-renewing organization (see Huse, 1975, for additional definitions of O.D.).

According to Huse (1975), there were two primary historical antecedents to O.D., both of which were initiated by Kurt Lewin. One was the National Training Laboratories T-group movement. In 1946, Lewin and his staff at Massachusetts Institute of Technology (M.I.T.) brought together community leaders to learn about group dynamics from first-hand experience. Members were placed in small groups and given personal feedback about their behavior in groups. This group became known as a T-group (training group). The National Training Laboratories were soon established and offered training to such organizations as the American Red Cross, the Episcopal church, and Republic Aviation. The idea behind such training was that, if people were brought together from different levels of the organization and given open and honest feedback regarding their behavior in groups, then communication on the job could be improved.

The other major historical predecessor of O.D. mentioned by Huse (1975) was Lewin's application of attitude-survey research and data feedback to organizational problems at the Research Center for Group Dynamics at M.I.T. and later at the Institute of Social Research at Michigan. In a typical application, attitude-survey data were collected from all members of an organization, with data grouped by hierarchical level within the organization. Then, starting with the top of the organizational pyramid, a small group of subordinates would meet with their superordinate to go over the data, discuss the issues raised, and decide on possible plans of action.

O.D. came to be identified as a distinct set of techniques in the 1960s, when T-groups and survey-data feedback were incorporated into systems interventions. For example, an O.D. effort carried out at Esso Refineries included training in problem-solving techniques for high-eschelon personnel and their subordinates to create a more open, trusting interaction pattern. *Intergroup labs* were also developed to clarify and resolve conflicts between different departments of the company.

T-group activities for teachers have been carried out since the mid 1950s, and in 1961, the National Training Laboratories began to offer lab training especially designed for educators (Schmuck and Miles, 1971). The first true O.D. project in education was carried out by Miles in the early 1960s. This three-year intervention applied data feedback, problem-solving workshops, and process consultation for work teams in two eastern school districts. In 1965, the National Training Laboratories began the Cooperative Project for Educational Development (COPED). This massive project brought together researchers and trainers from Boston University, Lesley College, Teachers College (Columbia University), Yeshiva University, Newark State College, The University of Wisconsin, The University of Chicago, and The University of Michigan to plan and carry out an O.D. project in twenty-three school districts. Different strategies were used in different locales, but the interventions included inservice education in problem-solving and action research, process consultation to groups of teachers and administrators, and training in-house change-agents to carry out these functions in their own schools. Unfortunately, the project funds were terminated after the first year of the intervention, but the project and the subsequent report had major effects on the development of O.D. in educational settings (Schmuck and Miles, 1971).

Many of the systematic O.D. efforts that have been carried out and documented since the COPED project are discussed in Schmuck and Miles (1971). Included are interventions using conflict consultation, training in confrontation, and student advocacy as a power manipulation, as well as more traditional O.D. techniques.

The contributions of O.D. theorists and practitioners in school consultation has been manifold. Three contributions of particular importance include the emphasis given group interventions versus individual interventions, the clarification of mechanisms of change within organizations, and new ideas about the causes of organizational problems.

Mental health professionals working in schools have traditionally worked with individuals. Even with an increased interest in group therapy, the focus of the counselor, psychiatrist, psychologist, and social worker typically has been the individual. This has been due, in part, to the influence of psychiatric theories suggesting that individual intrapsychic disturbances account for the origins of maladaptive behaviors. The literature on group interaction, however, has clearly documented that individuals have difficulties in work groups because of counterproductive interactions of group roles or dysfunctional communication patterns within the group (see Bales, 1959). As group-dynamics concepts have been refined by O.D. specialists, they have stimulated the development of a variety of group consultation interventions that have greatly augmented the options available to the school consultant. These techniques will be discussed in greater detail in Chapter Six.

Mental health professionals have repeatedly seen patients or consultees make healthy progress in a protected environment (a clinic, hospital, office, or retreat), only to see them return to old, maladaptive patterns when they return to their normal, day-to-day social routine. Early interventions with organizations had similar results; the group that functioned well in a T-group often could not maintain that level of performance on the job. It appeared that the main organization—its values, culture, and structure—created strong pressures on its members and subgroups to return to their original patterns of behavior. It is widely understood that organizations resist change (Moorish, 1976), but O.D. specialists did much to clarify this phenomenon with regard to consultation activities. They reasoned that the only way to produce meaningful change was to intervene with the organization as a whole; this became the essence of organizational development. O.D. focuses on the interactions of subgroups making up the system as much as on the individuals making up the subgroups. This aspect of O.D. has provided cues to effective techniques that may be used (and pitfalls to be avoided) in educational settings, and it has placed individual consultation in a broader perspective. When individual consultation is necessary, a great deal of work with the support systems of the organization must be done to ensure that individual change will not be thwarted by organizational pressures. When organizational consultation is possible, it is the intervention of preference—especially when all levels of the school can be involved.

Problems occur in organizations for many reasons, including poor lateral and hierarchical communication, poor conflict-management, a lack of sensitivity to changing organizational environments, and antiquated theories regarding worker motivation. Typically, school-based mental health professionals have tended to blame the poor performance of a particular school on the lack of skills or the intrapsychic conflicts of school personnel. Of course, these problems may exist, but viewing all school problems as resulting from these causes is myopic. The O.D. literature has introduced mental health professionals to management theory and the theory of complex organizations. This added knowledge can only improve the perspective and flexibility of the mental health professional's consulting skills.

Other Influences on School Consultation

Although both Caplan's model and organization development have influenced the development of school consultation,
neither was designed specifically for the schools. These approaches
fail to delineate various factors that are relevant to consultation in
the school. For example, O.D. has not systematized techniques appropriate for working with individual teachers. Although Caplan
has done this, he does not discuss several useful school consultation
techniques, such as interaction analysis, task analysis, or behavior
modification. However, other influential research has focused
specifically on the schools.

Irving Berlin (1956, 1962) was one of the first community
psychiatrists to stress the relevance of consultation to the schools.
He characterized the role of the consultant as helping the teacher
to understand himself as a teacher. In particular, he suggested that
the consultant help the teacher to clarify his or her feelings toward
the child. Like Caplan, Berlin described consultation as the communication of mental health principles to enable the consultee to
work more effectively.

Seymour Sarason has influenced the development of consultation as a viable role for mental health workers in the school.
Sarason developed a psychoeducational clinic at Yale University for
preventive mental health in the school and community (Sarason
and others, 1966). This early work was important, in part, because
Sarason described a psychological clinic that tried to break with the
tradition started by Witmer. Instead of having clients come to the
clinic, the clinic tried to help the client in the community. The clinic
took a strong environmental emphasis, focusing on student-teacher
interaction and classroom milieu.

Sarason recognized that consultation in the schools is different from consultation in other settings because of the unique
sociocultural environment in the schools. He elaborated this point
of view in a later work (Sarason, 1971), where he used a social
psychological orientation to analyze the culture of schools. He
demonstrated a variety of institutional norms, roles, and
communication patterns characteristic of schools, and he showed
how these factors can affect the role definition of psychological
consultants and other mental health workers in schools.

The work of Caplan, Sarason, Berlin, and the O.D. theorists was important for its development of conceptual models to guide the practice of consultation. Another important contribution was made by those who described consultation efforts in detail. Ruth Newman was one of the first practitioners to document her experiences as a consultant and leader of a team of consultants in the school. Her project began in the early 1960s as an extension of her work under Fritz Redl at the Child Research branch of the National Institute for Mental Health. Newman's consultation was psychodynamically based but interdisciplinary and preventive in orientation. Her writing demonstrated sensitivity to the problems of people in schools and provided a large number of practical hints for the consultant. For example, she suggests that the consultant begin consultation several weeks after the beginning of the semester and terminate consultation several weeks before the end of the semester, because these periods are particularly hectic for teachers. She provides advice for handling requests to sit in on parent-teacher conferences, for dealing with the expectation that the consultant will provide magical cures, and for ensuring the support of the administration. Many of these suggestions have been supported by the experience of other school consultants and have become part of the consultation lore.

Summary

School consultation began early in the twentieth century. During the first two or three decades, social workers, sometimes called *visiting teachers,* provided much consultation to schools, while psychologists and guidance counselors provided relatively little consultation to schools. Consultation efforts declined sharply during the 1920s, and by 1930, consultation was a very minor function of mental health professionals. This period of slow development in consultation lasted until the early 1950s, when new remedial techniques and new conceptions of the causes of maladaptive behavior in schools made consultation a more viable preventive and remedial function. Although mental health professionals working in schools have contributed much to the literature on consultation in the last few years, the major influences on consultation practice have been from disciplines outside of education, including psychiatry, social psychology, and group dynamics. Particularly noteworthy is the work of Gerald Caplan, Irving Berlin, Seymour Sarason, and Ruth Newman. The work of these individuals has changed the focus of consultation from advice giving in the early years to a more coordinate, expertise-sharing process. They have also augmented the consultant's knowledge of the school as a culture and as an organization. Finally, they have contributed a variety of techniques other than inservice education and case feedback, including group dynamics exercises, applied research techniques, theme interference reduction, organization development techniques, and conflict resolution procedures.

CHAPTER THREE

Interpersonal Processes of Consultation

▣ ▣ ▣ ▣ ▣ ▣ ▣ ▣ ▣ ▣ ▣

Throughout Chapters One and Two, consultation was presented primarily as a service delivery system. Moreover, chapters Five through Eight will consider various approaches to developing intervention strategies in consultation. However, consultation is difficult to implement effectively regardless of the quality of intervention plans. Therefore, our purpose here and in Chapter Four is to consider those factors that increase the probability that consultation strategies will be effective; these factors are often referred to as *the consultation process*. In this chapter we will consider consultation as an interpersonal process, along with implications for practice and research.

Psychotherapy, teaching, and supervision are a few of the many helping relationships that involve some type of interpersonal process. Consultation is similar to each of these techniques; however, there are important distinctions as well. For example, the goals of therapy and consultation are different: Consultation is limited to work-related problems and psychotherapy considers all

of the individual's personal problems. Also, consultation generally
concentrates on problem solving and educational techniques and is
based on an indirect, rather than a direct, service model.

Consultation has elements in common with teaching and,
under certain circumstances, uses the didactic strategy of teaching.
But unlike teaching, consultation focuses on interpersonal skill
development or the affect of the consultee. Furthermore, the processes of teaching and supervision are not synonymous with consultation since the consultant does not have any coercive power. (For
an extended discussion of how the consultation relationship differs from other professional relationships, see Caplan, 1970,
pp. 21–28.)

Since there has been so little research to date on the consultation process (Mannino and Shore, 1975), relevant ideas from
research on related interpersonal processes, such as therapy, have
been abstracted. Caplan (1970), for example, relied on concepts of
psychoanalytic therapy to establish his frame of reference. As a
result, he developed techniques for consultee-centered consultation that attempt to reduce cognitive distortion based on subjective,
affective involvement of the consultee (for example, a teacher). Of
course, he excluded many generalizations from psychoanalytic
therapy that did not fit the consultation situation. A similar analysis
of any current theoretical approach to consultation will reveal the
influence of theory and research from a variety of related interpersonal techniques. For example, Dinkmeyer and Carlson (1973) rely
on techniques derived from Adlerian counseling and therapy, organization development consultation (for example, Schein, 1969;
Schmuck and Miles, 1971; and Gallessich, 1972) owes a heavy debt
to small group process and organizational psychology for the frame
of reference, and Bergan's (1977) view of consultation process derives from operant conditioning.

Because there is no single theoretical position that conceptualizes adequately the process of consultation in schools, we will
broaden the consultation perspective by presenting four very different manners of conceptualizing the consultation process. Each
one may add to the development of process techniques since they
are each distinct from the orientations noted earlier. The four
viewpoints are diffusion research (research on the communication

of innovation), social-psychological principles of attitude change, transactional analysis, and derivatives of Rogerian counseling.

In one sense, this chapter may confuse the serious student of the consultation process, because it adds to the numerous perspectives already present in the literature. Such a student might ask why we did not synthesize the different generalizations instead of simply presenting additional points of view. We feel that, given the present state of the art of theory and research on the consultation process, synthesis is premature. Most researchers discuss a relatively small number of process techniques and provide empirical support for only a portion of them. Furthermore, the frames of reference of each writer—their assumptions, languages, and methods—are so different that common points among perspectives are difficult to find. Consultation theory is in the "preparadigm" stage (Kuhn, 1962), that stage of scientific development in which numerous approaches or perspectives exist, each looking at somewhat different aspects of the problem, with no one perspective more encompassing than another. We will not even attempt a synthesis of the four viewpoints presented here. Our purpose is to make readers aware of the complexity of the consultation process by indicating the variety of explanations of the process that are available.

Consultation as Diffusion of Innovations

During the past few years, a new area of research activity and study has developed that looks at the manner in which innovations are communicated to, and adopted by, social systems. *Diffusion* is the term describing the process by which new ideas are spread to members of the social system (Rogers and Shoemaker, 1971). Diffusion research has its intellectual roots in anthropology, general, rural, and medical sociology, communication, marketing, and education. It concerns such problems as: How do agricultural extension agents succeed in getting farmers to plant better hybrid corn seeds than they have traditionally planted? In what manner is new information about drugs and other pharmaceutical products best communicated to doctors? How long does it take for a new brand of coffee to be used widely by consumers? What are the characteristics of school districts that adopt new math versus those that do not?

From research about such questions has come a conceptual model of the manner in which innovations are communicated and a large set of empirically supported generalizations that strengthen the model. This conceptual framework and the generalizations derived from it appear to be relevant for school-based mental health consultants. The consultant's role was designed to hasten the diffusion of social science knowledge to school personnel. The consultant presents new information, a new perspective, or a new application of generally available information.

One area of diffusion research focuses on the role played by agents who enhance diffusion. In discussing the role played by such change-agents, Rogers and Shoemaker (1971) point out that the agent is a bridge between two systems: the system that produces a set of knowledge and seeks to create change by disseminating this knowledge, and the system whose function can be enhanced by using the knowledge. The latter, client system may understand the relevance of the production system's knowledge for its problems, or it may have to be convinced of the utility of the knowledge. The important point, however, is that the two systems represent two different cultures, each having different languages (technical jargon), different values, and different goals. To bridge the gap between these cultures, the change-agent (consultant) must be able to speak and understand the languages of both cultures and must be able to understand the values and goals of both cultures. The social worker who wishes to point out to educators the importance of environmental factors on the education of children reared in poverty must understand the culture of the school as well as his own profession.

Diffusion research offers many guidelines for the professional who must serve this bridging function between cultures. To illustrate a few of the ideas drawn from this body of research, we present an example discussed by Rogers and Shoemaker (1971, pp. 3–5):

> The public health service in Peru attempts to introduce innovations to villages to improve their health and lengthen their lives. . . . It encourages people to install pit latrines, burn garbage daily, control house flies, report suspected cases of communicable disease, and boil drinking water. These innovations involve major

changes in thinking and behavior for Peruvian villagers, who have little knowledge of the relationship between sanitation and illness.

Water-boiling is a necessary method of preventive medicine for these people. Unless they boil drinking water, patients who are cured of infectious diseases in village medical clinics often return within the month to be treated for the same disease.

A two-year water-boiling campaign [was] conducted in Los Molinos, a peasant village of 200 families in the coastal region of Peru.... From the viewpoint of the health agency, the local hygiene worker, Nelida, had a simple task: To persuade the housewives of Los Molinos to add water boiling to their pattern of existing behavior.

At the end of the two-year intervention, only eleven families had been persuaded to boil their drinking water. Insight into the reason for this failure on the part of the change-agent can be obtained by examining three types of clients with whom the hygiene worker dealt:

Mrs. C. rejected the innovation.

This housewife represents the majority of Los Molinos families who were not persuaded by the efforts of the change-agent during the two-year health campaign. Mrs. C does not understand germ theory, in spite of Nelida's repeated explanations. How, she argues, can microbes survive in water which would drown people? Are they fish? If germs are so small that they cannot be seen or felt, how can they hurt a grown person? There are enough real threats in the world to worry about—poverty and hunger—without bothering with tiny animals one cannot see, hear, touch, or smell.

Several housewives, particularly those of the lower social class, are rejectors because they have neither the time nor the means to boil water, even if they were convinced of its value. These women lack time to gather firewood and boil the water. The poor cannot afford the cost of fuel for water-boiling.

Mrs. A already boiled water.

Mrs. A is about forty and suffers from sinus infection. She is labeled by the Los Molinos villagers as a "sickly one." Each morning, Mrs. A boils a potful of water and uses it throughout the day. She has no understanding of germ theory, as explained by Nelida; her motivation for water-boiling is a complex local custom of hot and cold distinctions. The [basic] principle of this belief system is that all foods, liquids, medicines, and other objects are inherently hot or cold, quite apart from their actual temperature.

Boiled water and illness are closely linked in the folkways of Los Molinos; by custom, only the ill use cooked, or "hot" water. Once an individual becomes ill, it is unthinkable for him to eat pork (very cold) or to drink brandy (very hot). Extremes of hot and cold must be avoided by the sick; therefore, raw water, which is perceived to be very cold, must be boiled to overcome the extreme temperature. Villagers learn from childhood to dislike boiled water. Most can tolerate cooked water only if flavoring, such as sugar, cinnamon, lemon, or herbs is added.

Mrs. B was persuaded.

The B family came to Los Molinos a generation ago, but they are still strongly oriented toward their birthplace, located among the peaks of the high Andes. Mrs. B is marked as an outsider in the community by her highland hairdo and stumbling Spanish. She will never achieve more than marginal social acceptance in the village. Because the community is not an important reference group to her, Mrs. B deviates from group norms on innovation. . . . [Further], Mrs. B worries about lowland diseases which she feels infest the village. It is partly because of this anxiety that the change-agent . . . was able to convince Mrs. B to boil water. [Finally] Nelida is a friendly authority to Mrs. B (rather than a "dirt inspector" as she is seen by most housewives), who imports knowledge and brings protection. Mrs. B not only boils water but also has installed a latrine and has sent her youngest child to the health center for an inspection.

This unsuccessful attempt at innovation diffusion exemplifies many of the general tenets of diffusion research. For example, Rogers and Shoemaker (1971) report a number of studies showing that innovations compatible with the cultural beliefs of the social system are more readily adopted than those that are not compatible. In the current example, the idea of boiling drinking water was not compatible with the hot-cold distinction of the culture. Tradition linked boiled water with illness, in the sense that boiling removed the cold quality of water and made it appropriate only for persons who were ill.

Similarly, many psychological principles are in some ways incompatible with the traditions and cultural beliefs of educators. Mental health professionals typically have an individual orientation, for example, and educators typically have a group orientation. When the mental health consultant recommends that an individual child be treated in a special way, particularly if the treatment is seen as more lenient or as allowing the child more access to rewards and privileges than other children, teachers frequently object. Such recommendations run counter to their idea of what is just or fair. This value holds that rewards and privileges must be equitably distributed to all group members, or at least all group members must have an equal chance to obtain them.

Another principle of diffusion theory is that change-agent success is more likely when the agent has a client orientation rather than an agency or innovation orientation. The hygiene worker was innovation-oriented; her message was presented in terms of germ theory, which the villagers could not understand and did not need to understand. To make the message more client-oriented, the hygiene worker should have started where she found the villagers, with their understanding of the natural world, of disease, and of boiled water. Further, the message would have been more client-oriented if it had been stated in terms of their present needs and environmental demands rather than seeming to add to their environmental demands (increased effort to chop and collect wood for boiling water).

The behaviorist who goes to the school to consult on child management problems often is more innovation-oriented than client-oriented. Because of his or her extensive training, the consultant is often preoccupied with the philosophical, theoretical, or technical aspects of the knowledge base. Therefore, communications to the client may reflect this preoccupation. It may not be necessary, for example, to correct a client who uses the word reward in place of the consultant's word reinforcement. Although the distinction between these words is theoretically very important, the consultee need not understand these theoretical complexities to carry out the program adequately. Likewise, the parent or teacher who conceptualizes school phobia in dynamic terms need not be introduced to the subtleties of preaversive stimuli, avoidance learning, fear hierarchies, reciprocal inhibition, or systematic desensitization, as long as he can carry out the procedure stipulated by the consultant.

Diffusion research has indicated that to enhance the possibilities of adoption of the innovation, the change-agent must concentrate his energies on the opinion leaders in the social system he wishes to change. The hygiene worker did not seem to understand this concept, for she concentrated her efforts on socially marginal people. Mrs. A was marginal in the Los Molinos social structure because she was the "sickly one." She was defined as different, and her water-boiling behavior had no implication for the other healthy members of the village. Mrs. B was marginal because she was an outsider (despite having lived in the village for some time); her dress, speech, and values were those of a mountain village, not of the lowlands. She was not a part of the reference group of the village, and therefore her adoption of the innovation had little effect on other villagers.

Similar situations often occur during consultation experiences in schools. For example, Roy Martin was consulting in a parochial school that had agreed to accept university-based consultant trainees but had little idea of how the consultants could be helpful. During the first six-month period of the contract, the strategy for the consultants was to explain and demonstrate to teachers the variety of ways the consultant could be used. Particular emphasis was to be given to the principal and the teachers in the school who were leaders. However, one of the first consultees to seek help was a lay teacher who was afraid that her contract was not going to be renewed. The teacher had strong feelings about her work situation, she had feelings of failure, and she needed support in keeping her perspective on the situation. After approximately six weeks of consultation, the teacher actually received a termination notice. This increased her bitterness and feeling of inadequacy, and she continued to demand much of the consultant's time. This is consistent with Mann's (1973) finding that those low in the power hierarchy frequently seek consultation first.

Because the consultant was in this particular school only one-half day per week, and because this teacher's needs were so pressing, much of the first three months was spent with her. When the consultant finally was able to terminate the relationship, his help was seldom sought by other teachers, although the principal used his services quite frequently. Despite some awareness of the processes at work, the consultant was unable to change the role he had taken as the counselor of those who were dissatisfied with or outside of the "teacher system." For many reasons, including his failure to influence the important leaders among the teachers, the contract with the university was terminated at the end of the six-month trial period.

Rogers and Shoemaker (1971) list other generalizations from diffusion research similar to the three that have just been discussed. These generalizations relate to characteristics of the change-agent, the innovation, the client, the channel through which the message is communicated (person-to-person versus mass media), and the social system that adopts or rejects the innovation. A thorough study of these generalizations is useful for mental health professionals who serve as consultants, because they place the consultant's function in context. As our examples indicate, diffusion research demonstrates that mental health consultants have much in common with Peace Corps volunteers, agricultural extension agents, and salesmen. Consultation is not a new idea but a new variation on a very old idea. Understanding these related functions will stimulate consultants to use the principles illustrated in our examples: interventions that are compatible with the teacher's (or school's) cultural beliefs are the most widely adopted; the consultant will be most successful when thinking in terms of the teacher's (or school's) frame of reference rather than his own psychological frame of reference; and the consultant should focus his energies on the opinion leaders in the school. This sort of understanding will help consultants to avoid unnecessary mistakes, and it will prevent the wasted energy of reinventing the wheel.

Social-Psychological Principles of Attitude Change*

At some point in the consultation process, the consultant attempts to persuade the consultee that the consultant's knowledge and ideas are useful. Thus, consultation can be perceived, at least in part, as persuasion, and the extensive social-psychology literature on attitude change is relevant to this aspect of the consultation process. It is important for consultants to understand the types of persuasion that are most likely to bring positive results and the conditions under which these types of persuasion are most effective. Our purpose in the following discussion is to familiarize the

*This discussion is an abbreviated version of an article by Martin (1978).

consultant with some of this literature and to demonstrate the possible application of these ideas to consultation. We are aware that some of the ideas presented in this section may be controversial; consultants using an indirect orientation may interpret some of the concepts as either too directive or too manipulative. It is our opinion, however, that these ideas are both appropriate and important to the success of all consultants, regardless of how indirect their orientation may be. It should be the goal of future research to determine the ultimate applicability of these ideas.

Types of Power Not Available to Consultants. There are a number of classifications of social power, but one that has had a good deal of influence on psychological thought is the schema set forth by French and Raven (1959). These theorists identify five forms of social power: reward power, coercive power, legitimate power, expert power, and referent power. They postulate that all social change resulting from human intervention can be attributed to the operation of one or more of these forms of power. In French and Raven's conceptualization, power is the potential of one person to affect the attitudes, perceptions, or behavior of another. Influence is the result of the successful application of that power. We shall see that only the last two types of social power, expert and referent power, are relevant to consultation.

Reward and coercive power result when person A has control of resources that person B wants or needs. Person A has influence on person B when he provides or removes these resources contingent on changes in person B's behavior. Legitimate power accrues to person A when person B internalizes a norm, value, or role expectation that person A has the right to control his attitudes or behavior. In a democracy, for example, the populace has internalized the norm that persons elected to local, state, or national office have the right to control the behavior of the electorate through taxation, spending, creation of jobs, and so forth.

Reward, coercive, and legitimate power form the basis for line authority in our culture. For example, administrators and supervisors have these types of power in schools since they can control such factors as tenure, class assignments, and curriculum. In contrast, mental health professionals who serve as consultants do not have access to these forms of power. Rather than occupying line positions with superior administrative power, they occupy coordinate staff positions. Thus, their ability to produce change must be based on alternative processes.

Types of Power Used by Consultants. The remaining two types of power discussed by French and Raven (1959)—expert power and referent power—are available as a basis for consultant influence. Expert power results when person B attributes to person A knowledge or skill that person B feels he needs to meet his goals. Everyday experience indicates that this form of power is in operation whenever one person seeks help from another, for one seeks help from a person whom he perceives to have expertise in the area of his problem. Liberman (1965) has shown that nonprofessional neighborhood advisors are selected on the basis of expertise, and Goldstein, Heller, and Sechrest (1966) have provided extensive documentation that professional therapists are selected partly on this basis. It seems clear that consultants would be chosen largely because of their perceived knowledge or skill, although little empirical evidence supports the contention.

Since expert power is attributed to one person by another, it is important to discover under what conditions this occurs. The extensive literature on attitude change provides helpful clues in this regard. In reviewing this literature, McGuire (1969) shows that the older an individual is, the higher the level of his education, the greater the amount of his relevant experience, and, in general, the more indicators of social status the individual possesses, the more likely he is to be seen as an expert.

One of the major characteristics of expert power, according to French and Raven (1959), is that it is highly restricted in range; that is, expertise is usually attributed to any given individual in a small number of content areas. Further, these theorists hypothesize that whenever one attempts to exert any form of power outside the range attributed to him, this power is decreased. This characteristic of expert power is of particular importance to the consulting mental health professional because of the breadth of his training and the wide scope of problems he faces during a typical working day. Taken together, these factors make it likely that the consultant will be asked to provide advice in areas of only superficial expertise. If the consultant attempts to honor all such requests, there will be too many failures, and the consultant's overall influence will decrease.

If the French and Raven hypotheses are correct, they lead to two suggestions for increasing the consultation effectiveness of mental health professionals. First, the consultant should develop a small number of content areas of real expertise over and above the expertise developed in general training. This can be done through concentrated experience, self-instruction, supervision, or advanced education. Second, he must be more careful than has been traditional in the profession to limit consultation to those areas of real expertise. Third, consultation should be limited to those consultees who attribute relevant expertise to the consultant.

Although expertise is an important characteristic of a consultant, it is not sufficient by itself. In addition to developing such expertise, the consultant should develop referent power. The doctor who has a good "bedside manner," the neighbor who is easy to relate to, and the therapist who seems to understand his patients' problems have all developed referent power. Such persons are more sought after than those who do not have this characteristic, and they tend to be more effective (Goldstein, Heller, and Sechrest, 1966). The importance of rapport, or a feeling of oneness between consultant and consultee, has also been thoroughly discussed in the consultation literature (see Caplan, 1970; Dinkmeyer and Carlson, 1973).

The concept of referent power discussed by French and Raven (1959) provides a framework for understanding the manner in which this characteristic of a relationship produces change. Referent power accrues to person A when person B identifies with him. This identification is based on the perception by person B that person A manifests feelings, attitudes, and behaviors similar to his own, or that person A manifests feelings, attitudes, and behaviors that person B would like to possess.

The consultation literature has focused extensively on methods of building referent power, although this term has not been used. In fact, a criticism that might be leveled at much of this literature is its considerable focus on techniques consistent with referent power but virtually excluding consideration of expert power. A major tactic for accruing referent power is to get to know those whom one wishes to influence and to allow them to get to know you. In other words, the consultant tries to facilitate the consultee's identification with the consultant. This may involve spending time in teachers' lunch rooms, engaging in small talk at any opportunity, and helping with school projects unrelated to the mental health program. These informal settings facilitate the identification process, since the real attitudes and behaviors of the consultant and consultee may have more chance to be revealed. Also, these informal interchanges simply increase the number of opportunities for interaction between consultant and consultee, and this time alone can help facilitate the development of rapport as well as identification.

Relationship Between Expert and Referent Power. The most influential persons are those who have more than one source of power at their disposal. If expert and referent power were independent of one another, the goal of the consultant would simply be to foster identification and the attribution of expertise to the greatest extent possible. It appears that these forms of power, however, are not independent. Aronson, Willerman, and Floyd (1966) have demonstrated empirically that when a person is attributed a great deal of expertise, his overall attraction declines. They hypothesize that when a person is perceived to be highly expert, others find him so different from themselves that identification becomes difficult.

This line of reasoning indicates that consultants who are perceived as experts must balance this perception by accentuating areas of commonality between themselves and their consultees. This is particularly true for consultants who come from outside the organization of the consultee. Such consultants are often seen as highly expert, but they typically consult for periods so brief that the development of real identification is difficult. Caplan's (1970) emphasis on onedownsmanship and communicating to the consultee that the consultation relationship is coordinate reflects his understanding of the need for the external consultant to emphasize identification-building activities.

Meyers (1973a) was once involved in a consultation program that seemed consistent with this idea. In this instance, highly trained psychologists with either a doctorate or at least sixty credits of graduate work provided consultation to an alternative public school program. The program was designed for ghetto youths who were not succeeding in junior and senior high schools for a variety of interpersonal reasons. The teaching staff, though highly competent, did not have traditional teacher certification, and many had never completed college. Moreover, the staff was mostly black and dressed informally. When highly trained, white consultants entered this school with their jackets and ties and made highly intellectual recommendations, they were doomed to failure. Instead, each successful consultant had to take steps to decrease his image as a professional expert while increasing his identification with the staff. The consultants fostered identification in several ways. Some consultants attempted to dress more like the school staff, leaving their jackets and ties at home; others tried to involve themselves in a variety of nonacademic activities such as helping to move furniture; and in other instances the consultants involved themselves in the day-to-day teaching process.

The consultant who has accrued a good deal of referent power, however, may have to accentuate areas of expertise to maximize his influence. This situation occurs most often for consultants who work in the same organization as the consultee and who have frequent contact with the consultee. Many mental health professionals find themselves in this position, and it may be necessary for them to engage in expertise-building activities to maximize their influence. Such activities could include attending workshops, pursuing a higher degree, or reporting to the school faculty on mental health projects in other districts.

We have discussed several generalizations derived from the concepts of expert and referent power that have practical implications for mental health professionals who engage in consultation. These generalizations now need to be evaluated.

1. High-status consultants will be more successful than lower-status consultants, where status is measured in years of experience, years of education, consultation fee or general income, association with prestigious organizations, and so forth.

2. Younger consultants will seldom be as effective with older consultees as they will be with consultees of similar age and professional experience. (Referent power will be more easily accrued in a relationship with a younger consultee than in a relationship with an older consultee.)
3. External consultants and other consultants who have little contact with their consultees will rely more on expert power as a means of influence than referent power. (Referent power takes time to build.)
4. Internal consultants and consultants who have frequent informal and formal contacts with their consultees will rely more on referent power than expert power as a means of influence. (Very high ranges of expertise are seldom attributed to persons with whom one has frequent contact. Also, referent power has a wider range than expert power.)
5. Successful consultants will have a better balance between expert and referent power than less-successful consultants.
6. Long-term consultation will be more successful than short-term consultation. (Because of the wide range of reference power, the long-term consultant can influence a greater variety of consultee attitudes and behaviors than the short-term consultant. Also, if identification and expertise can be maintained, there is a linear relationship between exposure to new ideas, attitudes, and behaviors and change in these activities [Zajonc, 1968]).

Transactional Analysis and the
Consultation Process

Regardless of content or technique, consultation requires interaction and communication between a consultant and consultee. One of the basic tools of consultation is the interview technique (Newman and others, 1971). Consequently, models that focus on interaction, communication, and interviewing should facilitate the consultation process. Transactional Analysis (TA) is one such model.

Transactional Analysis is both a technique of psychotherapy and an original personality theory. TA began in 1954 with the writings of Eric Berne. His early thoughts on the topic were presented in a series of articles on intuition published in the *Psychiatric*

Quarterly between 1949 and 1962. It is not our intention to cover in detail this complex theory but to note its essential points and potential use for analyzing the consultation process.*

Berne (1964) noted that when two or more people meet, eventually one will speak or in some way acknowledge the second. The basic unit of such social intercourse he termed a *transaction*, which includes a transactional stimulus (behavior, verbal or otherwise, exhibited by an individual hoping to elicit a response) and a transactional response (the behavior of the individual who is reacting to a transactional stimulus). Berne indicated that the analysis of these transactions requires identification of the ego states of the speakers. Berne felt that each individual had three ego states, which he termed the *Parent* (P), the *Child* (C), and the *Adult* (A), and he suggested that each ego state was especially suited for specific situations. For example, the Child ego state is described as a source of intuition, creativity, and spontaneous drive and enjoyment. Although this state tends to be fleeting in adults due to social mores, it is apparent in such situations as sporting events, parties, and church revivals, where norms are not as restrictive. The Adult ego state is essentially a computer, which processes data and computes the probabilities that are essential for the proper observation and prediction of reality. Finally, the Parent ego state is made up essentially of behavior copied from parents or authority figures.

TA is concerned with identifying the ego state of the speaker who provides the transactional stimulus and identifying the ego state of the speaker who provides the transactional response. In other words, if person A speaks to person B, the first goal is to identify the ego state of person A (Adult, Parent, or Child). The second step is to identify the ego state of person B when he responds. Two related factors should be noted. First, the Adult ego state will be necessary when the person is attempting to cope with reality in a rational fashion. Second, transactional responses typically should be in the same ego state as the transactional stimulus to facilitate communication. In other words, if person A speaks in the Adult ego state, the response of person B should be in the Adult

*For more detailed consideration of Transactional Analysis, the reader is referred to Berne, 1964, Dusay and Steiner, 1972, and Jongeward and James, 1973.

ego state. These are referred to as *parallel transactions*. By analyzing transactions in this manner, people should be able to gain control of their behavior and thus use the ego state that is most facilitative to the progress of the social exchange.

Applying Transactional Analysis. TA has been used to assess the consultation process (Parsons and Meyers, 1978). First, it was postulated that communication during consultation would proceed smoothly as long as transactions were parallel. Specifically, it was predicted that successful consultative interactions would be characterized by a greater number of parallel transactions than unsuccessful consultative interactions. Second, since consultation is generally a reality-based, problem-solving situation involving the use of data and predictions about reality, it was predicted that successful consultation would be characterized by more Adult-Adult transactions than consultation judged as less successful.

An investigation was conducted with five consultation pairs who met once a week for seven weeks, and each of these seven sessions was tape recorded. At the conclusion of each consultation session, both the consultant and the consultee filled out a form providing their subjective evaluation of that week's consultation session. At the end of each session, data were collected representing the degree to which goal attainment had been achieved. Both the subjective evaluation scores and the degree of goal attainment were employed as criterion measures against which to assess the two predictions derived from TA theory.

Each consultation relationship investigated proved successful as noted by both phenomenal and behavioral measures of outcome. Using a scale of 1 (low in perceived success) to 4 (perceived as highly successful), the consultants and consultees consistently rated each session as highly successful ($\overline{X} = 3.5, sd = .35$). This perceived success is supported by the fact that as a group the consultees were very successful in obtaining their behavioral goals, with four of the five consultees attaining at least 80 percent ($\overline{X} = 89$ percent, $sd = 28.6$ percent) of their pre-set behavioral goals. Furthermore, the interactions between the consultants and consultees were highly parallel and Adult-Adult in nature. Of the 1,382 transactions sampled, 989 (72 percent) were parallel, and of these, 857 (87 percent) were Adult-Adult.

In an attempt to determine whether parallel transactions discriminated successful from relatively unsuccessful consultation relationships, the consultants were rank-ordered in terms of each outcome measure. Table 1 shows that, for the subjective evaluation score, the successful consultants (top two in rank ordering) had a considerably higher number of parallel transactions ($\overline{X} = 32$) than did the two least successful consultants ($\overline{X} = 23$). Similarly, Table 1 shows that, for the percent of goal attainment, the two most successful consultants had a considerably higher number of parallel transactions ($\overline{X} = 33.5$) than did the two least successful consultants ($\overline{X} = 25.5$). A similar rank-ordering/mean comparison technique was used to test whether successful consultants' interactions differed from unsuccessful consultants' interactions in the degree to which Adult-Adult transactions occurred. Table 1 reveals that, when the subjective evaluation scores were used as the criteria of success, the successful consultants had a higher number of Adult-Adult transactions ($\overline{X} = 28$) than did the least successful consultants ($\overline{X} = 19$). However, Table 1 shows that, when the criterion of success was the percent of goal attainment, the two most successful consultants had only a slightly higher number of Adult-Adult transactions ($\overline{X} = 28$) than did the least successful pair ($\overline{X} = 24$).

Although the data suggest a relationship between the TA process variables and the consultation outcome in the predicted

Table 1. Measures of Transactions Between Most and Least Successful Consultation Pairs

| | *Measures of Success* | | | |
| | Average Subjective Evaluation Score | | Average Percent of Goal Attainment | |
Transactions	*Most Successful* n = 2	*Least Successful* n = 2	*Most Successful* n = 2	*Least Successful* n = 2
	$\overline{X}$ SD	$\overline{X}$ SD	$\overline{X}$ SD	$\overline{X}$ SD
Total	41.1 1.2	30.6 0.4	48.0 5.9	31.0 12.0
Parallel	32.0 4.2	23.0 9.7	33.5 5.7	25.5 18.4
Adult-Adult	28.0 4.9	19.0 6.1	28.0 5.8	24.0 12.0

direction, the small number of subjects and the descriptive nature of this aspect of the study indicate the need for cautious interpretation.

Derivatives of Rogerian Counseling

Carl Rogers has had a significant impact on applied psychology in general and counseling psychology in particular. It is beyond the scope of this chapter to attempt to summarize this work, and the interested reader is referred to several sources (Rogers, 1951, 1957, 1959, 1961, 1967). However, of particular relevance to the consultation process was Rogers' (1957) suggestion that certain core conditions were necessary as a prerequisite to successful counseling. These conditions include genuineness, nonpossessive warmth, and accurate empathy on the part of the counselor.

Robert Carkhuff and his associates (Carkhuff, 1969a,b; Carkhuff and Berenson, 1967; Truax and Carkhuff, 1964) have attempted to extend Rogers' work by developing operational definitions of the core conditions, developing scales to assess these conditions, and conceptualizing a developmental theory for the process of helping. Carkhuff's ideas expanded upon Rogers' core facilitating conditions, and he has demonstrated (1969a,b) that the helper skills necessary for communicating these variables can be successfully trained. Also, some research has demonstrated that these variables can have a significant effect on outcomes. Carkhuff's work has been criticized (see, for example, *The Counseling Psychologist*, 1972, *3*, 31–79). However, there is sufficient evidence to suggest an investigation of the relationship between these variables and the outcome of consultation. Therefore, we will define three of these core conditions.

Genuineness is characteristic of a direct personal encounter in which the consultant is free to be himself. Also, the consultant acts in an integrated and authentic fashion so that his feelings are denoted clearly by both his verbal and nonverbal responses. In other words, the consultant's words must be congruent with his inner experience. Therefore, a genuine response would not include the denial of feelings, although there may well be instances when the consultant chooses freely not to express feelings in the relationship. Genuineness is particularly difficult to maintain in school consultation, because the consultant must act without defensiveness and without retreating into the facade of his professional role. Expectations regarding the roles of various professional personnel are defined rigidly in school, and they can inhibit genuine responses.

Nonpossessive warmth includes the consultant's ability to accept the consultee's experience without imposing conditions on this acceptance. The consultant should care for the consultee as another professional with human potential, and he should be willing to share the professional joys and aspirations as well as the depressions and failures of the consultee. Nonpossessive warmth involves valuing and prizing the consultee as a person without evaluating him or imposing conditions on his behavior. However, it should be clear that this characteristic does not imply that the consultant must approve of or like everything that the consultee does. On the contrary, nonpossessive warmth suggests that, regardless of the consultant's reactions to the consultee's behavior, the consultant still maintains basic respect and accepts the consultee as a person. Warmth is nonpossessive because the consultant's respect is extended regardless of the consultee's behavior.

Accurate empathy involves the consultant's ability to sense the consultee's private world as if it were the consultant's own world. Of course, unlike therapy, in consultation the term *private world* is limited to the consultee's perceptions and experiences of the teaching situation. Further, accurate empathy suggests that the consultant knows what the consultee means and has an appreciation and sensitivity to the consultee's current feelings. In fact, it implies the consultant's deep understanding of feelings and perceptions only partially revealed by the consultee. A key element of this concept is the consultant's ability to communicate this understanding to the consultee.

Carkhuff (1969a,b) has developed a scale to assess the degree to which any interpersonal process variable such as genuineness or accurate empathy is used. It is a 5-point scale, in which a level 3 response indicates the minimally facilitative level of interpersonal functioning with the process variable being assessed. A 1 represents the lowest level of interpersonal functioning, and a 5 represents the highest level of interpersonal functioning. Similarly, a 4 represents a positive facilitative response falling midway between a 3 and a 5, and a 2 represents a less than facilitative response falling between a 1 and a 3. This scale is highly subjective in nature and depends on the interpretation of the coder. This point has been acknowledged elsewhere (Carkhuff and Berenson, 1967), and as a result it is necessary that coders be well trained and that great care be taken to obtain adequate reliability.

The following list shows how this scale could be used to assess consultation types in terms of the genuineness of a consultant.

- *Level I:* The consultant's verbal expressions are clearly unrelated to other cues indicating his feelings, *or* the only genuine responses are highly negative toward the consultee and destructive in nature.
- *Level II:* The consultant's verbalizations are slightly unrelated to other cues suggesting his feelings, *or* the only genuine responses are negative toward the consultee, and these negative reactions are not used constructively as a basis for further inquiry.
- *Level III:* The consultant's verbalizations are not discrepant from any other cues indicating the consultant's feelings, *and* the consultant provides no overt cues to suggest a genuine response.
- *Level IV:* The consultant's verbalizations are congruent with other overt cues indicating the consultant's feelings, *and* these genuine responses are used in a nondestructive manner.
- *Level V:* The consultant is completely spontaneous and open to his feelings during the consultation interaction, *and* these responses are used constructively to encourage additional areas of inquiry.

Carkhuff (1969a, 1969b) and Gazda and others (1973) should be consulted by those interested in a more detailed presentation of how this scale can be applied to a variety of process variables.

A problem occurs when this type of scale is used to code every interaction with a score from 1 to 5. Consider, for example, an attempt to apply this scale to assess the level of accurate empathy of a particular consultant. Even though empathy is being coded, there will be some instances when the most appropriate consultant response would be either to provide direct information or to confront the consultee rather than to empathize with the consultee. If the empathy scale were used alone, such highly appropriate responses might be scored as 1, and the resulting impression might be that the consultant was not facilitating the interaction. To account for this when coding for variables such as empathy, we have found it useful to include a sixth category, which we label NR, to indicate those interactions where the consultant's response is *not relevant* to the variable being coded. Sometimes this eliminates some 1 scores and presents a more realistic picture of the consultant's functioning.

To assess accurate empathy in consultation, an additional modification should be made to the coding procedures by distinguishing clearly between the consultant's understanding of the *feelings* and *content* of the consultee. This distinction is relevant to school consultation, where frequently it will be facilitative for the consultant to communicate an understanding of the content of the consultee's statements. In fact, during consultation there may be instances where it would be unnecessary or even destructive for the consultant to communicate an understanding of the consultee's feelings. For this reason, we feel that research and training on empathy in consultation should use scales such as the *accurate reflection of feelings* scale developed by Ivey (1971), since this scale focuses separately on the consultant's understanding of the content and the feelings of the consultee.

Developmental Aspects of Consultation. A modification of the Rogerian model stresses stages of the counseling process. This model has been elaborated recently by Gerard Egan (1975), and it is relevant to consultation. The first stage of the developmental model is directed toward facilitating self-exploration on the part of the consultee. The process skills used by the consultant at this stage would include genuineness, nonpossessive warmth, and accurate empathy. The second stage is directed toward facilitating an integrative understanding of the problem by the consultee. Among the important process skills at this stage are advanced accurate empathy (that is, the consultant communicates an understanding of what the consultee implies in addition to what he says) and confrontation.

Confrontation is stressed primarily in the work that followed Rogers (see Carkhuff and Berenson, 1967). It appears to be one of the key variables in effective helping. Role expectations may, however, decrease the probability that school consultants will use this technique. Nevertheless, it is essential that school consultants become aware of the potential impact of confrontation as well as developing familiarity with the variety of confrontation techniques that are available. Confrontation will often consist of the consultant challenging the discrepancies and distortions in what the consultee says or does, but appropriate confrontation is not meant to be a punitive attack on the consultee. Instead, it should be an extension of advanced accurate empathy where, in addition to understanding the consultee at a deep level, the consultant uncovers some of the contradictions or distortions of the consultee's attitudes.

The third stage of the developmental model is directed toward facilitating action on the part of the consultee. At this stage, in addition to using some of the process skills noted previously in this section, the consultant would need to be able to collaborate with the consultee in setting up detailed action programs. These might include a behavior management program, developing plans for group discussions of important emotional issues, or implementing various group process techniques. This stage of helping is crucial for the effective school consultant.

Although the developmental model has intuitive appeal as an orientation with relevance for consultation, few relevant data are available to document this position. However, the successful research from other helping relationships (see Egan, 1975 for a summary) suggests the potential applicability of this model to consultation. Of course, the model is not likely to apply in its totality to all consultation relationships. For example, although the rapport-building techniques used at the first stage should generally be applicable, there will be certain consultation relationships where quick action is important and advanced empathy or confrontation would not be used. Consequently, the model is presented as a framework for understanding the consultation process in general rather than as a procedure to be followed in all instances.

Summary

In this chapter we have presented four different models to conceptualize the consultation process: diffusion research, social psychological principles of attitude change, transactional analysis, and a process model derived from Rogerian counseling. Each of these models is designed to increase the probability that intervention strategies will be implemented by the consultee. Since each model is a substantive topic in itself, we have not attempted to present them comprehensively. Instead, we have pointed out some of the ways that each could be applied to the consultation process, and we have suggested areas for further research.

The ideas presented from diffusion research have pragmatic implications; they increase the probability that interventions will be implemented and that resulting changes will be long-lasting. For example, concentrating on opinion leaders in the school will facilitate action by the consultee by helping to establish support systems that increase the likelihood that consultation effects will be enduring. Although some of these ideas have probably been used previously by consultants, we feel diffusion research represents a particular contribution because it has not been considered systematically as a framework for determining how to consult in schools.

The principles generated from the social psychology approach to attitude change provide a readily understood model for consultation process. Expert power and referent power are two types of power that the consultant can use to influence the consultee; they must be used with appropriate balance. While the consultant must be perceived as having expertise that the teacher does not have, the teacher must also see similarities with the consultant. For appropriate balance, the consultant must analyze his or her perceived power. In those cases where a high degree of expert power is attributed (for example, with a consultant who is external to the system), the consultant will need to establish increased referent power. When the consultant is not attributed much expert power (for example, with an internal consultant), he will need to increase his expert power.

Transactional analysis aims to facilitate verbal interaction between consultant and consultee with parallel, adult-adult transactions. Adult transactions should predominate because consultation is a work-focused problem-solving relationship that relies on rational processes. Parallel transactions should be the consultant's goal since responding in the same ego state (Adult, Child, or Parent) as that used by the consultee should maintain productive communication.

The process model derived from Rogerian counseling was presented as an alternative approach to increasing communication between consultant and consultee. This model suggests that three basic consultant attitudes—genuineness, nonpossessive warmth, and empathy—will help to develop the consultant/consultee relationship. By learning specific skills, which have been defined operationally, the consultant can communicate these attitudes to consultees. Implementing these skills early during consultation increases the probability that confrontation will be successful later.

All of these models conceptualize techniques that facilitate relationship building, but there are differences among them also. For example, some emphasize social-psychological factors and the culture of the school, while others stress the interpersonal process. Although these models were presented separately, with no effort to integrate them, such integration should be a goal of future research and theory development.

CHAPTER FOUR

Stages of Consultation

□ □ □ □ □ □ □ □ □ □ □

As we noted in our discussion of the developmental model in Chapter Three, the process of school consultation can be conceptualized in terms of stages. These stages include: (1) entry into the system, (2) orientation to consultation, (3) problem identification, (4) problem definition, (5) developing an intervention plan, (6) assessing the impact of consultation, and (7) concluding the relationship. Although these stages are defined discretely, they do not necessarily occur separately in practice, nor do they necessarily occur in an invariant order. Instead, a consultant may often operate at more than one stage simultaneously, and the consultation process may progress back and forth through these stages in a cyclical fashion.

Entry into the System

The process of entering the system involves two types of acceptance. First is the formal step of negotiating a consultation contract with the organization, which signals official sanctioning for this model of service delivery. The second type of entry involves obtaining acceptance by the caretaker (for example, a teacher). Although this second type of entry is less formal than the first, it is equally important. We will discuss each of these types in some detail.

The first step in establishing a school consultation program is to negotiate a contract with the relevant administrators. This could be a formal contractual negotiation associated with obtaining employment or a less formal negotiation establishing the mental health worker's role.

When negotiating with administrators, it is usually necessary to obtain sanction for the consultation role from the highest-level administrators. This will ensure that the proposed program or role has support from the top, and it will help to prevent resistance to a consultant's functioning from administrators. Of course, when openly obtaining such administrative sanction, the consultant runs the risk of alienating some teachers, who might view the consultant as being too closely aligned with the administration. This close alignment would be feared if teachers felt that the consultant would pass information about them to administrators, or if teachers felt that consultation would be forced upon them by administrators. To minimize this issue, the consultant can emphasize to all concerned that the consultation relationship is confidential, and that consultation is offered only to those who seek it. Further, when establishing a contract, the consultant should be sure that his role is clearly defined. Any resistance to the role-definition should be discussed directly. In particular, the consultant should often be leery of an easy and unquestioning acceptance of the proposed role. The following example underscores this point.

During one semester, when Meyers was simultaneously negotiating two different consultation programs, he first prepared a rationale and description of consultation as an approach to school psychological services. This included the following statement:

> Traditionally psychologists work by diagnosing an individual child in their office. Regardless of the adequacy or thoroughness of the diagnostic workup, the psychologist usually writes

a diagnostic report with recommendations which have no real meaning for the classroom. Even on those few occasions when the recommendations are potentially useful, the teacher is unlikely to implement them because of the lack of personal contact with the psychologist. Consequently, to develop remediation ideas which have practical utility for the classroom teacher it is essential that the psychologist leave his office and spend time in classrooms. In addition, to maximize the probability that the teacher will implement recommendations resulting from the diagnostic work it is essential to have both formal and informal contacts between teachers and the psychologist. Traditionally there is a long waiting list for psycho-diagnostic evaluations. One reason for this is that frequently a referral for testing is the only formal way in which a teacher can request a psychologist's help. Often when the psychologist can be available to talk to the teachers about issues relating to child management in the classroom, there is less need for diagnostic testing and thus waiting lists for such testing can decrease. In summary, a consultation-based approach to the delivery of psychological services in the schools can result in more efficient services with a more meaningful impact on the lives of our students.

In the first school district, a meeting was held with the assistant superintendent, as he appeared to be the individual who wielded power in this district. A modification of the statement was presented verbally, followed by an invitation for the assistant superintendent to present any reactions or questions he might have. He replied by stating that it sounded like an interesting program, and that certainly his district wanted any programs that could help the children and improve the functioning of the staff. The meeting was concluded with polite smiles and friendly handshakes, and the program was scheduled to begin the following week. Things seemed to be off to an excellent beginning.

The meeting in the second school district was entirely different. This meeting was with an imposing group, which included the superintendent, an assistant superintendent, the principal, a local school psychologist, and a counselor. The meeting lasted for an hour and a half, during which the consultant was questioned about the specifics of the plan. The assembled group wanted to know the precise steps for implementing the program, and they expressed many reservations about the utility of this approach in their school district. This experience was emotionally draining, and it did not appear that a productive relationship would develop.

In light of the two initial meetings, the year spent in these two districts proved to be instructive. Despite the initial reservations, the program ran very well in the second school district. Whenever problems or questions arose, the administration quickly confronted the consultants, and this provided an opportunity to work out differences so that the program could continue to function successfully. There was always an option for either the district or the consultant to renegotiate the contract, and the administration felt actively involved in the development of this program. As a result, the administration consistently provided support for the program's continued success and development.

In contrast, there were continual problems in the first district, despite the apparently positive beginning. There was no real support for the program from any administrator, including the superintendent and the principals. Although the program apparently had been supported enthusiastically in the beginning, the negotiation process was not carried out in sufficient detail to allow potential problems and objections to surface. During the initial meeting, no precedent was set for the open airing of differences, and it was not made clear that renegotiation of the contract could be initiated at any time during the program. Consequently, no effective effort was ever made to solve the problems that occurred.

Besides negotiating with relevant administrators, it is crucial during the first stage to determine the perceived needs of the school or school system and to use an understanding of these needs to develop an initial consultation contract. For example, a school system may feel a strong need for individual psychological services, such as individual counseling or individual diagnostic testing. When this is the case, it may be unrealistic to offer a consultation program emphasizing direct service to the teacher or direct service to the organization. In these instances, it will be preferable to establish a contract that is designed to meet the system's needs and is also acceptable to the consultant.

A third important point for the consultant to consider when negotiating the initial contract is to present clearly a rationale for the consultation approach. In this way, the consultant makes his or her frame of reference explicit, which places its focus on developing an indirect service delivery model. Thus, even when the contract negotiated calls for a strong focus on direct service to the student, it should be clear from the beginning that the consultant's long-range goal is to work preventively by providing indirect service to the child, direct service to the teacher, and direct service to the organization, where appropriate.

Finally, as underscored in Meyers' example, the consultant must establish open communication and encourage discussion of any reservations or objections from the beginning. This point is felt to be so important that, even when no reservations or concerns are raised, the consultant should raise typical concerns to be sure there are no problems. It is important in such negotiations to keep open the possibility of either the administration or the consultant renegotiating the contract. This makes it clear that the consultant welcomes feedback from the administrators, while also leaving the consultant a clear option to suggest change.

In addition to observing these four principles, the consultant can make several pragmatic suggestions during negotiation, which will often facilitate the consultant's entry into the system. First, it may help to set up group case conferences on a regular basis. These conferences could be attended by all personnel who work with a referred child, and the conference could focus on that particular child. Secondly, holding periodic inservice sessions for the entire school can be recommended. A third technique, which we have found to facilitate both the initial contracting as well as the acceptance of the consultation program by the staff, is to set up a fixed period of time each week for group consultation sessions. These would differ from the previous two conferences, in that the consultant would meet each week with the same group of teachers to discuss some predetermined topic or problem, or the conference could be open to discuss whatever is brought up by the group members. Fourth, a fixed period of time for individual teacher consultation can be established. In fact, this time could be set aside to discuss anything a teacher wants, with the added understanding that these discussions will not result in individual counseling or testing. When time is clearly allotted for this sort of indirect service, and when teachers know it is clearly available, the consultant's commitment to this approach becomes evident, and teachers are more likely to use the consultant's help. One final idea that we have found useful is to structure time for follow-up with teachers on individual cases where recommendations have been made previously by the consulting mental health professional. This should be routinely scheduled in a formal way as a part of the individual diagnostic case work or counseling that is done.

Entry with the Teachers: Orientation to Consultation

Just as it is important to establish a contract with the administration before implementing a consultation program, it is equally important to gain entry at the level of the teacher. The teacher needs to know what to expect from the consultant and the consultation relationship; thus, the initial negotiation should delineate the parameters of the consultive intervention. Further, as was the case when negotiating with the administration, there should be a clear understanding that both the teacher and the consultant are free to consider renegotiating the focus or method of service delivery established by this informal contract at any time.

In negotiating an informal contract with the teacher, one of the first steps should include a review of the process of consultation. From the onset, the consultant should make it clear that he will focus his attention on the teacher rather than the child. Even in instances where the child has direct contact with the consultant or is observed in the classroom, the focus of consultation will be on what the teacher can do to remediate the problem rather than on what others outside the classroom can do. It should be underscored that the relationship is confidential, and that no one in the school (including the principal) will be informed by the consultant of what occurs during consultation. The only time the consultant will share information with other school personnel will be when the teacher has given consent. By emphasizing the confidentiality of the relationship, the consultant can help to reduce any anxiety the teacher might feel about the consultant's alignment with the administration or others in the school.

The consultant should stress at the beginning of consultation that the teacher should feel free to contribute ideas and suggestions. In fact, this is the teacher's responsibility. For example, the teacher can be informed that recommendations developed in consultation are most likely to be implemented successfully when the teacher is actively involved in establishing these recommendations. Furthermore, the teacher should be encouraged to feel free to reject any suggestion that might be made by the consultant or to modify any suggestion so that it is more consistent with the teacher's style, schedule, personal characteristics, or the characteristics of the children the teacher is responsible for. Also, the teacher should be informed that sometimes just talking things over is enough to help him to develop his own strategy. This effect occurs frequently during consultation.

In one example, a teacher and her aide requested an interview with a consultant because one of the students (a boy who was reaching adolescence) was being overly flirtatious and physically affectionate toward the female aide. As the teacher and aide described the problem, they indicated that they were afraid to hurt the youngster, but they felt that something had to be done to control this behavior. As they discussed the problem, they decided to simply tell him directly when his behavior was off limits or when his verbalized fantasies about the aide were clearly untrue (for example, he could not marry her). After the conference, the teacher and aide felt much relief and were able to respond to this youngster more effectively for the remainder of the school year. It is significiant that they developed the intervention plans with practically no input from the consultant. In this instance, the consultant showed that he valued the teachers' independence as professionals, and that his primary goal was to support the teacher and aide in reaching their own solutions. This process helped to increase the probability that similar problems could be handled in the future without the help of a consultant.

Following an explanation and description of consultation, the consultant should attempt to verify that the description is consistent with the teacher's expectations. If there is any hint that the teacher may not have understood the process originally, the consultant should communicate that there is no obligation to continue the consultive relationship. Moreover, even if there is no hint of misunderstanding, it may often be a good idea for the consultant to state explicitly that there is no obligation for the consultee to continue if he has doubts about the consultation process providing the necessary help.

Facilitating Entry: Crisis Intervention. Entering the system is not complete after a contract is negotiated with the administration or even after the teachers have been oriented toward the consultation model. After these hurdles are passed, the consultant may still find that initially the consultees are slow to use his services. One means of entering the system is for the consultant to intervene in a crisis. The assumption is that the consultant makes an effort to act while the crisis is occurring rather than responding after the crisis has passed. This principle serves as a theoretical basis for the entire consultation approach, since the consultee may be most receptive to help when defenses are in disequilibrium.

The importance of intervening during a crisis to facilitate the consultant's entry into a system was described in some of Sarason's early work (Sarason and others, 1966). This example is so typical that it will be described here only briefly. Sarason described a consultant-trainee who had been previously exposed to more traditional psychological techniques and initially was more comfortable cloistered in an office than in the school facing the real educational problems of teachers and students. The consultant's entry into the system was not yet established. On one occasion, the consultant was walking through the halls and heard a student screaming. The consultant stood in the hall looking into the classroom and saw a child having a severe temper tantrum, while the principal and teacher were both unable to intervene effectively. As a consultant-trainee, the first impulse in this situation might be to run quickly and quietly back to the safety of an office. Another frequent response might be to stand in the hall debating with oneself about the merits of intervening. For example, the consultant might be afraid that his success in this situation might be perceived as a put-down by the teacher and principal, or the consultant might be afraid of showing inadequacy by failing to calm down the youngster. If this debating process were to occur, the consultant might choose not to intervene, or the consultant might take so long to decide that the crisis could end before a decision was made. Fortunately, in this situation, the consultant did decide to act, even though he had no idea what the correct approach was. The consultant simply entered the room, grabbed the child, physically removed the youngster from the room to reduce the disruption, and held the child until he calmed down. Although this intervention did not help reduce the general disruptive influence posed by this student, it did show that the consultant was human and willing to join in working with the real problems of the classroom. This action said much more to the teachers in this school than hours of words about the advantages of a consultive approach. Soon after this event, the consultant's position in the school began to change. More teachers began to seek help, and for the first time, the consultant became a real part of the school.

The authors have all experienced instances where intervention in a crisis facilitated their entry as consultants into the school. One of these examples should help to clarify this point.

In one of Parsons' earliest experiences as a school consultant, he was serving as a school psychology intern. He was assigned to work with a federally funded agency serving the psychoeducational needs of the private schools in the metropolitan Philadelphia area. Parsons had been experiencing a great deal of difficulty entering the system of the schools to which he was assigned, and he found that much of the resistance he faced stemmed from the administration and staff's perspective of the previous psychologist. The school personnel perceived the psychologist-counselor in the school as someone who saw children in his office but rarely got involved in the school. Further, these professionals were not perceived as being of any real service to the teachers. His experience during the first two weeks was uneventful (in fact, quite dull) with the majority of the referrals during this period being requests to use the school psychologist's office as a time-out room.

The internship was designed so that the consultant was to spend two and one-half days at school A and two and one-half days at school B. Of the two schools, B had been the most vociferous in questioning the utility of psychological services. During one of the days he was assigned to work in school A, he received a phone call from the principal of school B. Her voice was trembling and filled with much anxiety. She stated that two brothers (one in seventh grade and one in eighth grade) had been fighting in the schoolyard; they had both drawn knives and had attempted to "kill each other." The principal said that the teachers had been able to talk the boys into giving up their knives and had separated them. She felt, however, that unless something was done to diffuse their anger, the two would continue the fight after school, and she feared the potential consequences. Parsons stated that he would come over immediately and spend the remainder of the day with the two boys. Upon his arrival, he found both boys sitting in the principal's office spitting, screaming, and cursing each other, and apparently in no mood to be counseled. Confronted with this situation, and seeing the frazzled look on the principal's face, Parsons took both boys by the collar to the storage room, which was located directly across from the principal's office. He told the youths that they appeared really angry. He suggested that they fight it out and stop all the ridiculous name-calling. He said that knives and chains were used by people who felt they needed special help and unfair advantage. This last statement stimulated each boy to boast of his fighting abilities, and each said that he would need no special help against the other. Parsons produced two sets of boxing gloves (which were in the storage room) and suggested that he would referee while the two fought it out. The only rule would be that once they started, he would not allow them to stop until there was a winner.

At this suggestion, both boys started to calm down and began offering face-saving excuses as to why this was not a very good idea. They said that the principal would expel them, or "he may drip his blood on my good shirt," and so on. From the excuses, Parsons was able to suggest that perhaps a better way of defining who was best could be established. After some debate, it was (calmly) agreed that the boys would play a one-on-one game of basketball with the goal being twenty-one points; Parsons would referee. The result was that both played a good game and enjoyed it, complimented each other on the fine shots, and decided (before either reached twenty-one points) that it would be more fun to play against Parsons. Following this two-on-one game, the boys returned to their classrooms without further incident.

The immediacy of Parsons' response, along with its unusual

nature and its apparent success, became the key to his admission into the school. The following day, which was a day scheduled for school B, teachers and students were talking about the incident. The result was that Parsons received numerous requests from students for similar competition (an excellent opportunity for contact with the troubled students in the school) and from teachers for assistance in their classrooms.

Problem Identification

Once the initial entry into the system has been completed and staff acceptance begins to manifest itself by way of referrals, the consultant enters the next stage of consultation, problem identification. Following the reception of a referral or a request for assistance, the consultant's first task is to make sure that the teacher understands the consultive process and wants to proceed. Once this issue is settled, the consultant proceeds with the first interview. This session generally is devoted to gathering information. The consultant should be careful to avoid giving a diagnosis or specific suggestions during this first meeting, regardless of how obvious the case may appear, and regardless of the teacher's pressure for a solution. One reason is that a quick response could make the teacher feel foolish. If the solution is so obvious to the consultant, then the teacher might feel that it should have been obvious to him, also. Another reason to avoid making diagnoses or giving suggestions during this first session is that waiting gives the consultant and consultee a chance to reflect on what has occurred. The teacher has the opportunity to think about the first meeting and to develop greater acceptance of the recommendations that will evolve from consultation. By gathering data rather than providing quick answers, the consultant helps to maintain some of the consultee's anxiety, which should promote productive change by the consultee. As the Yerkes-Dodson Law (performance is related to anxiety in a curvilinear fashion) and Caplan's writings state, change is most likely to occur when an optimal level of anxiety is maintained (not too high and not too low).

By gathering additional data early in consultation, the consultant has an opportunity to determine all factors that may relate to the teacher's problem. The additional information may suggest a need to focus consultation efforts at a different level from what was initially intended. For example, additional information may make it clear that the most appropriate consultation approach is direct service to the teacher rather than direct service to the child.

An example of this occurred when a teacher asked for help in controlling the behavior of a youngster who was disobedient, acted out, and was the class clown. If the consultant had asked no additional questions, the teacher might have been told to reinforce appropriate incompatible behaviors, such as paying attention and following directions, and ignore the negative behaviors. This probably would have resulted in a reduction of the child's negative behaviors. However, this approach would have missed important issues relating to the teacher's overly strong need for control and her negative way of responding to the class as a whole. By spending some time discussing issues that were not limited to the referred child, the consultant developed a basis for talking productively to the teacher about her generally negative style of interaction with students.

Actually, the process of problem identification is partly how the teacher learns what consultation is really like, and it is important for establishing a relationship with the teacher. Consequently, although the relationship skills discussed in Chapter Three are always important, they are particularly important during this stage of consultation. Thus, the consultant should emphasize such interpersonal skills as open invitation to talk, accurate reflection of feelings, empathy, and genuineness. Using these skills will markedly enhance the process of entering the relationship with the teacher and will lead to the most adequate identification and definition of the problem.

One of the major tasks of the consultant during problem identification is to determine which of four levels of consultation is most appropriate in conceptualizing the problem. The specific consultation techniques will vary significantly, depending upon whether the consultant chooses to respond with direct service to the child (Level I), indirect service to the child (Level II), direct service to the teacher (Level III), or direct service to the organization (Level IV). These levels will be discussed in greater detail in the following chapters. Of course, in practice the consultant may work at more than one of these levels simultaneously. Nevertheless, a decision as to the appropriate level of consultation will help in focusing the consultant's efforts.

An example can help to illustrate this point. In one case, a teacher requested help in controlling two disruptive students in the classroom (Meyers, 1975a). The consultant offered some behavior modification-based suggestions regarding child management, thereby trying to provide indirect service to two of the students. Actually, the entire class was out of control, and the teacher really needed help with her teaching style. In other words, the third level of consultation, direct service to the teacher, would have been most appropriate. However, the teacher seemed insecure in relation to the consultant, and the initial informal contract negotiated with the teacher called for indirect service to the child. Further, the consultant initially felt that the teacher was most receptive to indirect approaches to working with an individual child. Starting this way helped the consultant to establish credibility and thus provided a foundation for the consultant to later renegotiate the contract to focus directly on the teacher.

Problem Definition

Having identified the problem and the level at which the consultant will attempt to provide service, the next step in the consultation process is to define the problem in detail. In all efforts to define the problem, regardless of the level at which it is considered, one consistent underlying principle is that behavior is a function of the person and his environment. Thus, for example, even when providing direct service to the child (Level I), the referred child is not thought to be the sole source of the problem. In addition to gathering adequate data about the individual child, it will inevitably be necessary to gather detailed information about the child's environment.

When defining the problem, the consultant will rely on many of the content ideas discussed in Chapters Five through Eight. Although these ideas will be discussed in detail later, some of the following ideas have particular relevance to our consideration of the consultation stages.

When the focus is primarily on the child and his environment (that is, on providing direct or indirect service to the child), then problem identification would include learning about the child's behavior—low achievement, acting out, dependency, rebellion against authority, apathy, withdrawal, and so forth. For example, when attempting to learn something about a child's acting-out behavior, the consultant might want to determine how often the behavior occurs, how long it lasts, how intense the behavior is, precisely what forms of acting out are included, under what specific conditions the behavior occurs, how the teacher responds to the behavior, how the classmates respond to the behavior, what incompatible behaviors occur, and how the teacher and peers respond to the incompatible behaviors.

When the focus of consultation is on the teacher, one step in problem definition is to determine whether the problem is an example of lack of knowledge, lack of skill, lack of self-confidence, or lack of objectivity. The implications of these categories for consultation are discussed in Chapter Seven of this book and by Caplan (1970). We have found that, when focusing primarily on the teacher, the consultant must discover any attitudes the teacher has that might interfere with the teacher's objective approach to the problem. These attitudes can be discovered by considering the teacher's statements in terms of content (the source, object, and nature of the feeling) and in terms of the process of expression (how is the feeling expressed in the interview and in reality, both verbally and nonverbally). Caplan describes theme interference reduction, consultee identification with the client or a related figure, and consultee transference as examples of the process of expression. Caplan also mentions stereotyped responses (for example, expressing racial or sexual stereotypes) as examples of the process of expression.

The content of teachers' expressions may be analyzed in at least three potential areas of conflict to facilitate problem definition. These include teacher anger, teacher dependency, and teacher feelings about authority. Anger might be a problem for teachers characterized by two extremes; one extreme includes teachers who are overly indulgent (unable to say no or to challenge misbehavior), and other extreme includes teachers who are overly hostile. Another way to categorize this problem is to consider the ways in which the teacher deals with anger. Again, two extremes can be conceptualized, inner-directed anger (which includes self-blame by the teacher) and outer-directed anger (which includes blaming others).

A second content area of potential conflict for teachers is dependency. Dependency might be perceived as a problem for those teachers who rigidly follow others' ideas or who interact with others in a timid and passive manner. A teacher's dependency could be directed toward a variety of school people, including the consultant, other teachers in the school, the principal, or previous professors. Often it appears that highly dependent teachers are so unsure of themselves that they cannot rely on their own judgment. It also seems that such dependency can be an indirect way of expressing a need for acceptance and even love from colleagues, students, and others.

A teacher's attitudes about authority can also influence the way he teaches and thus be a third content area indicating potential conflict. These attitudes can be particularly important for young teachers, who assume a position of professional authority for the first time. These teachers may need help in learning to be an authority figure. Teachers with this sort of problem again are characterized at two extremes; their classes could be characterized as too permissive and unstructured or as authoritarian.

The consultant would consider each of these possible conflict areas while interviewing the consultee. Then, as a particular area becomes identified as important, it would become the focus of discussion during consultation until some resolution or behavior change was achieved by the consultee. A variety of consultee statements can provide clues to the potential importance of the conflict areas. Some of these types of statements have been derived from a rational, emotive view of behavior as applied to the consultation process (see Ellis, 1963; Grieger, 1972) and are presented here: (1) statements that include absolute judgments or conclusions ("must," "nothing I can do," "terrible," "I can't stand," "I can't control my feelings," "I don't know," "he makes me," "I can't"); (2) condemning or blaming statements ("should," "ought," "there's something wrong with the child," "it's wrong to express negative feelings," "it's their fault"); and (3) statements reflecting confusion on the part of the consultee (statements that include conflicting and contradictory information indicating ambivalence; irrational statements that the consultant has trouble understanding; and physical indications of intense emotion).

When the focus of the consultation is on the organization, the scope of problem definition becomes much broader, as it may include any of the subgroups associated with the school (administrators, teachers, students, or parents). Diagnostic skills can be used to help the organization to develop effective intervention strategies by using interviews, surveys, and questionnaires. The effort to define the problem includes attempts to discover whether there are any impediments to communications, whether there is confusion about the organization's goals, and whether there is some significant weakness in problem solving. Generally, it is reasonable to expect two different types of problems to be defined for this type of consultation: the problem may pervade the entire organization, or the problem may develop around one specific issue or crisis. Techniques of analysis and intervention in organizations are discussed in more detail in Chapter Eight.

Consultation Intervention

For the purposes of the present discussion, we are separating consultation intervention as a stage independent of the other stages. Although there is some justification for the categorization of intervention as a separate stage, in some sense this is an arbitrary distinction. Actually, consultation interventions take place throughout the consultation process. For example, the process of problem definition may be enough to stimulate a teacher to begin making significant changes in the classroom with no further consultation. Yet, typically some time is devoted specifically to discussing intervention plans with the teacher.

As has been suggested in discussions of the helping relationship in general (see Carkhuff, 1969a, 1969b; Egan, 1975; Gazda and others, 1973), the stage of the helping process where interventions are discussed will often involve relatively less focus on such relationship skills as empathy, open invitation to talk, and accurate reflection of feelings. Instead, there is a greater focus on confrontation techniques and direct suggestions for change. Some direct-confrontation techniques are presented in Chapter Seven, and the possible types of interventions are discussed in the next four chapters. Other approaches to confrontation in consultation are being developed by Gross (1978).

Assessing Impact

Once the problem has been identified and defined, and once the teacher and consultant have agreed upon an intervention approach, the next step is to assess the impact of the intervention. It is our strong conviction that a consultation relationship should not end without attempting to assess its effects. When such evaluations are not made, the consultant may be misled into thinking that unsuccessful consultation was successful. Or, if the consultant avoids the objective evaluation of his services, then he runs the risk of evaluating his services in terms of the number of cases completed or carried during a given period of time rather than in terms of his effectiveness.

For many practitioners, the suggestion of doing evaluative research may sound strange. However, the practitioner should view evaluative research as a means of improving consultation skills and developing a data base from which to demonstrate the utility of consultation techniques. This last point may prove especially valuable when negotiating a consultation contract. Assessing consultation impact is discussed more fully in Chapter Nine.

Concluding Consultation

One of the principles of consultation noted previously is that the teacher has complete freedom to discontinue the consultation relationship at any time. However, in those cases that proceed through the stages of entry, orientation, identification and definition of the problem, determination of intervention plans, and evaluation, the process of ending consultation should be handled carefully. At the conclusion of a consultation relationship, the consultant should be careful to leave the teacher with an open invitation to seek further consultation if the problem recurs or if any other problem emerges. One way this availability may be conveyed to the teacher is for the consultant to make occasional follow-up visits to the teacher's class to see how things are doing and to demonstrate the consultant's general interest in the teacher. This sort of follow-up seems to have a positive impact on teachers. Another way is to tell the teacher directly that there is always an option to seek further consultation and that it is the teacher's responsibility to take the initiative in requesting such help.

One of the potential problems that may be fostered by the availability of the consultant is consultee dependence. Although there are some instances where dependence is appropriate for the early stages, it is not an appropriate result of consultation. A major theoretical basis for consultation is the idea that, following consultation, the consultee becomes more capable of handling similar situations in the future without the assistance of a consultant. For this to occur, the consultee must become independent of the consultant and feel comfortable relying on his own judgment. Throughout the consultation process, the active participation of the teacher and joint consultant-consultee responsibility should be encouraged. However, it is especially important during the concluding stages of consultation that the consultant make specific efforts to encourage the consultee's independent problem solving.

A Flow Chart: The Consultation Process

The consultation process is dynamic, as it continually moves through the different stages that we have described. One key decision that affects this process is determining the level at which the consultant will work (direct service to the child, indirect service to the child, direct service to the teacher, or service to the organization). In view of the preventive goal of attempting to reach the largest number of children possible with relatively long-term effects, it is generally more desirable for the consultant to operate at the indirect levels of functioning (indirect service to the child, direct service to the teacher, and service to the organization). Furthermore, since it is likely that organizational factors can interfere with the short- or long-term effectiveness of consultation, organizational consultation should be the consultant's first choice when the problems are relevant. Once organizational factors are ruled out, preventive efforts should focus on teacher-related problems. The order of priority for choosing the various levels of consultation at the various stages of the consultation process are depicted in Figure 1.

Whereas other writers (for example, Reschly, 1976) have described many of these different approaches to consultation as separate models, our viewpoint is that, for maximally effective consultation, these different approaches must be integrated into one cohesive model. The flow chart in Figure 1 helps to demonstrate the integrated way in which we view the consultation model.

After negotiating a contract, the consultant may have to begin working at one of the levels of consultation lower on the chart than seems optimal. However, it should be clear from the chart that the consultant always has the option of renegotiating to gain sanction to function at some of the higher levels. Frequently, this renegotiation will be most successful when there is failure to solve a consultation problem (indicated as "ineffective" on the chart) or when it does not appear that any of the sanctioned approaches are appropriate to the problem being referred.

Although we feel that it is always most appropriate to begin working at the highest levels on this flow chart, this does not preclude working at some of the lower levels. For example, a consultant might respond to a referral for direct service to a student by working on a broad problem of communication within the school organization, if this broader problem was part of the request for direct service. According to the flow chart, once this problem is solved successfully, the consultation is ended and the consultant seeks new referrals. In this instance, the new referral may be the initial problem that initiated the organizational consultation, and the consultant would then focus on direct service to the child. In this way, the consultant could move from a high level on the chart to a lower level on two successive, yet related, cases.

Stated another way, the flow chart emphasizes two points. First, it is of primary importance to deal with any problems relating to organizational functioning or teachers' lack of knowledge, skill, or objectivity. These should be handled before providing indirect or direct service to the child, to increase the probability of success

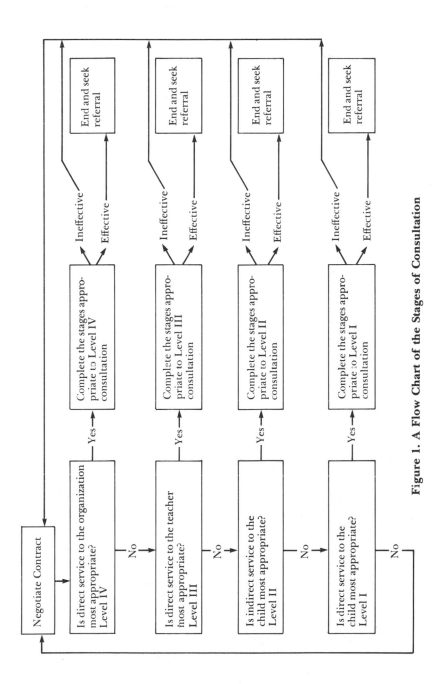

Figure 1. A Flow Chart of the Stages of Consultation

with these latter approaches. Secondly, the roles of other psychologists, counselors, and social workers who work in the schools should be restructured to change their emphasis. Instead of the bulk of their work involving direct service to the student, they should focus on the other, more indirect approaches to consultation.

Although not necessarily reflected in the chart, some additional points should be clarified. First, as noted in the chart, one section under each level of consultation indicates that the stages appropriate to each level need to be completed after the appropriate level of the problem has been identified. Generally, these stages are the same ones for each level that have been described in this chapter—the first stage is problem identification; the second stage is problem definition; the third stage is developing consultation interventions; the fourth stage is assessing the impact of consultation; and the final stage is concluding consultation.

Another point is that the consultant must decide to what extent he will communicate his expertise to the consultee and to what extent he will attempt to establish identification with the consultee. We believe that both of these factors are important for successful consultation. A general principle underlying our view of consultation is that the consultant and consultee share a joint responsibility for outcome. However, despite this general rule, in practice the consultant's choice regarding the degree of responsibility he will take depends on the consultee's characteristics. For example, with some highly dependent consultees, it would be almost impossible to establish a relationship, unless the consultant is willing to make some decisions and to assume a high degree of responsibility at the beginning. Also, the degree of responsibility the consultant takes may vary at different stages of consultation. In some instances, the consultant might choose to take on relatively higher responsibility early in consultation, and during the latter stages the goal would usually be to encourage the teacher to take on greater responsibility.

Another decision the consultant must make is the degree to which empathy and other relationship-building skills should be used, and the degree to which confrontation should be used. Some of the literature describing helping relationships suggests that, early in the helping relationship, relationship-building skills are relatively important, and, later in the helping relationship, confrontation skills become more important.

One further decision the consultant frequently has to make is whether to gather more information or to give recommendations. This issue is usually pretty clear in a first interview, when it is not appropriate to give recommendations, and it is also fairly clear at the intervention stage, when recommendations are the natural focus. However, there are a number of points in between when the decision will have an important bearing on the outcome of the consultation process.

A Case Presentation with Flow Chart Analysis

While working as a psychologist in a community youth counseling center and functioning as a consultant to a number of the community's private elementary schools, we experienced a situation that exemplifies the process of consultation previously depicted.

One of the feeder schools to the youth counseling center had shown only a moderate interest in our center's resources. Their referrals to the center always focused on direct service to the child—that is, diagnostic evaluations and therapy. Further, they declined all invitations to use the center's staff at some other levels of consultation involvement, for example, teacher training. Approximately eighteen weeks into the academic year, our staff noticed a radical increase in this school's number of referrals, which jumped from an average of two per week to fourteen per week over a two-week period. The overwhelming increase of referrals, along with their similarity in nature—all primarily classroom management problems—suggested that the direct service model would no longer be efficient. Thus, a conference was scheduled with the principal in order to propose a new method of service delivery (entry-negotiating consultation contract). The consultant told the principal about the nature and format of consultation and its procedures. He emphasized that the staff would employ indirect service to the child, with the hopes that such service would have a widespread influence on other potential problem areas and thus be cost efficient. Although the principal wanted the children removed from the classroom for their help, the possibility of reaching more children for less money interested her. Further, she wished to avoid placing twenty-eight new referrals on a lengthy waiting list. Throughout the presentation of the rationale and role definition, the principal stated her serious doubt about the potential effectiveness of this novel approach. Clearly, program evaluation techniques had to be built into the consultation program.

From discussion with the principal, the consultant decided that the primary problem was the teachers' lack of good classroom management skills (problem identification). The principal suggested that perhaps if we observed the referred children in the classroom we might better determine what specifically needed to be done (problem definition). We thanked the principal for her invitation and praised her apparent insight. Next we suggested that, in order to enter at such a level of consultation (Level II; indirect service), we would need to enlist the teachers' assistance. At a meeting we explained what consultation was all about, noting the responsibilities of the teachers as consultees (entry-teacher acceptance).

From the teachers' questions and critical comments it was apparent that they felt they could not possibly be expected to gather baseline data since they did not have a single extra moment in their busy day. They made it clear that any attempts at Level II consultation would be ineffective (assessment); the consultant attempted to reenter at another level. Their general complaints eventually led to specific criticism of the school's organizational and administrative system (problem identification). However, the teachers showed some apprehension about elaborating upon their complaints. The consultant then distributed a questionnaire on which the teachers could anonymously identify what they considered the most pressing need for the consultants to address (problem definition).

Their answers indicated that the teachers viewed the school as too impersonal, mechanistic, and punch-clock oriented. They felt overworked and little appreciated by the administration and noted that the atmosphere was basically cheerless and strictly work oriented. The teachers were frustrated about the lack of opportunity to associate with their fellow workers and to make decisions.

This dissatisfaction was expressed by the teachers' high rate of turnover—only three of eighteen teachers in the past three years stayed more than one year, a high degree of teacher absenteeism, and emotional outbursts in the classroom.

After analyzing the questionnaires, the consultant met with the principal to renegotiate the original consultation contract (entry). The consultant explained that, because the teachers spent the entire work day in their classrooms (even eating lunch there with the students), it was impossible to discuss cases or provide feedback to them. He requested that the school's schedule be slightly modified to start class on Fridays one hour later (service to the school—intervention). This minor revision in the traditional structure was met with a great deal of resistance from the administration, but, because the consultant had proven helpful in working with problem children (direct service to the child), the administration agreed to the request.

Initially, the teachers were required to attend the 8 to 9 A.M. "free period" on Fridays, and the principal noted their promptness and attendance by recording their names and arrival times on a work sheet. This formal stipulation made the first few sessions extremely forced, artificial, and generally unproductive. However, the consultant attempted to establish a congenial, informal atmosphere by providing coffee and donuts, informally joking with the teachers and principal, and acting as a role model, often entering and leaving the meeting room. After these initial meetings, the consultant met with the principal; during these feedback sessions the consultant emphasized the importance of voluntary participation and the need for establishing a nonthreatening atmosphere. By the third such meeting, faculty members started bringing their own baked goods, which acted as a catalyst for jokes, a mock baking competition, and informal recipe sharing, all of which created a sense of ease and informality. Similarly, by this third week the principal appeared without her roll book and generally began to relax.

These weekly sessions soon became a major mechanism for teacher-to-teacher communication and the development of a sense of community, a means for ventilating the everyday normal frustrations of a classroom teacher and for airing faculty concerns to the principal. This one minor modification in the rigid structure of the school diffused tension among school personnel and fostered the development of a supportive comradery.

As a result of this strategy (assessing impact) teacher turnover reduced (only four teachers left, two because of pregnancy), teacher absenteeism decreased throughout the remainder of the academic year, and teachers' reports reflected feelings of belonging to the school body and that their contributions were meaningful. Further, the number of referrals for psychoeducational diagnosis or therapy dropped from ten to fourteen per week to an average of one per week over the next five weeks.

Since the specific circumstance—the twenty-eight referrals —that generated the intervention strategy was no longer a concern, the consultant ended his involvement (concluding consultation). However, the weekly coffee klatch continued and the consultant visited these Friday morning sessions to demonstrate his availability and to seek new referrals.

With the success of this intervention plan, the consultant was able to redefine his service orientation and to take an almost exclusively indirect service delivery orientation. The results of this service helped pave the way to future requests for similar, more specific types of intervention and services to the school. In this particular situation, the consultant's next request for service (re-entry) involved presenting an inservice (Level III) training program on rational-emotive principles within the classroom (Parsons, Stone, and Feuerstein, 1977).

Summary

The literature on consultation has generally concerned itself with the philosophy, role definitions, and techniques to be employed. Such a level of concern has enabled mental health workers to identify that what they are doing *is* consultation. However, this focus falls short of assisting them in knowing *how* to do it successfully.

The present chapter focused on the how-to aspects of consultation and offered a model for guiding practitioners through the various decision points that characterize the dynamic nature of the consultation process. School consultation was discussed in terms of seven stages marking the development of a consultation program. Although not necessarily occurring separately in practice or necessarily occurring in an invariant order, each of these stages has special significance for the development of successful consultation. Each stage was discussed as a discrete unit, with its own unique demands and restrictions on the consultant and its own special techniques and consulting skills required to ensure success. Finally, the chapter presented a flow chart and case illustration of the use of the stage model to demonstrate the integrated way we view the consultation model.

CHAPTER FIVE

Direct Service to the Child

▣ ▣ ▣ ▣ ▣ ▣ ▣ ▣ ▣ ▣ ▣

Delivery of psychological services in the school has traditionally involved direct service to the child. Counselors, psychologists, social workers, and other mental health professionals in the past have generally focused on the troubled child and the intrapersonal factors that were thought to have created the problem. The two most frequent types of direct service provided by mental health workers in schools have been individual psychodiagnosis and counseling. As we pointed out in Chapters One and Two, this individual, direct-service approach has begun to give way to a more indirect service orientation, and consultation is one major aspect of this orientation.

Our historical account of the emergence of consultation might seem to indicate that direct service and indirect service are incompatible or mutually exclusive categories of professional activity, but we would not support such a view. Indeed, some authors have excluded direct service from their discussion of consultation

(Alpert, 1977; Dworkin and Dworkin, 1975; Gallessich, 1973; Reschly, 1976). Those who are against including direct service in a consultation model typically argue, as Reschly (1976) has, that if the term *consultation* is "used to refer to practically any function traditionally performed by school psychologists" and is simply a means of "repackaging traditional roles," then its utility is lost. Gallessich (1973) states that consultation has come to include such diverse functions as "testing and diagnosis, planning research activities, or working with school personnel in preventive mental health," and she argues that this broad use of the term is inappropriate.

Other authors see direct service as an integral part of consultation and therefore classify direct service as one aspect of consultation (Caplan, 1970; Mannino and Shore, 1975; Meyers, 1973b; Woody, 1974). In this view, which we support, when direct service is applied appropriately, it invariably involves consultive aspects; thus, to exclude direct service from consultation would be artificial. Let us examine this issue in more detail.

All psychological or educational interventions, whether direct or indirect, involve a diagnostic phase and a remedial phase. Typically, direct service involves formal individual diagnosis of the child and remediation of the child's problem. Similarly, consultation always involves a diagnostic phase. The consultant spends some time with the consultee trying to come to an understanding of the consultee's problem. When the consultee and consultant come to a consensus regarding the nature of the problem, they begin to discuss possible remedial strategies. Eventually, a remediation plan is devised. Thus, it is clear that there is a similar diagnostic-remedial process both in traditional psychodiagnostic approaches and in the more indirect methods that characterize consultation.

It could be argued that the term *consultation* does not apply to those situations where the mental health professional engages in active and direct diagnosis of the child. Such an argument would indicate that a consulting mental health professional could talk to a teacher about a child's abilities, for example, but could not find out directly what the child's abilities were. In other words, the only permissible data on which to base consultant-teacher conversation are the teacher's perceptions of the child. Although the teacher's perceptions are important, it is often important for the consultant to gather data directly from the child. Defining consultation in such a narrow sense would tend to place unnecessary restrictions on the consultant's activities.

Another argument, which could be offered, is that direct service cannot be considered consultation, because it focuses on the child's problems and not on the teacher's problems with the child. However, this dichotomy does not exist in reality, because the child's problems are no longer defined as intrapsychic but rather as interactions of the child and his environment. Direct service is simply one aspect of consultation, because focusing on the child's problem is just one stage of the broader process of helping the teacher to solve similar problems in the future.

If diagnosis, case work, and counseling cannot be distinguished from consultation in the ways just described, and if these direct services do involve consultation aspects, then how can direct service be differentiated from consultation? As the definition in Chapter One points out, the essence of consultation is collaboration, or the process of sharing expertise to solve problems. If a mental health professional makes a diagnosis of a child based strictly on his interaction with the child, no consultation has taken place. If the diagnosis leads to a categorization, and, based on this categorization, the child is placed in an institution or a special class or is simply transferred to a different teacher, no consultation has taken place. If therapy is recommended for a child (with or without formal diagnosis) with the assumption that the therapy will change the deviant behavior of the child, then neither the recommendation nor the therapy has any consultive aspects. If a social worker makes contacts with community agencies to obtain services for a child, then he is engaging in a liaison function, not consultation.

For direct service to be considered consultive, it must also include an interaction between the caretaker and the mental health professional. This process involves more than a diagnosis and a treatment. It involves a process of give and take, in which the social-science knowledge of one professional and the pedagogical knowledge of the other are brought to the problem. Interaction of this type may be prolonged and frequent. Its focus is on producing change in the environment, particularly the social environment, of the child. If these criteria are met, then the direct service is consultive in nature. There seems no reason to exclude direct service from a discussion of consultation. In fact, it is one of the most frequent forms of consultation that mental health professionals perform.

Rather than consider direct service and consultation as mutually exclusive categories, it is more useful to think of direct service and consultation as being at opposite ends of a continuum.

Consultation

◄───►

Direct Service	Indirect Service
Crisis emphasis	Preventive emphasis
Intrapersonal focus	Environmental focus
Child focus	Caretaker focus

The ends of the continuum represent abstractions that rarely occur in pure form in the day-to-day work of mental health specialists. Most mental health activity is some combination of these functions. Individual case work, for example, is typically classified as direct service, because it is usually carried out in response to a crisis, it is designed partially to diagnose and treat intrapersonal conflicts, and it is child-focused. However, in reality it often incorporates indirect service, which has preventive aspects, deals with environmental factors, and makes some attempt to change the behavior of caretakers.

As the pendulum of psychological thought in recent years has swung toward the indirect, preventive end of the continuum, proponents of this emphasis have talked of direct service as if in practice it always or usually consisted of the pure form found at the extreme end of the continuum. This argument may have helped to make a case for a change from traditional, individually focused psychodiagnostic approaches to indirect, preventive approaches. However, this argument ignores the reality of practice. Viewing service delivery as a continuum should help to dispel this false dichotomy and bring theory closer to practice.

Regardless of how one views service delivery, practical considerations demand that the aspiring consultant accept the organization as he finds it before attempting to initiate change. Public schools have historically viewed special-services personnel as providing direct services to individual children that the classroom teacher cannot provide. This conception is deeply rooted. A mental health professional who wants to take a more preventive approach and focus on teacher behavior will encounter major resistance, unless he understands the school's expectations and moves in small steps to change these expectations. If a school psychologist is required to handle eight cases per week, it will be impossible to find the time for classroom observations or meaningful teacher conferences. The school psychologist must then push for a small reduction to about six cases, for example, so he can spend the remaining time engaged in those indirect activities that seem appropriate. Similarly, if a counselor is involved in group testing, keeping attendance records, and individual and group counseling, with little time for parents or teachers, he must fight for small increases in time for consultation with parents and teachers. In both cases, professionals can successfully facilitate appropriate role-changes by using their understanding of the organization. The school should be thought of in the same light as an individual who has not yet learned a skill. Learning theory has taught us that one begins teaching the student where one finds him, not where one would like him to be. This point has been made by consultation theorists (for example, Caplan, 1970), but it is often overlooked.

Consultation and Formal Psychoeducational Diagnosis

Considerable criticism has been aimed at the psychoeducational diagnostic model in recent years. Much of this criticism may have been poorly conceived, in that some shortcomings may be attributed to poor application rather than to the model itself. But too often, practitioners and school administrators, who define the role, have restricted their conceptualization of psychoeducational assessment to the use of standardized testing procedures. Although this approach may result in a large number of completed evaluations with clinically appropriate diagnostic labels and erudite recommendations, there is often little pragmatic help for the classroom teacher. The assessment model is often seen at its worst in large urban school systems, where psychoeducational assessment is usually limited to a Wechsler Intelligence Scale for Children (WISC) or a Stanford-Binet Intelligence test.

Another criticism directed to this model is that results of diagnosis are often labels with potentially negative impacts from expectancy effects (see Rosenthal and Jacobson, 1968). This problem is exacerbated in a model emphasizing testing and deemphasizing collaboration with teachers; labels are less desirable than specific interventions as the end result of services.

An alternative model would require the diagnostician to reduce the amount of time spent in testing, increase classroom observation, and foster indirect delivery of remedial procedures through the teacher. Within this framework, diagnosis would still need to be accurate. However, rather than providing a label, it would provide accurate data as a basis for meaningful intervention.

In practice, it can be difficult to implement this broadened consultive-diagnostic approach for many reasons. First, unrealistic case loads and quota-filling criteria for evaluating job performance foster speed in diagnosis rather than accuracy or meaningful intervention strategies. Second, on those occasions where time is allotted for extensive diagnosis, and forethought is given to developing meaningful recommendations, the psychologist is often frustrated by the inability or disinterest exhibited by the caretaker (teacher, parent, or administrator) in implementing the recommendations. Frustration and feelings of impotence may result because of the lack of attention paid to consultation values.

The primary distinction between the traditional model and the indirect, remedial model is that, instead of expecting the mental health professional to arrive at a diagnosis and recommend an intervention plan on his own, the teacher or other important caretakers share the responsibility for diagnosis and remediation with the mental health professional. The rationales for sharing this responsibility with the teacher and others are: (1) teachers and others know important facts about a particular child that are important to the case, and many of these facts are difficult to obtain if one does not have long periods of contact with the child; (2) since the remediation activities will involve the caretaker in some way, the consultant must understand the problem as perceived by the caretaker; (3) a direct assessment of the classroom environment, including the teacher-student interaction, is impossible without teacher cooperation and support; (4) remedial recommendations that come partly from the teacher are less likely to be resisted than those generated solely by someone else; and (5) the mental health consultant cannot know what kinds of remedial adjustments the teacher is willing and able to make without interaction and meaningful communication about the recommendation.

Collaboration During Diagnosis

In traditional psychoeducational diagnosis, the mental health professional evaluates the client in isolation. This one-to-one evaluation process is based on the assumption that the questions asked or the answers given in response to psychometric instruments will be misunderstood by those who lack knowledge about such devices. Further, it is felt that the presence during diagnosis of one or more of the significant others in the client's life would inhibit or otherwise affect the responses of the client. The assumption is that the mental health professional will set up a warm, accepting atmosphere, which optimizes motivation to perform and to talk about personal feelings and attitudes.

Without denying the importance of this approach in some instances, the diagnostician who operates from a consultive point of view conceptualizes the process in somewhat different terms. Primarily, he believes that, unless the consultee makes a significant contribution to the diagnostic process, he or she will distrust it, perhaps misunderstand it, and in many cases reject the evaluation. Collaboration of consultee and consultant during diagnosis does not preclude the use of specialized instruments, about which only the consultant has significant expertise. Collaboration does imply, however, that at a minimum the consultant and consultee discuss the diagnostic process, so that both understand the rationale for each step in the process.

Consultant-consultee collaboration during diagnosis might be handled in a number of ways. The teacher might be present during an evaluation of the child and share in the interviewing process by collecting medical, developmental, and educational history. During the formal, psychometric aspect of the evaluation (if one is carried out), the teacher could take notes on the client's reactions to the examiner or the tests being administered. Sometimes it may be appropriate to switch roles, so the teacher does some testing and the consultant observes. After the client is dismissed from the evaluation, the teacher and mental health professional would compare notes on what had happened and would begin to form a common opinion about the client. This sort of collaboration provides observations that are potentially significant, and it demystifies the assessment process. This can be important, since much of the resistance of educators to typical psychological evaluations may result from a lack of understanding of what the process actually entails.

One technique, which can aid in developing a collaborative spirit during diagnosis, involves the mental health professional engaging in informal teaching. Hammill and Bartel (1975) have recommended this activity as highly appropriate for psychoeducational diagnosis, because it demonstrates directly how the child approaches new learning tasks and interacts with the teacher. From a consultive point of view, this technique has the added advantage of allowing the mental health professional and the teacher to share their observations about the child's approach to learning. In this discussion, the teacher is the natural leader, since he or she has previously observed the child in such situations, and because the child's approach to learning is the teacher's area of expertise. This kind of discussion helps to balance those discussions of behavior and feelings that may be more in the mental health professional's area of expertise.

The collaborative spirit of the diagnosis can be maintained, even if some aspect of the diagnosis has to be carried out without the teacher. A teacher might not have sufficient time free from classroom duties to participate in the process. In such cases, the rationale for the diagnostic methods should be discussed with the teacher, and the data from the diagnosis should be presented to the teacher (in appropriate form), so that he or she can aid in making diagnostic decisions.

The consultation model as applied to the diagnostic process proscribes a greater focus on environmental factors, and, for this reason, observation of the child in the classroom is a necessary part of the evaluation. This is one stage of the diagnostic process where

the shared responsibility of the consultant and consultee is particularly clear, since the consultant physically enters the teacher's area
of expertise.

Many systematic classroom-observation systems exist, but
few mental health professionals are aware of them or are comfortable using them. The reasons for this may be (1) these instruments
or techniques were typically developed by researchers, (2) direct
application to individual, client-centered diagnosis and remediation is not always apparent, and (3) these skills have not been emphasized sufficiently in training. Also, psychologists, counselors,
and social workers may feel that such observation would be unduly
time-consuming. Many professionals are not aware of the research
suggesting that even very short observations, if carried out over a
period of time and appropriately spaced, can be valid and reliable
(Powell, Martindale, and Kulp, 1975).

The mental health professional has a very wide range of
observational instruments and techniques from which to choose.
The event-measurement, trial-recording, time-sampling, or
interval-recording techniques used by behavior modifiers provide
one set of options (see Kazdin, 1975, for a discussion of such recording devices). Also available are the wide variety of instruments
used by educational psychologists and teacher trainers. An anthology of these instruments is presented by Simon and Boyer (1970),
and many of the instruments reported have direct application for
client-centered consultation. For example, the system outlined by
Brophy and Good (1969) records every interaction that occurs between a teacher and an individual student. With about two hours of
training, the mental health professional can use this instrument to
ascertain the nature of the dyadic interaction between teacher and
student, which can be so important in consultation.

It is clear that, in all these observational systems, the teacher
is being observed as well as the child. This type of observation, of
course, cannot be implemented successfully or ethically unless the
teacher feels that he or she has some responsibility for participation
in the diagnostic process. Specifically, the teacher must understand
that the client-centered diagnosis is going to have a consultive-
preventive component, in that the teacher's behavior toward the
referred child and other children may be one of the subjects of
discussion. If this fact has been worked through in the referral and

diagnostic stages, then it comes as no surprise when the consultant and consultee begin to discuss changes in consultee behavior during the recommendation stage.

The final aspect of consultant-consultee collaboration during diagnosis is arriving at a description of the client and a conceptualization of the possible causes of the inappropriate behavior. Even if the teacher has not participated actively in the process to this stage, it is almost always possible to foster participation in the formulation of a diagnosis. The process involves the mental health professional presenting his findings to the consultee and seeking feedback on each aspect of the behavior description and diagnosis. The consultant needs to maintain an image of a professional with expertise who has something to offer. However, the mental health professional should present any findings tentatively. An important goal is to communicate that the diagnostic process is ongoing, that the consultant is open to new data and alternative explanations, and that the opinions and observations of the consultee are much desired.

Diagnosis typically involves two kinds of statements: statements that describe the characteristic behaviors, attitudes, feelings, or abilities of the client, and statements that present a cause-and-effect analysis of this description. "Johnny is an underachiever" is an example of the former kind of statement; "he is an underachiever because his parents communicate conflicting expectations regarding academic achievement" is an example of the latter type of statement. The consultant must not proceed with remedial recommendations until he and the consultee have come to general agreement about both aspects of the diagnosis. It is generally easier to agree about behavior descriptions than causes, but divergent causal explanations cannot be brushed aside, since conceptualization of cause usually forms the basis for deciding appropriate remedial action.

Collaboration During the
Recommendation-Remedial Phase

Historically, the primary diagnostician in the school has been the school psychologist. Because school psychological services are expensive but are mandated by law in most regions of the country, school districts tend to spread the psychologist's services so thin that he or she has little time to interact with the parents or teachers of the referred child. This practice has numerous adverse consequences for diagnosis (for example, it creates an image of the psychologist as an IQ-tester), but it is most disadvantageous during the stage of the psychoeducational diagnostic process when recommendations for remedial action are made.

The terminal phase of a diagnosis is typically handled by attaching a list of written recommendations to the diagnostic report. Such recommendations have been criticized extensively by educators as vague, unrealistic, and filled with jargon that is incomprehensible to educators (Buktenica, 1964; Forness, 1970). Most of those who criticize these recommendations state or imply that the fault lies with the psychologist's writing technique. If he could only refrain from using technical language, be more specific, and understand the operation of the classroom well enough to make realistic recommendations, the recommendations would be better received. Toward this end, manuals have been written to provide suggested recommendations for specific problem situations (for example, Blanco, 1972), and elaborate diagnostic-prescriptive schemes have been devised to match remedial suggestions with specific diagnostic patterns (for example, Valett, 1968). This criticism can be used as a basis to suggest that school psychologists, counselors, and social workers should be trained initially as educators, so that more specific and realistic recommendations can be written in language compatible with the educator's point of view.

There is an alternative analysis of the difficulty with most written recommendations; their failure may not relate as much to the technical inadequacy of the writer as to the model of service delivery implied by such recommendations. The typical psychodiagnostic process is based on what Schein (1969) has called the *doctor-patient model*. In this model, the psychologist is expected to examine the client and then prescribe a remediation. The sole responsibility for this prescription lies with the "doctor." This model works moderately well in medicine, because the patient plays a predominantly passive role in the remediation, and because the prescription is highly technical. A patient for whom medicine is prescribed does not have the technical knowledge to share in the prescriptive decision; further, he must only agree to take the medication regularly to carry out the remedial program. A similar process occurs when surgery is the remedial strategy. The process breaks down in medicine when the remedial strategy requires substantial patient participation, such as in weight loss, reduction of smoking, preventive dental care, or exercise prescriptions.

Similarly, this model of service delivery has serious flaws when applied to psychological and educational remedial programs, because the remediation requires a great deal of caretaker participation. For these reasons, remedial strategies cannot be the sole responsibility of the mental health professional; they must be a joint product of the mental health professional and the teacher or parent. Moreover, it is virtually impossible for a mental health professional to know enough about curriculum to be able to make sufficiently specific educational recommendations for children ranging from preschool to high school, and yet the curriculum must often be a focus of intervention. A consultant who tries to write recommendations in isolation from the teacher cannot possibly know what the teacher has tried before the referral was made, and he cannot know what adjustments the teacher is willing or able to make. Manuals of prescriptions or diagnostic-prescriptive schemes cannot possibly be applicable to all situations, no matter how refined they are, because the attitudes and motivations of the teacher are a crucial element. Further, extensive educational training and experience on the part of the mental health professional is not the answer. The value of consultation is that it brings together persons with different points of view. The binding force that holds the consultation relationship together is, in part, the enjoyment of sharing one's expertise with another person. If the consultant is also an educator, his relationship with the consultee may tend to become that of a supervisor, because he has expertise in the consultee's field; this could undermine the consultee's feeling of contributing actively to the solution of the client's problem.

There are several different techniques for fostering the consultive process when making decisions regarding remedial strategies. One technique is presently being used by Martin in a diagnostic training-clinic for school psychologists. The clients in the training-clinic are children who have been referred by their parents because of academic, social, or emotional problems. At the termination of a lengthy diagnostic process, a feedback session is held, in which the clinicians make remedial suggestions to be carried out by both the parents and the teachers of the child. After the diagnosis has been outlined by the clinician, instead of offering a remedial suggestion, he or she asks the parents to suggest some solutions to the problem. Since most parents come to the clinic with the expectation that they will be passive recipients of remedial suggestions, they are usually taken aback by the procedure, and the clinicians always have some suggestions ready if the parents are unable to respond. Given a little time, however, most parents do make some kind of suggestion. When necessary, the clinician's job is to modify the parent's idea in a manner consistent with the psychological principles that are the basis of his expertise. The parent then is encouraged to react to the adjusted remedial strategy and to suggest alterations if needed. In this way, the remedial suggestions are negotiated from the needs, knowledge, values, and abilities of the parties concerned. This process can be broadened by requesting suggestions from the child when appropriate.

Consultation as Part of the
Counseling-Therapy Process

The recent focus on preventive mental health and the indirect delivery of psychological services has resulted in criticisms of counseling and therapy (the terms will be used synonymously here) that are similar to the criticisms of traditional diagnostic procedures. For example, therapy is thought of as being too time-consuming, considering the limited professional manpower available, and as focusing on the wrong unit of analysis (the individual child) and the wrong psychological phenomena (intrapsychic conflicts). Furthermore, many critics have pointed to the lack of empirical support for traditional psychotherapeutic techniques. While these points have validity, they are directed most frequently at long-term, insight-oriented psychodynamic therapies. This approach to therapy, however, is rarely used in pure form in the schools. Often these arguments overlook the mounting research in support of a variety of therapies, particularly those based on behavioral principles.

Despite the importance of preventive work, there will be times when some form of therapy will be the best alternative, and it is our opinion that the appropriate use of the therapy can be consistent with a consultation model. The argument that therapy cannot be consistent with a consultation model conceptualizes psychological services in black and white terms. In other words, it rigidly conceptualizes mental health services as direct or indirect, preventive or crisis-based, and individually or environmentally focused. This ignores the continuum of psychological services from direct service to consultation discussed earlier in this chapter. These criticisms ignore the fact that the present emphasis on developing elementary school counseling programs is based on preventive principles. The arguments also ignore the varieties of group and family therapies that are specifically based on the rationale that the social environment has important effects on individual behavior and that the proper unit of analysis is the interaction between individuals (Yalom, 1975). Further, these arguments overlook the possibility that the information gained from therapy with a child can be used as a basis for developing classroom interventions through teacher consultation. The experience of one of the authors will help to clarify this point.

Mark was referred to Parsons for counseling to help him "remove the chip from his shoulder." Mark was a bright, conscientious, eleven-year-old black male attending an inner city parochial school. Since the beginning of the academic year, he had been talking back to the teacher, mumbling under his breath, and declining in his academic performance. Through individual counseling, it was learned that, during the summer, Mark had become very aware of his own black heritage and the general plight of the black man throughout the history of the United States. A result of this summer research was that Mark had set goals for the upcoming academic year to excel in school and to continue his historical investigations. Mark's teacher had taught first and second grades in suburban schools for twenty-five years and was teaching in the last year before retirement. She tended to address the students as "boys" and "girls" and generally treated them on a somewhat infantile level. Mark was acutely aware of the demeaning connotations of the term *boy*. Consequently, he was extremely sensitive to her teaching demeanor, and he responded quite negatively toward the teacher. This information became known during individual counseling, and a decision was made to consult with the teacher regarding the negative connotations of the term *boy* when used in reference to a black, adolescent male. As a result, the teacher had a productive discussion with the class about this problem, she tried to reduce the frequency with which she used the words *boy* and *girl*, and she conducted discussions after class on black history. The information gathered from the direct contact with Mark enabled the consultant to facilitate change in the teacher, which in turn not only remedied the specific referral problem (Mark's negative attitude), but also led to a much more positive rapport between the teacher and the class as a whole.

This example clarifies how the information obtained through counseling can be used appropriately in consultation. It would be a mistake to exclude direct counseling services from our definition of consultation. There will undoubtedly be many instances when the integrated implementation of therapeutic and consultation services will provide the best possible help to children, even though there is little doubt that, at present, there is a need to deemphasize such direct service.

Summary

Direct service to children is the predominant form of service offered by mental health professionals in the schools. This form of service has a long history and will continue to be an important part of school mental health services for the foreseeable future. It is clear, however, that psychologists (of all types), counselors, and social workers must overcome the expectation on the part of school personnel that their predominant function is to provide direct service. At the level of the individual school district, this can be done by obtaining a thorough understanding of the expectations for services held by the district. If direct service is overemphasized, the mental health professional must work in a step-by-step fashion to instruct and guide the system toward more preventive approaches. One of the strategies that can be used for this purpose is to incorporate consultive functions into direct service. This can be done by having educational personnel (particularly the referral source) participate in the diagnostic-remedial process with the mental health professional. Such sharing can take the form of collaboration during the diagnostic process and collaboration and negotiation of remedial strategies. Techniques for facilitating the diagnostic process include consultee obervation during psychometric evaluations, informal teaching by the mental health professional, various forms of classroom observation, and collaboration during diagnostic decision-making. Important opportunities for consultation also present themselves as part of the counseling-therapy process. The goal in all these strategies, however, is to augment the information base and the problem-solving skills of the caretaker, so that future problems can be remediated without referral for direct service.

CHAPTER SIX

Indirect Service to the Child

◙ ◙ ◙ ◙ ◙ ◙ ◙ ◙ ◙ ◙ ◙

When providing indirect service, the consultant uses someone else to gather data from the child for defining the problem (via observation by teachers, other students, or the client) and uses a caretaker (a teacher, for example) to carry out the derived intervention plan. Indirect service is often an economical and efficient use of the consultant's time. The primary goal is to change the child's observable behavior (in the classroom or at home) and his attitudes. Consequently, diagnostic techniques are related directly to remedial programming for specific children as was the case with Level I consultation discussed in Chapter Five. However, consultation based on indirect service to the child (Level II) emphasizes extrapersonal factors in the child's environment, leading inevitably to questions about the curriculum, teaching techniques, and teacher behavior at the child's school (Oakland, 1969).

In practice, there is often overlap between the different categories of consultation, especially when attempting to distinguish between direct and indirect service to the child. A brief review of the case of Mark, presented in Chapter Five, along with the following list should help to clarify this distinction.

Level I	Level II
Data Gathered Directly by Consultant	*Data Gathered by Other Personnel*
(a) Projective testing	(a) Behavioral recordings (antecedent, event, and consequences) by teacher
(b) Clinical interview	(b) In-class observation of teacher-child interaction by paraprofessional
(c) In-class observation of teacher-child interaction	(c) Classroom observation by the referred student
(d) Counseling	(d) Observation by other students in the class

In Mark's case, the problem behavior was elicited by the teacher's verbal cues—using the word *boy*. The consultant responded to the teacher's referral by scheduling an interview and an initial counseling session with Mark. During the meetings with Mark, the consultant acquired the essential data used to understand the problem and develop an intervention strategy. The principle concern was to identify and remediate the child's behavior problems. Because the primary data collection was done directly by the consultant, the case was considered appropriately as direct service to the child. However, if the consultant had responded to the initial referral by asking the teacher to record antecedent and consequential conditions of the child's behavior, the consultant could have avoided meeting Mark in a counseling session. The teacher's observations might have suggested the importance of her language in triggering the problem behavior, and the appropriate classroom recommendations might have become apparent.

If the recommendations about the teacher's use of the word *boy* had resulted from such indirect contact, then this consultation would have been labeled appropriately as indirect service to the child. Such an approach might have been more economical in terms of consultant time and energy, and, as suggested in Chapter Four, this should always be a consideration of school consultants. We believe that school consultants must consider the Law of Parsimony when responding to referral problems by making an effort to determine the approach that will lead to the most effective change from the most economical use of the consultant's time. Therefore, the consultant needs to be sensitive to those occasions when the data essential to diagnosis of the classroom problem may be available from interviews with the consultee or from classroom observation. By focusing on observable school behavior, the consultant may be more likely to inquire about methods for changing behavior, rather than probing for the presumed intrapersonal causes of this behavior. This orientation is consistent with the notion that complex diagnostic testing is not always necessary for the development of relatively uncomplicated remedial techniques (Wolfensberger, 1965). Similarly, it is congruent with the characteristics of consultation noted previously, including a focus on reduced time in testing, emphasis on observable behavior and environmental causes, and personal contact with school personnel.

We will focus in this chapter on two different approaches to providing indirect service to the child: task analysis and behavior modification. Task analysis techniques provide a productive approach to assessing academic behavior, and behavior modification techniques can be used to identify and remediate children's socioemotional behavior. (Both academic behavior and socioemotional behavior can also be explored through techniques appropriate to direct service to the child.) There are other relevant indirect service approaches—the mental health approach, group processes, and affective education, for example—and information about them can be obtained from other sources (see Ginott, 1972; Schmuck and Schmuck, 1971, 1974). Rather than present an all-inclusive list of the variety of techniques that are consistent with indirect service to the child, we concentrate on demonstrating two approaches to consultation.

Task Analysis

Task analysis represents a logical educational technique for describing the subskills and subconcepts a student must acquire in order to master a complex skill or an interrelated set of concepts and principles and for effecting change in conceptual and skill development. We will sketch the orientation and procedures required to perform task analysis briefly, in an effort to demonstrate their application within Level II consultation. The interested reader is referred to other efforts that have focused specifically on task analysis in more detail (see Anderson and Faust, 1973; Sulzer-Azaroff, McKinley, and Ford, 1977).

Problem Identification Phase. The first step would be to identify appropriate behavioral objectives with diagnostic techniques related directly to the school curriculum. These diagnostic tests would be administered by the classroom teacher or aide. In contrast to the norm-referenced tests used in traditional psychoeducational test batteries, task analysis is designed to examine the child's progress in relation to some goal. The goal of task analysis is to identify the child's existing skills along with those required for obtaining the program's stated objective.

The next step after identifying behavioral objectives is to define clearly both the prerequisites for and the criteria indicating the attainment of these goals. This analysis should be complete, with relationships among component skills and concepts clearly specified and the circumstances under which each component skill is to be performed clearly identified.

In identifying the subskills involved, task analysis lends itself to event recording, where the operationalized subcomponents are simply listed with spaces in which "present" or "absent" can be noted. For finer analysis and recording, the component tasks can be noted on a scale—for example, 1 = none, 2 = some, 3 = all; or 1 = if the target behavior does not occur, 2 = if it occurs sometimes but not throughout the period, and 3 = if it persists throughout the entire period.

Numerous charts, tables, and devices have been employed to assist in recording the component tasks, and again the interested reader is referred to those texts specifically written on the subject of task analysis.

Once the specific behaviors comprising the subobjectives of the task have been identified, the task analyzer must decide on the order of presentation. That is, the task analyzer must determine the sequence of experience that leads to proficiency in that particular task. This determination of the hierarchy of subskills is the critical issue, one to which the psychoeducational consultant may bring his or her special skills.

Intervention Phase. The utilization of task analysis techniques will lead to the development of specific academic programs that are focused in terms of the child's current behavior, regardless of chronological age or grade level. By considering skills directly related to the classroom tasks, specific academic recommendations emerge with clear relevance for the teacher.

At the intervention level, the consultant is needed to collaborate with the consultee in determining those variables affecting the learning and to provide a means of manipulating those variables to increase the probability of evoking the correct response. For example, variables such as brightness, material, function, size, texture, position, and color may all be used in cueing the desired behavior. The task for the consultant will be to identify what might be manipulated and to blend this with the teacher's knowledge of what can be manipulated to produce the desired results.

A Case Example. The following brief case example is offered to clarify the role of the consultant using task analysis for Level II consultation.

Johnny was referred by the teacher to the consultant because he "may be learning disabled." Prior to meeting with Johnny, the consultant interviewed the teacher and discovered that Johnny was apparently unable to "do math." Rather than respond at Level I consultation, which would require psychodiagnostics, the consultant suggested that perhaps by looking over Johnny's previous homework sheets and test papers, the teacher and the consultant might be better able to determine what skills Johnny demonstrated and which ones he needed to develop.

Through this conference, the original referral problem of being "learning disabled" was more specifically defined as being unable to subtract two two-digit numbers requiring regrouping, without the use of concrete objects. The subobjectives to this goal were established through consultant-consultee collaboration:

1. Provided with the two-digit numbers, the student renames the larger number in the manner of tens plus units.
2. The student renames the smaller number in the same manner.

3. The student then regroups the units column of the larger number, borrowing one ten from the tens column and adding it to the units column.
4. The student then subtracts in the units column.
5. The student then subtracts in the tens column.
6. The student renames the answer, adding the units and tens.
7. The student reads the answer.

The overall educational objective established at this time was, given two two-digit numbers written on a paper, the student will correctly subtract the smaller number from the larger number eight out of ten times.

In discussing these subobjectives, the teacher indicated that Johnny had demonstrated on his homework and previous tests that he was capable of performing the first two. Therefore, it was decided that the intervention procedures would begin at subskill three.

The consultee was pleased and somewhat relieved following this session, feeling that Johnny was not as hopeless as she first felt and that a blueprint for her teaching had been established via the task analysis. A follow-up visit revealed that the teacher was employing similar task analysis procedures for defining and remediating other students' academic problems. This was one occasion when the potential educative-preventive nature of a consultation encounter was achieved.

Behavior Modification Consultation

The most often reported consultation techniques providing indirect service to the child are those using behavior modification for classroom management (for example, Bergan and Caldwell, 1967; Dustin and Burden, 1972; Hall and others, 1970; Hall, Lund, and Jackson, 1968; Kennedy, 1971; Morice, 1968; O'Leary and O'Leary, 1972; Randolph, 1972; Stephens, 1970; Thomas, Becker, and Armstrong, 1968). The development of a technology of behavior modification, the growing use of observational instruments, the focus on behavioral objectives, and the growing dissatisfaction with traditional psychological services noted earlier have all contributed to the development of formal behavioral consultation methods (Bergan, 1977; Bergan and Caldwell, 1967; Bersoff and Grieger, 1971; Goodwin, Garvey, and Barclay, 1971). These authors and others provide an extensive body of research suggesting that behavior problems in the school can be changed efficiently through systematic observation and subsequent modification of the reinforcement contingencies controlling the child's behavior. Although we refer in this chapter to some of the relevant research that has been conducted, we make no attempt to review the wide variety of research or applications in this area, since this task has been accomplished in several other sources (for example, Axelrod, 1977; Bergan, 1977; Hall, 1971; Neisworth, Deno, and Jenkins, 1969; O'Leary and O'Leary, 1972; Piper, 1974).

It has been demonstrated repeatedly that behavior modification techniques can successfully change behavior when administered by a trained professional, and these techniques are also applicable to a consultation model (Bergan and Caldwell, 1967). Recently, evidence has accumulated demonstrating that a consultant can influence children's behavior by helping teachers to implement behavior modification strategies (for example, Bergan, 1977; Cooper, Thomson, and Baer, 1970; Cossairt, Hall, and Hopkins, 1973; Hall and others, 1970; McNamara, 1971). Since this chapter focuses on indirect service techniques, our discussion of behavior modification will stress observation and intervention ideas that can be implemented directly by the teacher with the assistance of a consultant. We will not consider techniques that are so complicated that they can be implemented only with the direct assistance of the consultant in the classroom. The reader interested in such direct techniques is referred to Hall (1971), O'Leary and O'Leary (1972), and Piper (1974).

Behavioral consultation proceeds in a series of steps, which involves: (1) defining the problem in observable terms; (2) collecting baseline data; (3) developing an intervention plan; (4) implementing the intervention, and (5) evaluating the intervention by continuing data collection. The first four of these steps will be considered as substeps of the problem identification stage and the intervention stage, which were presented in Chapter Four.

Problem Identification Stage of Consultation

Defining the Problem. The first step in problem identification is for the consultant and consultee to agree on a clear and specific definition of the problem. A consultant using a behavior modification orientation will attempt to develop a definition based on directly observable behavior that can be charted or counted readily. Furthermore, the definition will often emphasize the antecedent and consequential conditions that may control behavior. The conceptualization underlying this sort of definition will emphasize extrapersonal factors influencing behavior, and often this orientation may conflict with the teacher's emphasis on intrapersonal factors influencing behavior. Thus, rather than being specific and behavioral, the teacher might report that the child is emotionally disturbed, learning disabled, lazy, or even wicked. Such definitions of the problem are too vague. Often an important task of consultation is to reconcile the difference between consultant and consultee in their orientation to defining the problem, resulting in an emphasis on the environmental factors (particularly the classroom factors) that can be manipulated in an effort to help the child.

Collecting Data. One part of defining the problem will include observation of student behavior. The use of objective data facilitates the development of specifically defined goals, which leads clearly to treatment and intervention plans. Furthermore, this observation is often a meaningful intervention with the teacher in itself, and it provides a basis for evaluating the effectiveness of the consultation effort.

When using a behavioral approach to Level II consultation, the observation and collection of data are completed by the teacher, the referred child, or the child's peers. Several sources on observational techniques should be examined by any behavioral consultant (for example, Bergan, 1977; Hall, 1971; Neisworth, Deno, and Jenkins, 1969; O'Leary and O'Leary, 1972; Piper, 1974). In this section, we will describe a few of these techniques, which can be implemented by the classroom teacher with minimal difficulty. These techniques have been adapted from Piper (1974).

1. When possible, the teacher should record behaviors that leave written evidence—for example, the number of work sheets that have been completed. This sort of behavior can be counted easily by the teacher without any interference with classroom routine.

2. Some behaviors, such as in-seat behavior, can be observed and recorded at intervals. For example, rather than keeping a narrative account of how often a particular child is in-seat, a kitchen timer can be set for intervals of five, ten, or fifteen minutes. The child's in-seat behavior would be observed by the teacher only when the timer rings, thereby minimizing disruption of the teaching process. When this sort of procedure is used, the children will often enjoy it as a game.

3. Sometimes the children can help count behaviors that are well defined. In fact, good students could be permitted to earn the privilege of being the behavior counter for the day.

4. When reinforcing behavior with tokens, stars, or checks, the reward system can be used as a method of observing behavior as well. When using this technique with an entire class, the record sheet can cover the bulletin board, and when using this technique with an individual child, the record sheet can be taped to the top of the child's desk. In these ways, the observation and reward systems will be clearly brought to the child's attention.

5. Some behaviors occur on a regular basis throughout the day, and so an accurate record is not dependent upon observations made throughout the entire day. For example, a teacher might get an accurate reading of some frequent behaviors by observing for only one-half hour per day.

Intervention Phase of Consultation

Developing an Intervention Plan. Just as the consultant and teacher must collaborate to develop a consistent conceptual understanding of the problem, it is essential that they collaborate in developing the intervention plan. This collaborative process should involve both consultant and teacher in generating intervention ideas, and it should blend some of the consultant's theoretical knowledge with the teacher's awareness of what is possible in the classroom. The consultant needs to be aware of the capabilities of the teacher, relevant aspects of his or her personality, the teacher's expectations for the child, and the general ecology of the classroom and school while generating such intervention plans.

Behavior modification interventions are based on the concepts of reinforcement, punishment, generalization, discrimination, shaping, fading, and extinction, and these concepts are discussed at length in the sources referred to at the beginning of the section on behavior modification consultation. One of the major problems is to find a variety of rewards that really have the potential to change the child's behavior (for example, foods, points, stars, tokens, classroom jobs and privileges, parties, honors, and positive notes to parents). Frequently, teachers are most amenable to using verbal praise as well as nonverbal (hand-shake, pat on the back, hug, or smile). However, sometimes more powerful reinforcement systems such as token economies are necessary to modify behavior that is more difficult to change. Practical examples of both of these types of reinforcement are presented in the cases at the end of this chapter.

Implementing Intervention. Once the problem has been defined clearly and an intervention strategy generated, the plan must be implemented, and the consultant should provide regular follow-up contact to ensure that the intervention is implemented successfully. Meeting regularly to discuss the case's progress, providing support and reinforcement for the teacher's effort, adjusting the intervention plan as needed, and assisting in the interpretation of the data collected during treatment are all essential consultant behaviors during this phase of consultation.

Case Examples. The following case should help to illustrate Level II consultation using a behavior modification approach. Anthony was a well-proportioned six-year-old who was referred to Parsons for a psychodiagnostic evaluation because of his apparent inability to cope in the classroom. The first step was to meet with the teacher to define in specific detail the referral problem. Anthony's teacher reported that he was a poor learner who was easily distracted and generally overactive, and he was becoming an unbearable disruptive influence on the class. When asked to pinpoint the behavior (problem identification) that needed to be changed, the teacher indicated that Anthony talked too frequently without raising his hand or being recognized in any way. Therefore, it was decided that an appropriate goal would be to have Anthony raise his hand and be recognized by the teacher prior to talking in class. Both the consultant and teacher agreed that it might be possible to modify this behavior without a formal psychoeducational assessment.

The second step in the process was for the teacher to observe Anthony's responding behavior in order to make some baseline observations (collection of data). These observations were made during two thirty-minute periods (one before and one after lunch) for the next two days. Typically, this would not be sufficient time for baseline observations. However, pragmatic limitations in the school situation led to the shortest possible baseline. During the observation period, the consultant noted that the teacher was an active, energetic instructor who posed questions consistently and encouraged active participation from the students. During the teaching process, the children would raise and wave their hands vigorously to have the opportunity to report the answer. Anthony, like the other children, often raised and waved his hand and attempted to obtain teacher attention. However, unlike many of the other children, Anthony was not called on once during the consultant's observation period. Following the discussion periods, when the teacher was introducing a new topic or when the children were to do seat work, Anthony would talk to himself or attempt to distract a neighboring student. The teacher's inevitable response was to come over to Anthony's seat and reprimand him. The close connection between the observed behaviors and the reinforcement contingencies suggested the hypothesis that Anthony's increase in inappropriate behavior (in-seat talking out) was attributable to the teacher attention given in the form of a reprimand, which inevitably followed the inappropriate talking behavior.

The third step in the behavioral consultation process was to determine an appropriate intervention plan. To do this with maximum involvement on the part of the teacher, the consultant asked the teacher to tape record her class with an audio cassette. The audio recording was to be done during the same periods of time in the day that she had previously used to record Anthony's inappropriate behavior. Furthermore, the teacher was asked to try to stay in front of the room as much as possible during the tape recording, so that she would have to recognize the children by name frequently. The consultant and the consultee reviewed the tapes, and in the process the teacher noted, half-jokingly, that "Anthony sure is popular, always getting teacher attention!" One important strength of this particular case was that the teacher made this observation herself with the facilitating help of the consultant.

This active involvement on the part of the teacher is likely to increase the probability that the teacher will implement some change effectively.

Following the review of the recording, the consultant discussed how the teacher's observation paralleled his own. Together they developed a program in which Anthony's talking in-seat would be ignored, and his first attempts at appropriate in-seat behavior (hand raised, waiting to be recognized) would be reinforced with teacher attention. In addition, the teacher would say, "Thank you for waiting to be called on before answering, Anthony" or some other cue of similar specificity.

The fourth step in the process of behavioral consultation was to implement the intervention, and this was done for a two-week period with no modification necessary in the program. During this period, the consultant met with the teacher, reinforced her efforts, and encouraged her to continue, noting that his support and assistance would be there if needed.

The last step of the process was to evaluate the impact of the intervention by continuing to collect data. In this instance, the continued data collection was performed by the teacher as she continued to tape record her lessons. She reported that things had changed for the better, and this was confirmed when the consultant returned to listen to a taped segment of one hour. To the delight of both the consultant and the teacher, a total absence of reprimands was noted, an absence of inappropriate talking-out by Anthony was noted, and a number of positive reinforcements for appropriate behavior were observed. A further result of this intervention was that the tape recording became a part of the teacher's procedures for checking her interaction with other students on her own. She noted that listening to the tapes gave her insight into how she often "played her favorites." The teacher was now pleased with Anthony's classroom behavior, and the case was closed.

The school consultant might use behavioral strategies with a variety of other caretakers in addition to teachers. For example, parents (Hawkins and others, 1966), paraprofessionals (Parsons, 1978), and even other children in the class (Surratt, Ulrich, and Hawkins, 1969) can be effective in implementing behavior modification strategies. Involving other caretakers besides the teacher helps to broaden the consultant's potential impact.

The following example demonstrates this latter point as well as suggesting the practical effects that can be obtained by using a token economy. R. Parsons (1978) trained a high school secretary to help implement a token economy using a check-mark system. The program was designed for ninety-six tenth-, eleventh-, and twelfth-grade males who had demonstrated a high rate of unexcused absences during the previous academic year. The target behavior was to increase class attendance as well as arriving on time. It was decided that the students would be reinforced for this behavior with tokens administered in the form of check marks. The schedule of reinforcement was that for each class period the student attended during a day (six possible periods), he would receive 1 point, and an additional point per class would be awarded if the student was punctual. Both tangible rewards (gifts from the students' store, lunch tokens, bus tokens) and in-school privileges (early admission to the lunch room, hall passes) served as back-up reinforcers.

Following the development of the program plan, Mrs. Ellis (the secretary) met with the boys and explained that she would record their daily attendance and punctuality. For each class attended and for each class attended on time they would be awarded a point (maximum = 2 points per class). She indicated further that points would be recorded with a check mark, and the continuing total of points accrued would be posted on a special chart hung outside the guidance center. She also instructed the boys that once a week (Friday) they could exchange the tokens for various gifts and privileges. Mrs. Ellis explained the exchange rates and procedures for exchange to be followed, and then she began the program. The token group demonstrated a reduction in violations of attendance (either unexcused absences, tardiness, or both). In addition to the actual reduction in attendance problems, the anecdotal reports from both the participating students and the secretary were very encouraging, resulting in the expansion and continuation of the program.

Summary

The techniques we have discussed under Level II consultation (task analysis and behavior modification) assist the consultee to

become a mediator of change. At this level of functioning, therefore, the mental health specialist removes himself from assuming
the principal responsibility for the child and provides the means
for the teacher to continue as the primary caretaker for the child in
the school. In fact, the data gathering for this type of consultation is
done by the consultee (or others) rather than the consultant. Also,
Level II consultation (as Level I) emphasizes intervention strategies
that are implemented by the consultee with collaboration and support from the consultant. The potential problem with this approach to service delivery is that it is difficult to ensure that the
consultee will cooperate in implementing the program. For this
reason, collaboration and active involvement of the teacher are
emphasized. It has been noted that, in many instances, strategies
aimed at remediating the referral problem have been developed
only to prove ineffective, because the consultant failed to develop a
supportive, collaborative relationship with the consultee (Grieger,
1972; Parsons, 1976). Thus, it is essential for the consultant operating at this level of consultation to be aware of the potential factors
working to undermine the relationship with the consultee as well as
procedures for overcoming such resistance. Many of the issues to
be considered in developing such a relationship have already been
noted in Chapter Three.

CHAPTER SEVEN

Direct Service to the Teacher

□ □ □ □ □ □ □ □ □ □ □ □

We have been stressing the importance of environmental factors that influence behavior in the classroom. Obviously, one such factor is the teacher, who is central to understanding and remediating many classroom problems. Psychological services with a preventive orientation should be available to the teacher to improve his or her ability to function effectively with all the children in the classroom. Direct service to the teacher is an investment in teacher change as a means of establishing classroom conditions conducive to preventive mental health. Although the consultation methods described previously (Levels I and II) may improve the teacher's general functioning, this third level is distinct, in that the consultant's *primary goal* is to promote change in the teacher's behavior rather than the child's behavior. Changing the child's behavior becomes a secondary goal of Level III consultation.

There are times when it may be difficult to distinguish between direct service to the teacher (Level III) and indirect service to the child (Level II). Many of the teacher skills that a consultant may stress at Level III may also be recommended as a part of an intervention effort directed toward the child at Level II (for example, behavior modification techniques, teacher effectiveness training techniques, affective education techniques, teacher-student observation techniques, and group process techniques). However, at Level II, the focus of the consultant's intervention is to change the behavior of a specific child or group of children; at Level III, the focus is to change the teacher's behavior so that his or her interaction with children will be different in the future.

The primary methods we recommend to provide direct service to the teacher are derived from Caplan's consultee-centered case consultation techniques (Caplan, 1970). Interviewing techniques are used by the consultant to determine whether the problem is relevant to any of the categories requiring direct service to the teacher. These categories of teacher problems include lack of understanding, lack of skill, lack of self-confidence, and lack of objectivity (Caplan, 1970). Once the consultant establishes whether the problem lies in one of these categories, then he would choose from a variety of intervention techniques, including didactic information giving, theme interference reduction, direct confrontation, or emotional support. The diagnostic and remedial techniques used most frequently for each category of direct service to the teacher will be defined and illustrated further in the sections that follow.

Lack of Understanding

Often, the teacher draws erroneous conclusions about (or simply lacks the psychological knowledge to draw conclusions about) a child's unusual behavior (Fine and Tyler, 1971). In these instances, the consultant in the school can share his knowledge and expertise regarding child development, interpersonal dynamics, and the teaching-learning process. Didactic exchanges on these topics may help a teacher to recognize that what was apparently deviant behavior falls within normal limits for a given level of development or for the particular ecological factors affecting the classroom. This sort of information exchange will often free a teacher to try a variety of options that were not available previously.

There are numerous possible causes of lack of understanding. For example, a teacher might misinterpret some data in a child's cumulative folder, a psychological evaluation, or a previous teacher's report. As a result, the teacher might jump to invalid conclusions or develop inappropriate expectations for the student. The consultant should be available to provide the appropriate information to help clarify such situations. The effectiveness of the teacher is not only a function of his or her content expertise, but is also a function of the awareness of variables affecting the delivery of such content. The consultant can use his knowledge of methods for assessing and modifying interactional processes to help the teacher establish conditions that will facilitate learning. Some of these conditions that might be considered include flexibility, cooperativeness, and democratic attitudes (Gordon, 1970; Hamacheck, 1968; Rogers, 1969). Often, the lack of understanding regarding the behavior of a child or a group of children or the inadequate understanding of variables affecting the interaction of teacher and students can concern several teachers. As a result, there will be times when it is most advantageous to do this sort of consultation in a group. Some examples should help to clarify this approach to consultation.

In one example, Meyers was consulting with a teacher who had training and experience working with brain-injured children, but who had no exposure to emotionally disturbed children. This teacher was working with a seven-year-old youngster who was emotionally disturbed and showed many autistic behaviors. Unsure of her understanding, and particularly unsure of her approach to dealing with this youngster, she referred the child for a psychological evaluation. Discussions with the teacher revealed that she was reluctant to try ideas that she thought might be effective because of her feeling that she lacked the expertise to work with an emotionally disturbed youngster.

Consultation consisted of providing as much information as possible to the teacher, so that she could feel more comfortable in her understanding of the child. One step in this process was to provide some reading material on emotionally disturbed and autistic children. A second step was to help the teacher set up a day when she could visit another program that dealt with similar children. The third step was to meet with her and discuss important concepts related to the etiology and treatment of such children. As a part of this discussion, one of the most helpful consultation techniques was to explain that this seven-year-old youngster was actually much younger in social-emotional maturity. The consultant knew from previous conversations that this teacher had a young child at home who was not yet one year of age. Consequently, the consultant tried to explain that, in many social-emotional ways, this student needed to be treated more like her own young child.

As a result of this discussion and the other interventions, the teacher no longer felt that the child was strange, and her desire to avoid this youngster diminished. Instead, she seemed to think of him more as a normal human being who happened to be slow in developing social-emotional skills. As a result, she was free to do many things she had wanted to do all along. For example, after consultation, she was observed holding and rocking this child in her arms. In addition, she set up a system in which she devoted specific times of each day to working individually with him, when she would do things like play with him on a big toy truck or rock him in the baby cradle.

Another example was Sister Anna, an eighth-grade teacher in an inner city parochial school, who became very upset over the constant fighting, criticizing, teasing, and generally unkind behavior that was exhibited by her eighth-graders. Sister Anna had taught the same group of students in seventh grade, and she was confused and frustrated by the apparent metamorphosis of her seventh-graders, who had been sensitive and caring but now appeared insensitive and hypercritical. Parsons discussed this situation with Sister Anna and found that most of the insensitivity was related to issues of physical appearance (dress, mannerism, physique, and so on). Following a brief discussion regarding adolescence as a period of development, he suggested that Sister Anna view a film-strip series prepared by Human Relations Media Center (1977) on adolescent development. The following day, prior to the start of classes, Sister Anna, who was smiling sheepishly, apologetically asked if she had really been as upset the day before as she was now remembering. Parsons gave assurance that her concern was real and was nothing to be ashamed about, and he reiterated that adolescence is a trying time for both the adolescents and those around them.

Sister Anna stated that she now recognized (after reading the suggested materials and viewing the film strips) that the turbulance she was observing stemmed from the students' own sensitivity to what they probably felt were faults in their own bodily appearance that could not be remediated. Subsequently, she used these and other materials she obtained to help her students become aware that adolescence is a shared experience and can be viewed less emotionally. She also initiated discussions to help them express their sensitivities in a more constructive manner. The result of the consultation with Sister Anna was that she was able to view the classroom more positively and develop strategies to foster a healthier emotional climate for her students.

Lack of Skill

Often, the teacher is quite knowledgeable about the factors that affect the teaching process. However, while being aware of the empirical literature on the subject and the relevant theory, a teacher might still lack the skill or ability to implement this knowledge effectively in the classroom. Therefore, the consultant should be aware of the various methods and techniques that are available for the analysis of classroom factors affecting the overall environment, teacher-student interaction, and student development (see Amidon and Simon, 1965; Flanders, 1970; Ginott, 1972; Gordon, 1974).

Since consultation focuses on the environmental factors affecting the behavior, learning, and social development of children in the classroom, one important consultation goal is to develop teachers' skills in the systematic observation of the classroom environment. A second important goal is to develop teachers' skills at intervening in the classroom environment based on observations that have been made, whether by the teacher, the consultant, or someone else.

In addition to observation tools, other techniques have been noted as appropriate for consultants to help teachers improve their skills. For example, it has been argued that sensitivity training and encounter sessions (Grossman and Clark, 1967; Hyman, 1971) can help to promote teachers' sensitivity to the needs of pupils; that preparing and presenting formal reviews of the literature can stimulate the use of specific techniques and the development of related skills (Heisey, 1967); and that suggesting specific techniques for communications, such as Gordon's (1974) teacher effectiveness training or Gazda's (1973) empathy training, can improve teachers' relationship skills.

Although systematic classroom observation is a primary technique for improving teacher skills, most descriptions of school consultation ignore these techniques. Two notable exceptions include consultation based on a behavior modification approach (O'Leary and O'Leary, 1972) and consultation based on a group process approach (Schmuck and Schmuck, 1974). Both of these orientations emphasize detailed intervention plans based in part upon systematic observation of classroom behavior. Additional observation techniques have been developed specifically for analyzing the behavior and interaction of teachers and students in the classroom. Simon and Boyer (1970) provide an anthology of the most widely used observational techniques. However, these have not generally been considered as specific tools for teacher consultation. One notable exception is Hyman's (1972a) discussion of the use of observation techniques in teacher consultation. He suggests that the teaching process should be examined systematically in three areas: cognition, affect, and management.

Observing Cognitive Factors. Hyman (1972b) notes that Sanders (1966) has utilized Bloom's (1956) work to develop a manual for the analysis of the seven levels of thinking, which are inferred by answers to questions asked by teachers. The levels include memory, translation, interpretation, application, analysis, synthesis, and evaluation, in ascending order. Davis and Hunkins (1966) have found that patterns of teaching generally feature questions by the teacher that require the lower levels of thought. For example, a teacher's question is more likely to involve memory than analysis. If a teacher lacks skills in facilitating the higher levels of thought, the consultant can observe teacher-student interaction with Sanders (1966) scale. Such observation would provide the basis for suggesting teaching techniques for stimulating higher levels of thinking.

Observing Affective Factors. Of several systems for analyzing teacher-pupil interaction in terms of affective dimensions, the Flanders Interaction Analysis categories is one technique that has been used a great deal in classroom research (Amidon and Simon, 1965; Flanders, 1970). The categories are broken down into four areas. Indirect teacher talk includes the first four categories: (1) accepts feelings, (2) praises or encourages, (3) accepts or uses ideas of students, and (4) asks questions. Direct teacher talk includes the next three categories: (5) lectures, (6) gives directions, and (7) criticizes or justifies authority. Student talk includes the next two categories: (8) student response and (9) student initiation. Finally, the last category (10) is coded for silence or confusion.

Flanders' (1970) review of the research that has been done with this technique is encouraging. However, one recent review of the conflicting research (Rosenshine and Furst, 1971) concluded that neither direct nor indirect teaching styles produced superior achievement. There is more consistent evidence that indirect teaching styles result in gains for students in cooperativeness, ability to work independently, and feelings of intrinsic rather than extrinsic control of their behavior (Hyman, 1964, 1972a). These are important goals independent of achievement, because they relate to preventive mental health in the schools. Although not conclusive, the research literature with the Flanders categories points to a trend sufficiently so that the consultant can confidently use this technique as a basis for effective feedback to teachers regarding their skills in the process of teaching.

More recently, Jere Brophy and Tom Good have developed a system for studying teacher-child dyadic interactions (Brophy and Good, 1969; Good and Brophy, 1970). Rather than focus on the interaction between the teachers and the class as a unit as Flanders (1970) did, the technique developed by Good and Brophy (1970) focuses on the interaction between the teacher and the individual child. Moreover, Brophy and Good (1970) have suggested this technique as a useful tool for teacher consultation because of its ability to focus intensively on the relationship between the teacher and the individual child. Of course, like many other classroom observation techniques, a significant body of research regarding its use in consultation has yet to emerge.

To examine the relationship between children's coping behavior and teaching style, Spaulding (1967) has devised a set of instruments referred to as the Coping Analysis Schedule for Educational Settings (CASES) and the Spaulding Teacher Activity Rating Schedule (STARS). These systems can be used together to code teacher and student behavior, or they can be used separately. STARS provides a measure of the teacher's techniques for establishing control in the classroom by the use of such categories as setting performance goals, prescribing certain actions, approving student behavior, and disapproving student behavior. CASES provides data about all classroom behaviors of students; essentially, it is designed to provide information about students' behavioral styles. Behavioral styles are assessed by observing behavior in thirteen categories. Some of these categories are: aggressive behavior; negative attention-getting behavior; manipulating, controlling, and directing others; resisting; and self-directed activity. The utility of this system is that, while providing objective measures of students' social-emotional coping styles in the classroom, there is the chance to observe simultaneously how the teacher interacts in terms of these socio-emotional coping behaviors. Therefore, this system has particular utility for providing assistance to a teacher who may be having some difficulty with children who present social-emotional problems.

Observing Management Factors. The third area of classroom observation discussed by Hyman is the study of general classroom management. Jacob Kounin (1970) has developed a method of identifying six different teacher styles for managing behavior: (1) withitness; (2) overlapping; (3) momentum; (4) smoothness; (5) group alerting; and (6) accountability. *Withitness* is defined as a teacher communicating to the children that he knows what the children are doing. *Overlapping* refers to what the teacher does when he has to attend to two different things simultaneously. *Momentum* concerns the behaviors of teachers that affect the rate of flow of activities. *Smoothness* delineates behaviors initiated by teachers that interfere with the flow of movement in academic activities. The last two categories, *group alerting* and *accountability*, both relate to the extent to which the teacher maintains a group focus during recitations in contrast to becoming immersed in a single child. An emerging body of data suggests that these categories of teacher behavior affect classroom discipline (Kounin, 1970; Hyman, 1972a, b).

Both Hyman (1972a, b) and Marino (1975) have used this technique in teacher consultation. Based on applied use of the scale, Hyman concluded that Kounin's system can be used as a basis to help teachers change their classroom behavior. Marino (1975) investigated the utility of this technique in teacher consultation. He found that consultation resulted in a significant reduction in teachers' classroom-management errors, with concomitant reductions in the negative classroom behavior of students (however, the change in student behavior was not significant).

Improving Teachers' Knowledge and Skills

Martin (1974) has outlined a procedure for improving teachers' skills, which is illustrated in Figure 2. The procedure is based on the idea that teachers' behavior in the classroom might be inappropriate for a number of reasons, including lack of awareness of classroom behavior, inability to demonstrate teaching behavior consistent with teaching ideals, lack of understanding of what is considered to be ideal teaching behavior by educational and psychological experts, or lack of congruence between what the teacher considers ideal teaching behavior and what educational and psychological experts consider ideal teaching behavior. Further, Martin's procedure is based on the hypothesis that self-correction is easier and more fruitful than consultant-produced correction. The consultant essentially provides a mirror for the teacher to see his or her own behavior. Data are communicated to the teacher to provide objective, nonevaluative feedback, and the teacher is encouraged to respond in the way that he or she feels is best.

The first step in the process, after observations are made, is to ask the teacher to estimate the frequency of the various categories of teacher behavior that were observed. The teacher is then told the observed frequencies of the behaviors. If the estimates are poor, the teacher is observed again, and the process is repeated.

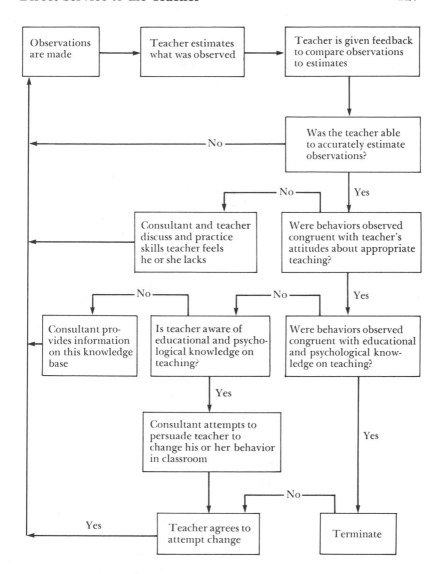

Figure 2.   Stages of Consultation When Using Classroom Observation to Change Teacher Behavior Toward Students.

If the estimates are good, the second step is begun, in which the teacher is asked to compare the observed behavior with what he considers to be appropriate or optimal teacher behavior in this situation. If these frequencies are not congruent, the consultant and teacher work on the skills necessary to produce the appropriate behavior, and the observation process, including comparison with teacher estimates, is repeated.

If the teacher felt that the behavior observed was congruent with his ideas about teaching, then the third step in the process is initiated. In this step, the teacher's behavior is compared with theoretical and empirical knowledge regarding appropriate teacher behavior. If what is observed is not congruent with the body of knowledge, the consultant then determines whether the teacher is aware of this knowledge; if not, the consultant provides the relevant knowledge base.

If the teacher is aware of the relevant theory but does not agree with it, the consultant tries to convince him to try some new behaviors based on this knowledge. If the teacher agrees, the process of observation and comparison with estimates, personal norms, and professional norms is repeated. The process is continued until the teacher is aware of his own teaching behavior, the teacher's behavior is congruent with his own norms, the teacher's behavior is congruent with the current professional knowledge base, or until the teacher feels comfortable with his own behavior and does not want to change it.

It is our feeling that most people who observe teacher behavior move directly from observation to the step in which they attempt to produce change in teachers' beliefs and behavior by imposing their personal or professional values. Not surprisingly, this approach results in much resentment and little change.

Although the model we have outlined is theoretical, in the sense that the entire model has not been tested, the first step in the model has been investigated (Martin and Keller, 1976). The purpose of this research was to ascertain to what extent teachers are aware of the quantity and quality of their contacts with individual students in the classroom. Thirty elementary teachers were observed for one day using the Brophy and Good observation system mentioned previously in this chapter. At the end of the day, teachers were asked to estimate the quantity and quality of their interaction with individual children during the day. It was determined that most teachers are unaware of many kinds of interaction they have with students. This research provides at least partial support for the model. If teachers are not sufficiently aware of their teaching behavior, then nonevaluative feedback to generate self-awareness in teachers is a potentially important consultation procedure.

Lack of Confidence

Teachers are challenged constantly by the disparate personalities of their children; they are bombarded with literature describing technological advances in curriculum materials; and they are subjected to mass media criticism of education. Such challenges can shake a teacher's self-confidence and self-esteem (Fine and Tyler, 1971). Poor self-esteem is a problem that is likely to emerge with new teachers who have not yet developed a style with which they are confident—however, it can occur with all teachers. In those instances where there appears to be reduced self-confidence, and where there is no lack of objectivity apparent, the teacher may simply need ego support. In these cases, the consultant can help by demonstrating a willingness to listen while the teacher describes the situation and his approach to dealing with it. It can be helpful simply to support the good ideas of the teacher. Another type of support that may be provided is to help the teacher resist the apparent attacks on his self-esteem.

Parsons was involved in one case, where the faculty of an urban, private elementary school, with a majority of novice, first-year teachers, was suffering from a lack of self-confidence (Parsons, Stone, and Feuerstein, 1977). The school environment had become tense, because the self-confidence of a large number of new teachers had been undermined as a result of normal classroom frustrations. There was a great deal of screaming and teacher-student conflict. Consequently, an effort was made to bolster the confidence of the group of teachers by presenting a rational-emotive approach to the classroom (Ellis, 1963). It was hypothesized, for example, that many of these teachers, who were still somewhat uncomfortable with the subject material, might view thought-provoking questions by the students as a threat to their professional integrity. This could result in angry, sarcastic, and generally inappropriate responses by the teacher. It was as if the novice teachers were saying to themselves, "As a professional educator, I should know" or "To be worthwhile, I must be perfectly competent, and therefore, if I don't know the answer, I'm not worthwhile." The goal of the workshop was to suggest that the teachers' internal feelings of incompetence and worthlessness were generated from irrational self-talk rather than from the specific questions posed by the students. Thus, an effort was made to show the teachers that they themselves had helped to cause these feelings, which had resulted in inappropriate teacher comments such as "Not now!," "Don't interrupt," and so forth. The teachers were shown that they could help to reduce the generally tense, negative learning environment. The consultants introduced the basic principles underlying rational-emotive therapy and encouraged the teachers to apply the Ellis "A-B-C" theory to their classroom experiences. Furthermore, it was suggested that the teachers could generate rational alternatives to their described reactions within the setting. Pretest and posttest questionnaires on the teachers' level of rationality and self-confidence in classroom management, along with anecdotal data and the reduction in teacher referrals, indicated an increase in the self-confidence of teachers during the consultation experience.

Lack of Objectivity

Occasionally, the teacher may have the understanding and skills necessary to work with a particular child but be inhibited from using his professional skills because of personal, affective involvement with the child. Caplan (1970) notes that this can occur when a consultee fails to maintain the proper professional distance from a client. The result is a clouding of the consultee's judgment regarding the client.

Caplan's (1970) effort to define lack of objectivity has been an important contribution to consultation theory and practice. By emphasizing that a lack of teacher objectivity can interfere with teaching, Caplan has broadened the scope of mental health services significantly. Yet, few professionals attempt to increase teacher objectivity using Caplan's techniques, partially because the structure of schools and of most psychological service delivery systems does not encourage such interventions. For example, there are few places where a teacher and psychologist can speak in privacy, and, in addition, the teacher has little time free to talk to a consultant. However, Caplan's work has had a large audience, and, despite the interfering factors, a growing number of mental health professionals in the schools are aware of the potential help they can provide by increasing teacher objectivity.

Caplan has developed a system, based in part on his psychoanalytic background, for understanding four different causes of lack of objectivity—direct personal involvement, simple identification, transference, and characterological disturbance. In addition, Caplan (1970) places considerable emphasis on one specific type of transference, which he labels *theme interference*. We will define briefly each type of lack of objectivity. These definitions are taken from Caplan (1970), and the reader is referred to Caplan for more detailed definitions.

Direct personal involvement occurs when the consultee (teacher) changes his professional role with the child and evolves instead a personal relationship.* Under these conditions, the teacher allows the direct expression of his own personal needs in the work setting. Examples of direct personal involvement include a teacher developing a maternal relationship with a student, a teacher responding to a student based primarily on racial prejudice, or a teacher falling in love with a student.

Simple identification is a mild form of identification, where the teacher identifies with the child or with someone related to the child, such as the mother or a sibling. The teacher does not distort reality seriously, as there is some obvious similarity between the teacher and the person with whom he identifies. As a result of this identification, the teacher's judgment is disturbed. The teacher may describe the person with whom he identifies in very positive terms and describe others who interact with this person in very negative terms.

Transference is a form of identification involving more distor-

*This discussion will use the word *teacher* rather than *consultee* for clarity. However, readers are reminded that many school personnel other than the teacher could be a consultee.

tion of reality by the teacher. When transference is involved, the teacher forces the drama surrounding the child's life to fit some aspect of his own life. In doing this, the teacher transfers attitudes and feelings that derive from past relationships and/or fantasies onto specific aspects of the work situation.

Characterological distortions of perception and behavior involve an even more serious distortion of reality in the work situation. Here, covert or minor disturbances of work performance occur because of enduring emotional disorders.

Theme interference is the last category related to lack of objectivity. Caplan describes theme interference as a special type of minor transference reaction. He suggests that major transference reactions (which we just defined) usually involve either disturbed individuals (teachers) or organizations with inadequate administration or supervision. However, there will be occasions when theme interference will impede the functioning of almost any professional. It occurs when an unresolved personal problem is expressed indirectly on the job, and the result is temporary ineffectiveness and emotional instability. In other words, a teacher who is generally effective finds a professional situation to be confusing and upsetting.

Caplan notes that, since a theme usually involves some unresolved problem, it will involve negative feelings and a rigid pattern of thinking. The rigidity will usually be represented syllogistically with an "inevitable link" between two thoughts. According to Caplan's definition of a theme (1970, pp. 145–146): "Statement A denotes a particular situation or condition that was characteristic of the original unsolved problem. Statement B denotes the unpleasant outcome. The syllogism takes the form, 'All A inevitably leads to B.' The implication is that . . . everyone who is involved in A inevitably suffers B."

The following example of a theme is taken from consultation with a middle-aged female teacher. The teacher referred a fourth-grade youngster who had just begun to show emotional problems that the teacher found confusing. She was unsure of the best approach to handle this child. The teacher reported that this student's parents had been divorced recently, and the mother had returned to work to support the family. During the course of interviews and some informal discussions, it was learned also that this teacher's parents had been divorced, the teacher's mother had been forced to return to work, and the teacher had developed some emotional difficulties in relating to peers in school. Furthermore, it was learned that the teacher, who had two school-aged children, was contemplating separation from her husband. Apparently, her present life situation, in conjunction with the recent classroom situation, had stimulated the reemergence of an unresolved conflict. The resulting theme was conceptualized by the consultant as follows:

Initial category: "A divorced woman with two children works a full-time job."

Inevitable outcome: "She will have children with emotional problems who will inevitably have difficulty getting along with peers."

One of the appealing features of Caplan's consideration of themes is that it is one of the few problems discussed in the literature of consultee-centered consultation that has clear implications for intervention. Caplan describes two possible intervention strategies—unlinking and theme interference reduction. Briefly, *unlinking* involves an effort to convince the consultee that the referral problem does not fit into category A. *Theme interference reduction* represents an effort to accept the problem referred by the consultee as fitting into category A, but arguing that it does not lead inevitably to outcome B in this case. Caplan suggests that the more appropriate strategy is theme interference reduction, since he feels this will result in more lasting change. This technique can be demonstrated through our example. First, the consultant would accept the initial category—that is, the consultant would agree that this child's mother was a divorced woman with two children and worked a full-time job. Then, the consultant would attempt to reduce the theme by denying the inevitable outcome. In this instance, the consultant would show how the referred child had only just begun to show signs of emotional difficulty, and he would indicate the probability that the observed problems were only transitory.

In addition to his specific discussion of theme interference reduction, Caplan describes some general intervention techniques, which can be used by the consultant to increase the teacher's objectivity and restore the appropriate professional distance. These techniques are summarized as follows. First, the consultant can act as a role-model for the teacher by gathering data and describing positive as well as negative aspects of the case in an objective manner. Second, the consultant can discuss the teacher's affective involvement with the case in an indirect manner. For example, the consultant could discuss the teacher's overinvolvement indirectly by describing or explaining a similar interpersonal problem existing in a child rather than by discussing the teacher's problem. Yet another way to discuss the teacher's overinvolvement indirectly is to use the technique Caplan refers to as the *Parable*, where the consultant invents an anecdote that is similar to the teacher's present situation. For example, the consultant might describe a similar situation encountered at another time in an effort to decrease the teacher's affective involvement in the present situation and increase his objectivity.

Despite its important contribution, Caplan's system for conceptualizing lack of objectivity has some weaknesses, especially in relation to school consultation. First, Caplan's distinction between four different types of lack of objectivity may not have sufficient practical value. These categories differ, at least partially, in the degree of distortion of reality and the degree to which the teacher meets some personal need by interacting with the student. Although this concept may be useful at times, the different categories do not appear to lead clearly to different consultation techniques. Furthermore, Caplan devotes a great deal of emphasis to his consideration of themes and theme interference reduction, perhaps because there is a clear connection between the identified theme and the specific consultation technique (theme interference reduction). However, despite the connection, so far there is little evidence to support the effectiveness of theme interference reduction. Moreover, there is almost no evidence indicating the success of any of the other techniques he describes. It has been our experience that, often, more direct intervention techniques than those offered by Caplan are warranted. Some emerging evidence supports the use of direct confrontation as a consultation technique (Meyers, 1975a; Meyers, Freidman, and Gaughan, 1975), and direct confrontation is specifically avoided in Caplan's discussion of interventions. Furthermore, theme interference reduction is an indirect procedure, in which the consultee is not informed about the goal of the intervention. The consultee does not have the opportunity to give informed consent. Such a procedure can be questioned on ethical grounds; we wonder also about the efficacy of such secret techniques.

Caplan's work has one other important weakness. The psychodynamic notion of looking for themes, simple identification, and transference all imply that there is something *internal* to the teacher that is *wrong*. This assumption seems to be further supported in Caplan's notion that the consultant must confront the teacher indirectly. The teacher's internal problems are assumed to be too serious to approach directly without destroying the teacher's defenses. Generally, we think that it is more useful to respect the teacher as a professional and as a person. The consultant should accept the teacher's emotional strength and trust his or her ability to handle appropriate confrontation. More readily implemented and effective techniques might become apparent if the teacher's lack of objectivity were defined in more objective and behavioral terms. The resulting consultation techniques should be related directly to the problem definitions, and they should be more straightforward and more readily understood by both consultant and consultee. This approach is more consistent with the idea that environmental factors influence behavior. Although consultants advocate this principle when helping teachers to understand the environmental factors that can influence students' problems, this principle seems to be ignored in Caplan's ego-based conception of teacher problems. It needs to be made clear that the teacher's lack of objectivity can be helped, not only through intrapersonal clinical techniques and insight, but also through modifying the teacher's school environment. Sometimes more direct confrontation techniques would provide a way to help increase teacher objectivity by changing the teacher's environment.

Our developing system for analyzing lack of objectivity in the teacher strives to make two important improvements on Caplan's approach. First, we define types of problems in objective terms with a link to intervention strategies based on direct confrontation. Second, our definitions are more behavioral, and we stress the environmental factors that may be linked to the problem.

As noted earlier, Caplan conceptualizes lack of objectivity in terms of the consultee's degree of identification with the client (or some person connected with the client). Instead, it may be useful to consider the conflicts that contribute to the consultee's lack of objectivity. One type of conflict involves the teacher's need to maintain control by assuming the role of classroom authority versus his distaste for an authoritarian, undemocratic role. This conflict may be especially common in recent years, when preservice teacher education has emphasized open classroom approaches to teaching. Also, some teachers prefer to maintain a relationship with students in which the teacher is perceived more as a friend than an authority. Naturally, the teacher needs to maintain an appropriate balance between an authoritarian and open atmosphere.

Another teacher conflict involves the teacher's need for both independence and dependence. Frequently, a teacher who has not resolved this conflict will demonstrate a rigid approach in the classroom by demanding excessively dependent and submissive behavior from the students. A further indication of this conflict occurs when the teacher simultaneously acts in an overly dependent manner with the consultant, who is expected to provide definitive answers.

A third area of teacher conflict involves feelings of anger and hostility versus the teacher's need to be valued professionally and liked personally. These feelings might be directed toward other school staff, the parents, or even the children. This conflict can be expressed at either extreme, by expressing unreasonably severe anger or by refusing to acknowledge any angry feelings.

A final area of teacher conflict is Caplan's concept of identification with the student or someone closely related to the student. Although it may not be necessary to distinguish between simple identification and transference as Caplan has done, there are clearly instances where the most direct way to conceptualize the teacher's lack of objectivity is in terms of his or her identification with the client.

When teacher conflicts are conceptualized in the ways we have described, clear problem definitions are facilitated. Also, there are objective ways to identify teacher conflicts, and these signs have been discussed by Caplan (1970). For example, one sign includes nonverbal expressions of affect such as increased speed of talking, flushing, and various gestures or body movements. Another way the existence of a conflict may be indicated is through the expression of contradictions. There may be a contradiction between what the consultee says during consultation and how the consultee behaves during consultation; there may be a contradiction between what the consultee says during consultation and how the consultee behaves in the classroom; or there may be a contradiction between what the consultee says at one time and what he says at another time during consultation. Finally, the presence of a conflict may be indicated by absolutes, such as *always* and *must.* Usually, these signs will reflect conflicts that influence the teacher's classroom behavior, and these signs can be identified clearly through behavioral data.

Not only can these conflicts be identified and defined readily, but they also lead to clear intervention strategies. The first part of the intervention strategy is for the consultant to determine a meaningful way to make the teacher aware of the conflict he may be experiencing. The second part of the intervention is for the consultant and teacher to consider strategies for overcoming this conflict. Often, the teacher can implement some specific change in the classroom environment. Interventions developed in this manner would include the teacher directly as a part of the process and would obviate the use of the indirect strategies discussed by Caplan. The development of direct intervention strategies should become clearer through the following examples.

The first example helps to differentiate our direct approach from Caplan's indirect approach. Moreover, this case involves a teacher whose conflict was the teacher's identification with a student. Mr. O'Reilly was a fifth-grade teacher who sought assistance from Parsons to stop the boys in his class from physically and psychologically abusing a small boy named Freddy. Mr. O'Reilly reported that the boys picked on Freddy, calling him "shrimp," "four-eyes" (he wore glasses), "twirp," and various other maligning names. When the consultant asked if the children had hurt Freddy physically, Mr. O'Reilly stated that they had not, but, "I know they will, such bullies always do." When observing Freddy interact with his peers in the school yard, the consultant noted that the children treated Freddy much like any other fifth-grader, sometimes asking him to join in, sometimes deliberately excluding him. On those occasions when Freddy was excluded from participating, he would often resort to name-calling and would threaten to tell Mr. O'Reilly! This would exacerbate the name-calling and teasing by the other boys, who would call him a "sissy" and a "teacher's pet." The consultant also noted that Freddy was quite similar to Mr. O'Reilly in physical appearance and social demeanor.

The consultant reported his observations that the peer interactions appeared essentially normal. However, Mr. O'Reilly retorted that he knew better and that he was well aware of how it feels to be isolated socially and called names. He added, "I went through hell when I was his age!" Mr. O'Reilly's referral to his own youthful school days offered the consultant an opportunity to discuss directly the possibility that Mr. O'Reilly might be identifying with Freddy. The consultant suggested further that Mr. O'Reilly might be reacting from his own fears rather than actual situations being experienced by Freddy. Rather than presenting these observations indirectly by discussing conflicts in the youngster, Parsons mentioned the possible identification directly to the teacher. Only after Mr. O'Reilly understood his own subjective involvement in the case did the discussion focus on strategies for helping Freddy. These discussions included techniques to facilitate proper social interaction and emotional sensitivity among all the students.

The second example is another case where it was deemed important to identify, define, and confront the teacher directly regarding a conflict. In this case, the teacher's conflict involved ambivalent feelings about being the authority in the classroom. This example is also noteworthy because it is one of a small number of empirical investigations of consultee-centered consultation where there is direct observation of behavior (Freidman, 1977; Meyers, 1975a; Meyers, Freidman, and Gaughan, 1975).

Meyers was consulting with a teacher, and they first developed a treatment plan for a student named Donna, in which verbal praise was administered for appropriate behavior, and inappropriate behavior was ignored whenever possible. Furthermore, when punitive statements were made, this was done in a nonemotional manner. This treatment was assessed using a reversal design. The results are illustrated in Figure 3, which shows a change in Donna's disruptive behavior that could be attributed to the treatment program. Thus, the first part of this consultation project involved the apparently effective delivery of indirect service to the child through a behavior modification program (Level II consultation).

Although the reinforcement program was apparently successful in modifying Donna's behavior, the entire class remained at a high level of disruptive behavior throughout the baseline, treatment, and reversal conditions. The consistently high level of disruptive behavior was noted during informal observation by both the observer and the teacher's supervisor. Moreover, conversations with the teacher's supervisor revealed that not only the teacher but also the school administration was seriously concerned about the high level of disruption in this classroom. It was thus determined that, in addition to the treatment program for Donna, something had to be done for the classroom as a whole.

The teacher had ambivalent feelings about being an authority figure, and it was hypothesized that these feelings might inter-

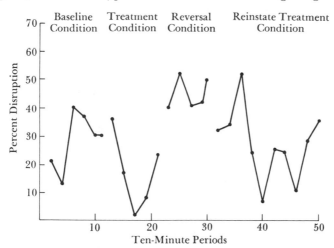

Figure 3. Percent of Disruptive Behavior During the Four Experimental Conditions for Donna.
Note: Each point represents the combination of two observation periods.

fere with her ability to control the class. For example, it was noted that the teacher treated her class in an apologetic manner, often explaining and excusing her actions. It appeared that she was not comfortable in the role of the authority figure, and during one consultation conference the teacher responded to a suggestion by saying, "The children would never let me get away with that."

The consultee-centered consultation procedures included discussions in which the consultant mentioned observations regarding the teacher's feelings about being an authority figure and sought the teacher's reactions. Following this direct confrontation, they discussed the teacher's role in the classroom, and the consultant reinforced the idea that, as the teacher, she was the authority in the classroom. These discussions helped the teacher to express her feeling that she had not felt comfortable as the authority figure and that this discomfort had interfered with her ability to teach. Throughout these discussions, the consultant attempted to clarify what the teacher said about her feelings as an authority figure. In addition, the teacher was praised for verbalizing her feelings. Three consultee-centered consultation sessions, lasting from fifteen to forty minutes each, were devoted to the teacher's conflicts about being the authority figure, and they took place during the first two days of the reinstatement of treatment condition for Donna.

Throughout the consultation focused on Donna, data were collected for another child named Frank. Figure 4 reveals that, during Donna's baseline, treatment, and reversal periods, Frank's behavior remained unchanged. These data indicate that the treatment directed toward Donna had no effect on Frank. However, the data also suggest that consultee-centered consultation with this teacher decreased Frank's disruptive behavior significantly. Thus, Figure 4 shows that, subsequent to the consultee-centered consultation (during the reinstatement of treatment condition), both the level and the variability of Frank's disruptive behavior decreased sharply. Since Frank's behavior had not been changed by the original treatment condition for Donna, it can be argued that Frank's behavior would have remained unchanged also in response to the reinstatement of the same treatment condition for Donna. The only other factor that was systematically manipulated during the

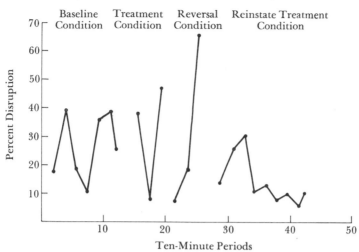

Figure 4. Percent of Disruptive Behavior During the Four Experimental Conditions for Frank.
Note: See Figure 3.

reinstatement of treatment condition was consultee-centered consultation. Therefore, consultee-centered consultation may have been responsible for the observed changes in Frank's behavior.

Anecdotal observations of the class provided additional information suggesting that consultee-centered consultation was successful, since the dramatic decrease in Frank's disruptive behavior appeared to characterize the class as a whole. This general decrease in disruptive behavior included less inappropriate talking, more in-seat behavior, and fewer fights. For the first time, the students would respond to the teacher's directions consistently. In one instance, the entire class sat quietly, listening attentively to the teacher read a story for fifteen minutes. This sort of control had not been observed previously in this classroom. There were also changes in the teacher's behavior, which supported the conclusion that consultee-centered consultation was successful. One of the observed changes occurred during the consultation conferences, when she indicated that her feelings about being an authority figure had changed. During the last session, the teacher mentioned that she had just begun reading a book that made an analogy between the home and the classroom, which had particular meaning for her. She said she needed to develop the feeling that the classroom was her castle in order to establish the type of control she wanted. Changes in the teacher's behavior in the classroom were also observed, such as a reduction in her shouting. Following the consultation, a word from her would be enough to inhibit disruptive behavior during class time.

Both of these examples underscore key issues regarding our view of consultee-centered consultation. First, two types of teacher conflict are illustrated: *Identification* with a student interfered with teacher objectivity in the first case, and ambivalence over being an *authority* figure was the key conflict in the second case.

Each example demonstrates a technique for identifying teacher conflicts. The absolute statements of the first teacher indicate his conflict as he said, "Such bullies *always* do." The contradictory statements of the second teacher indicate her conflict regarding authority. There were many occasions when she indicated that she was in charge of her students. However, she sometimes responded to consultant suggestions with such comments as, "They would never let me get away with that." In contrast to Caplan's focus on indirect confrontation, each of these consultants used direct confrontation once a conflict was identified. The resulting increase in teacher objectivity had slightly different effects for each teacher. After objectivity was increased, the first teacher was able to consider intervention strategies productively, while the second teacher began to develop her own strategies.

Finally, generalization is one of the key goals of effective consultation, and increasing teacher objectivity may be one way to achieve this goal. In the second case the initial behavioral intervention with Donna did not generalize to other children in the class, but when objectivity increased, the teacher quickly implemented changes that affected the whole class. These examples demonstrate that techniques designed to increase teacher objectivity are powerful tools for the prevention of mental health problems in the schools.

Summary

In this chapter we have considered a variety of consultation procedures designed to provide direct service to the teacher. The four major categories of problems appropriate for this level of consultation were defined as lack of objectivity, lack of professional self-confidence, lack of skill, and lack of knowledge. Techniques were described for evaluating the teacher's problems. While some of these techniques assessed classroom behavior, others examined the teacher's feelings regarding teaching. In addition, this chapter pointed out some of the strengths and weaknesses of Gerald Caplan's work, especially his approach to lack of objectivity. His work on theme interference reduction was described as a model approach to the specific description of intervention procedures in consultation. Moreover, Caplan's approach to indirect confrontation was contrasted with more direct confrontation techniques.

CHAPTER EIGHT

Service to the Organization

□ □ □ □ □ □ □ □ □ □ □

The mental health specialist who provides direct or indirect service to children or direct service to teachers often finds that the realities of the organization do not permit some interventions, or that the client's behaviors soon revert to the old patterns, because the new behaviors are not supported by the organization. If the mental health specialist attempts to change such organizational factors, he or she is intervening at the fourth level of consultation, the organization level.

Although some organizational interventions may be initiated by the mental health professional, a more desirable situation occurs when the organization itself recognizes the existence of some problem and seeks a counselor, psychologist, or social worker to help remedy it. Such problems may include communication breakdowns between subgroups of the organization, a crisis caused by outside pressures that will demand changes in organizational procedures, or simply a failure of the organization to meet its goals.

Although many of the skills described in previous chapters

for interventions at the individual or small-group level are necessary for effective consultation at the organizational level, our discussion in this chapter will be limited to organization development techniques. As discussed in Chapter Two, organization development is a set of techniques and theories based on the application of group dynamics, social psychology, and organizational theory. Techniques derived from these theoretical bases supply the single most useful set of tools for consultation at the organizational level.

Because O.D. theory and technology developed in industrial settings, we will use examples and terminology that are not specifically related to educational settings in our overview of O.D. at the beginning of this chapter. Educational application will be discussed after the necessary theoretical basis is presented.

Traditional Bureaucracy

According to O.D. theorists, many of the problems associated with modern organizations result from the bureaucratic "machine" model of organizations. As described by Bennis (1969), a bureaucracy has the following characteristics: a well-defined chain of command, a system of procedures and rules for dealing with contingencies related to human activity in the organization, a division of labor based on specialization, a reward system based on technical competence, and a style of human interaction that emphasizes rationality and impersonality.

Argyris (1970) points out some of the psychological effects of working in such organizations. First, the highly specialized, fractionated contribution of any one worker reduces the likelihood that the worker will have the psychological experience of success associated with completing a larger task on his own. The classic example of this type of division of labor is the assembly line. Assembly-line workers each contribute such a small amount to the products they produce that they often feel that they make no real difference to the quality of that product; therefore, they derive little satisfaction from such work. Education is also becoming the domain of specialists, each of whom has responsibility for only a small part of the growth and development of the child. In addition to subject-matter specialists who only teach one area of knowledge, the modern school is staffed by many types of curriculum specialists, remedial specialists, medical specialists, administrative specialists, and mental health specialists. Such specialization reduces the probability that any one specialist in the school has the same feeling of pride watching students progress as the teacher in the one-room school house did when only one person was responsible for the child's education.

A second effect of traditional bureaucracies on workers is that the well-defined chain of command means that evaluation, distribution of rewards and penalties, and responsibility for all important changes in procedure (hiring, firing, moving employees, changing work descriptions) resides with management. This results in a feeling of dependence and submission on the part of the worker. It also means that the worker will feel little responsibility for meeting organizational goals.

Today's teacher exists in an extensive organizational hierarchy. This hierarchy usually extends from the school board through the superintendent, assistant superintendents, a principal, and in some cases a department head to the teacher. The result is the teaching staff feels dependent on others over whom they have little control. When important organizational goals are not met, the probability is that the teachers will pass responsibility to others along this chain of command. The process also works the other way; that is, administrators can assign responsibility for failures to meet organizational goals to other administrators or to the teaching staff.

These characteristics and others typical of most bureaucracies lead to what Argyris calls *adaptive antagonistic activities* on the part of the worker. These include trade unions, absenteeism, turnover, apathy, alienation, and increasing demands to relate financial compensation to degree of job satisfaction. Argyris' analysis and predictions fit education well, for it is virtually impossible to pick up any daily newspaper in this country and not find reference to the union activities of the teaching profession, the high turnover in teaching positions (particularly in the largest city school districts), and the frequent expressions by teachers of low job-satisfaction, indifference, and alienation.

Instead of focusing on the structural characteristics of bureaucracies, McGregor (1960) looked at the motivational assumptions held by those in power in such organizations. McGregor labeled *Theory X* that set of assumptions which is most common in large organizations. This theory is based on the idea that most people are inherently lazy and will not work unless they have to. People are incapable of self-control and self-direction and therefore are incapable of working on their own toward the goals of the organization. There are, however, some people (the elite) who are industrious and capable of taking responsibility. Thus, proper management involves selecting the elite and putting them in positions of power in the organization, so that they can supervise, evaluate, and in other ways control the workers. There is the additional assumption that, since the workers lack self-control, they will be unresponsive to the intrinsic rewards of working toward the goals of the institution and therefore must be controlled extrinsically, principally through financial rewards and penalties. Such assumptions, according to McGregor, create the very worker behavior predicted and lead to the feelings of antagonism and apathy described by Argyris.

In place of Theory X assumptions about worker motivation, McGregor suggests an alternative, which is labeled *Theory Y.* This theory is based on the idea that people, whether workers or managers, will work to meet their personal goals. If their personal goals can be met while working toward the goals of the organization, an effective organization will result. Theory Y assumptions imply that people at all levels of an organization should participate in the decision making, planning, and problem solving to the extent of their ability to make a contribution. Further, when workers contribute to the overall functioning of the organization, their personal needs will have a greater chance of being met. This set of assumptions about worker motivation has provided the rationale for many interventions used by organization development specialists.

Another important aspect of traditional bureaucracies is that they have difficulty coping with change (Beckhard, 1969; Schein, 1969). Because traditional bureaucracies rely on standard operation procedures, they adapt to novel occurrences very slowly. "We have never done it that way before" or "We are not allowed to do that" are typical reactions to suggestions for new procedures. Also, as organizations become larger, managers are increasingly remote from line workers, who are dealing with the environment on a day-to-day basis; in the words of organizational theorists, the worker, not the manager, is on the *organizational-environmental interface*. Since the chain of command concept is most functional in downward communication, workers at the lower levels who sense changes in the environment find it difficult to communicate about problems and possible solutions upward through the chain.

Another factor contributing to poor communication within organizations is that, with worker specialization, personnel begin to form professional associations and alliances instead of an allegiance to the organization. Thus, communication within a professional organization or labor union becomes easier and more meaningful than communication within the organization.

In summary, if one studies the kinds of problems encountered by traditional bureaucracies, a number of common problems will be observed. These problems include slow response to internal crisis and to changing environmental situations, poor communication between individuals and subgroups, antagonism between subgroups, a failure of individuals to take responsibility for meeting organizational goals, and a general feeling among workers of alienation from important organizational processes, which in turn produces apathy or antagonism. Many of these problems result from inherent structural properties of organizations and the assumptions about human motivation held by their directors.

Interventions

In contrast to the assumptions of Theory X, organization development specialists advocate a theory of human motivation emphasizing the satisfaction of personal needs in the work situation through participation in all aspects of the organization. O.D. specialists attempt to change the negative aspects of bureaucratic structure by increasing worker participation in decision making and by opening channels of communication, so that individual and subgroup interaction is frequent, authentic, and personally meaningful. O.D. specialists and others who have used O.D. methods have applied a wide variety of techniques to produce these organizational changes. We will discuss three types of interventions: laboratory training, data feedback, and process consultation. The methods discussed are intended to be suggestive of the kinds of interventions that can be used. Those seeking more comprehensive descriptions are referred to Beckhard (1969); Bennis (1969); Blake and Mouton (1976); French and Bell (1973); Lawrence and Lorsch (1969); Schein (1969); Schmuck and others (1972); Schmuck and Miles (1971); and Walton (1969).

Laboratory Training. The technique most closely associated with organization development is laboratory training—specifically, sensitivity training or T-group training. This close connection between organization development and laboratory-training techniques exists because sensitivity training was developed by the same social psychologists who later founded organizational development (Lewin, Benne, Lippitt, and others).

Laboratory training is an educational process for learning about human interaction through experiencing such interactions. The concept of laboratory training is very broad, encompassing a variety of techniques. Since most mental health specialists are familiar with the rationale for and operation of T-groups or sensitivity groups, we will not discuss them here. Instead, we will discuss a few examples of short-term exercises designed to enhance communication, conflict resolution, and decision making in groups.

Before describing such techniques, however, it is important to note that, despite the close relationship between laboratory techniques and O.D., any one technique or any set of these techniques is not in itself organization development. Laboratory training, as applied in training institutions like the National Training Laboratory, for example, is carried out in groups of strangers, whereas in an organization development program it is carried out in groups made up of *cousins* (people from the same organization who do not work together) or *families* (members who come from the same work group). Also, the emphasis of laboratory training in organization development is on applying the training in the work group, and frequently, real work problems are systematically dealt with. Finally, such training is seldom applied in organization development in isolation. Usually, the exercises are applied with survey feedback, process consultation, or other techniques (Schmuck and others, 1972).

The following exercises are examples that are used to help

people in a work group find out more about each other and to explore the reactions of others. Such exercises are often used at the beginning of a group experience to develop a norm of open communication.

Exercise 1	Who am I? [Schmuck and others, 1972, p. 67]
Procedure	On a standard sheet of lined paper, each participant writes ten answers to the question, "Who am I?" Participants then pin their answers on their chests and go around reading each other's answers. No verbal communication is allowed. After ten minutes or so, the participants are instructed to go back to two or three people that they found most interesting and to ask them questions which would not be easy to ask under normal circumstances.
Consultant	The consultant's role in this exercise is simply to instruct the participants in what to do, and to encourage in both phases of the exercise the divulging of and asking of personally significant material.
Exercise 2	Giving and receiving feedback [Schmuck and others, 1972, p. 59]
Procedure	Participants are divided into three-person groups. Each member in the group is assigned one of three roles: to give feedback, to receive feedback, or to act as an observer. The person giving feedback is asked to describe two helpful behaviors and two behaviors that are not helpful that are characteristic of the person receiving feedback. The person receiving feedback attempts to clarify the communication by summarizing and paraphrasing what was said. The observer makes sure the feedback person is clear and the receiver is listening and clarifying when necessary. After the four behaviors are communicated, the participants switch roles and continue the exercise.
Consultant	The consultant's role in this exercise is primarily to back up the observer in his consultation to the feedback receiver and giver.

The following two exercises are useful in helping a group to develop better methods of conflict resolution. The purpose of the first exercise is to uncover conflicts in peoples' perceptions regarding organizational power and influence. The second exercise helps to uncover much the same kind of conflict in groups.

Exercise 1	The influence line [Schmuck and others, 1972, pp. 156–157]
Procedure	Members of the organization are simply asked to form a line with the person who is most influential being at the head of the line and the person who is least influential at the end of the line. Since conflicts in perception are almost inevitable, the group begins to discuss the reasons for the differences in perception and the effects these differences might have on organizational behavior.
Consultant	The consultant observes and records some of the most important differences in perception. He also fosters an open discussion of the feelings of the participants about influence and the conflicts their differing perceptions may cause.
Exercise 2	
Procedure	Two work groups are asked to develop a description or image of itself and of the other group. The description is to be divided in half; the first half consisting of a favorable description and the second half consisting of an unfavorable description. When the four descriptions are completed they are posted and read by all group members. Then the group being described is asked to sit in a small circle while the other group sits in a circle around them. One by one a member of the outer circle reads a descriptive phrase which is then paraphrased by the person in the middle. After this procedure has been carried out for both groups, the two groups separate and prepare a list of behaviors that they exhibit which confirms the image held of them by the other group. They come back together in the concentric circle pattern and discuss these examples of behavior as before. Finally, points of conflict are discussed and possible remedies are developed.
Consultant	The consultant explains the exercise and its purpose. He or she then helps the groups develop clear behavior descriptions of one another and of behaviors that confirm the other group's image. He also aids the receiver of descriptions in paraphrasing the descriptions. Finally, in the last phases, he aids the group process in the development of remedies for the conflicts that have been clarified.

The final exercise we will describe is designed to allow a group to experience one type of decision-making process—

consensus formation. In addition, feedback on the adequacy of the decision arrived at through this process is provided to see if consensus resulted in the most appropriate solution.

Exercise Lost on the moon [Developed by J. Hall, presented in Schmuck and others, 1972, pp. 273–275]

Procedure Each individual in a group is asked to imagine that he is in a space ship which is to meet with a mother ship on the moon. Due to mechanical difficulties, the space ship in which he is riding lands 200 miles from the mother ship and most of the supplies and equipment are destroyed. However, the following items are left intact: a box of matches, food concentrate, 50 feet of nylon rope, parachute silk, solar-powered portable heating unit, two .45 calibre pistols, one case of dehydrated Pet milk, two 100 lb. tanks of oxygen, stellar maps of the constellations of the moon, self-inflating life rafts, magnetic compass, five gallons of water, signal flares, first aid kit containing injection needles, solar powered FM receiver-transmitter. Each individual is given the task of ranking these items in order of importance in case all items cannot be taken on the trip to the mother ship. When individual lists have been prepared, the group is given 45 minutes to come to a decision as to the item priorities. When consensus is reached, three scores are prepared. The mean rank ordering of items prior to the consensus discussion, the consensus rank ordering, and the best individual ranking as compared to the correct ordering. The group then receives feedback as to which of the three scores was actually the best, and discusses why their group did or did not arrive at the best solution given the information and skills of their group.

Consultant The consultant must arrange for the secretarial functions involved in the exercise, such as preparing the lists to be ranked by the individuals, and coaching or actually developing the scores. However, the major function of the consultant occurs when the exercise is over, when he encourages open communication about the experience and helps the group see what processes facilitated and impeded them from using their resources in the best way. Finally, he aids the group in tying this experience to decision-making processes that are used by the group in their work.

Survey Feedback. Survey feedback, as applied in organization development, consists of collecting data via a questionnaire, interviews, direct observation, or a combination of these techniques, then tabulating the data and presenting the results to those from whom they were obtained. With the help of a consultant, the group discusses the data, comes to agreements on the meaning of the data, and plans strategies for solving the problems revealed by the data. Roughly three different processes take place in the prototypic survey feedback intervention: data collection, data feedback, and process consultation around data feedback meetings.

During the data collection phases, the major decisions to be faced are, what kinds of data are to be collected and from whom? In O.D. applications, this decision is discussed collectively, and a decision is arrived at through interaction with the client system and the consultant. Most data are of the soft variety; that is, questions are asked about supervisor and subordinate attitudes and feelings. Typical questions focus on perceived problem areas, employee satisfaction, adequacy of decision-making procedures, perceptions of unspoken rules, and so forth. However, some hard data may also be collected, including rates of absenteeism and turnover or various measures of the extent to which the organization is meeting its goals.

Although a consultant may collect data relating to problem areas as seen by those who have asked for his help, the specific questions asked will be determined by the theory the consultant has (or the theory the organization has presented) about why its problems exist. For example, O.D. practitioners typically focus on questions related to decision making (assuming that the more the subordinates are involved in the process, the better the process), to atmosphere (assuming that most organizations with a democratic, person-oriented atmosphere are better than those with an authoritarian, task-oriented atmosphere), and to communication (assuming that open, authentic, and confrontive interaction is better than less-straightforward interaction). Consultants working from different theoretical models might probe into different areas of organization life, even if the problems presented were the same.

The next question to be addressed by the consultant in the data collection phase concerns the people from whom the data are to be collected. Two basic plans have been tried. In one plan, the entire staff of the unit, subsystem, or organization under study provides information. In another plan, the managers collect data from among themselves or from lower levels without contributing themselves.

Feedback of the data can be handled by the consultant, but most O.D. practitioners, consistent with their emphasis on involving the client system at every possible chance in the development process, usually prefer to have supervisors provide feedback. Data feedback in O.D. is often done in *family units* consisting of one supervisor and his immediate subordinates. Feedback then proceeds from the top to the bottom in what is called the *waterfall* procedure. That is, people who were subordinates in the first meeting provide feedback to their subordinates in the second meeting, and the process continues in this fashion to the bottom of the organization. Huse (1975) feels, however, that greater commitment to the project and to the plans for change can occur if just the opposite tactic is used—that is, by working up from the bottom of the organization.

In the process-analysis phase of survey feedback, the consultant's activities become those of a process consultant. That is, as the meetings around the data continue toward trying to decide on remedial steps and planning of the initiation of remedial steps, group processes take on increased significance and become increasingly clear. This opportunity is taken by the consultant to bring to the awareness of the group the processes that are operating to aid and impede the appropriate functioning of the group. (For an example of survey feedback in an O.D. program in a school, see the summary of McElvaney and Miles [1971] presented later in this chapter [Case 1].)

Process Consultation. Although O.D. interventions were primarily thought of as an extension of laboratory techniques and survey feedback early in their development, process consultation has come to be the primary tool of the organizational consultant. This is particularly true of those who approach organizational consultation from a mental health viewpoint, since process consultation bears a striking resemblance to the therapeutic process utilized by mental health professionals.

Process consultation, according to Schein (1969, p. 9), is "a set of activities on the part of the consultant which help the client to perceive, understand, and act upon process events which occur in the client's environment." Process consultation, by this definition, is an insight-oriented technique, in which a consultant brings to the attention of the client certain individual, interpersonal, and intergroup processes that the client may not have attended to before the intervention. Second, the consultant gives meaning to these events by providing an interpretation based on psychological theory and the consultant's experience. Finally, the consultant helps the client in changing his own behavior or that of a group, based on these interpretations.

What kinds of information about processes does the consultant bring to the attention of the client system? Schein (1969) has listed six processes that he considers most important for organizational health: (1) communication, (2) member functions and roles in groups, (3) group problem solving and decision making, (4) group norms and growth, (5) leadership and authority, and (6) intergroup cooperation and competition.

Considering *communication,* Schein points out that valuable information can be provided for a working group by simply plotting such data as the number of times each individual in the group talked during a given meeting. Other data that can be collected include the duration of time each person had the floor during a meeting, the content of the communications (task leadership versus process leadership, for example), frequency and duration of communication dyads (who communicates with whom), who interrupts whom, who supports whom, and so forth. Often, such data are collected and fed back to the group, and the meaning of the data is discussed. Finally, if communication problems are found, plans are made to remedy these difficulties.

One of the most significant things about groups is that the people making up the group serve different *functions and roles.* There are many ways of categorizing roles and functions within a group, but Schein (1969) chooses a classification system that reflects the developmental nature of task groups. The main tenet of this system is that early in the development of a work group the members are primarily self-oriented. Later, as this preoccupation declines, members can begin to attend to others and to the task at hand. During the initial period, four different problems must be resolved: each individual must determine his identity in the group; each individual must determine the amount of control and influence he can and wants to exercise in the group; each individual must determine if the group's goals are the same as his personal goals; and each individual must achieve a satisfactory level of acceptance by the group.

During the process of coping with these problems, group members are said to respond typically with three response styles, the response style chosen being determined by his past history and other factors such as group norms. He may try to fight or rebel (tough response), be supportive and compliant (the tender response), or be passive and indifferent (the denial response). The importance of coping styles is that they are to be expected, and members should be encouraged to express them openly, so that the underlying issues they reflect can be resolved.

The role of the process consultant during this initial phase of group development is (1) to be aware of these processes and not to become concerned about the lack of work progress early in the group's development, (2) to help the group understand that these processes are normal and necessary for future healthy group functioning, and (3) to give feedback to group members concerning their behavior when it will be constructive and will contribute to the individual's and the group's growth.

The second major phase of group development represents the mature phase, in which members focus on the task and on group maintenance functions. Schein lists nine task functions that must be served if the group is to make progress in meeting its goals. They are: initiating, opinion seeking, opinion giving, information seeking, information giving, elaboration, summarizing, and consensus testing.

One of the major focal points of all organization development activity, not just process consultation, is the processes the organization uses to solve its problems and to plan and initiate action. *Problem solving and decision making* can be handled at the organizational level or at the small-group level. The process consultant intervenes primarily in decision making at the small-group level.

The tasks of the consultant in the decision-making process are manifold. First, he must be aware that there are numerous ways to make group decisions (rule by authority, majority rule, consensus, unanimous vote, and so forth). Second, he should be aware of the positive and negative attributes of each type of decision-making process. Schein (1969) takes the position that no one decision-making procedure is best in all situations. Rule by authority, for example, is fast, but it may cause resentment and lack of commitment to the plan. More participatory forms of decision making avoid these problems but may require protracted lengths of time to accomplish. Some organization development practitioners would not agree with Schein's appraisal and see as one of their primary tasks the replacement of authority- and minority-based decision-making procedures with more participatory forms (Schmuck and Miles, 1971). Finally, if the consultant feels that members of the group are uncomfortable with the decision-making style of the group, and if the decision-making rules have not been formally decided upon, he focuses the attention of the group on this fact and encourages them to establish a definite policy on the matter.

Regarding *group norms*, it can be said that all groups have rules for their operation. Some of these rules are explicit, such as the stated policy of most personnel committees that the proceedings be held confidential. Many rules governing member behavior are implicit, however. Examples of implicit norms might include members being on time to meetings or the authority of the leader not being questioned. The role of the consultant in intervening in the process of norm formation is much the same as it is with regard to communication, decision making, or any other facet of group behavior. First, he must become aware of the norms that are in operation. Second, at appropriate times, he makes the group aware of the implicit norms he feels he has observed in operation. Finally, he helps the group to decide whether these norms are useful to the group and meet the needs of its members.

Another crucial aspect of group behavior that process consultants deal with is *leadership*. In fact, process consultation began primarily as a management-consultant technique. For a group to function, one person or several people must perform the task of coordinating and integrating the functions of the members. Several of the tasks outlined in the section on group functions and roles must be performed by leaders. A task leader, for example, would initiate more, seek opinions more, give opinions more, and attempt more summaries than other group members. In fact, the leader is often defined, in situations where spontaneous leadership is allowed to develop, as the person who performs these functions the most.

Leader behavior can be categorized in many ways. One way is according to the assumptions about leadership that the person serving as the leader seems to exemplify. For example, a leader may think of himself primarily as a group motivator, an emotional leader, or a leader who establishes the conditions for the group to lead itself. Once the consultant has diagnosed the style of the leader, he may find it desirable to discuss this style with the leader. If the leader and consultant agree as to the behavior of the leader and are clear as to the assumptions it is based upon, and if the leader feels that this is the best way to proceed, the consultant may terminate his intervention or may try to convince the leader that other styles can be adopted. In many cases, the leader desires a different leadership style from the one he is manifesting. Or the leader may be unaware of his own style, in which case the consultant provides feedback and tries to help the leader change his behavior.

In concluding this discussion of intervention techniques, let us note that the three types of interventions discussed—laboratory training, data feedback, and process consultation—have much in common although they are designed to remedy organizational problems in different ways. First, they are all based on the assumption that full participation by every member of an organization in the group processes of the organization is essential to individual fulfillment and organizational vitality. Second, the three sets of techniques are primarily exercises designed to increase the individual's awareness of his own feelings, attitudes, and behaviors and of the feelings, attitudes, and behaviors of others. These techniques are based, then, on the assumption that awareness goes a long way toward creating change at the individual and organizational level. Third, these techniques are all "love-cooperation" interventions as opposed to "coercive-competition" interventions. That is, an assumption is made that if people get to know one another, they tend to like one another and, in turn, tend to work cooperatively toward the mutual satisfaction of important individual goals through appropriate adjustments of organizational goals. Coercive-competition strategies assume that the goals of some individuals or groups cannot be met and that the goals of some individuals or some groups are antagonistic to those of others. Such assumptions produce strategies of organizational change based on adversary relationships. These strategies have not played a significant role in traditional O.D. applications.

Educational Illustrations of
Organizational Consultation

We devote the remainder of this chapter to the presentation of three case examples of organizational consultation in educational settings. The first two cases utilize typical O.D. interventions, but the third does not. Despite the fact that different intervention techniques are used in each example, an overall similarity in general approach to organizational problems is apparent.

The cases illustrate several issues regarding organizational consultation that cannot be dealt with in detail. For example, in each case, the reader should be aware of the method used by the consultant to obtain sanction to engage in the intervention. One of the most important questions in the consultation literature is why some organizations permit and seek out consultation and others do not. Does the nature of the initial approach to the organization significantly affect the likelihood of being given sanction to intervene? (For further discussion of this issue, see Caplan, 1970.)

Two of the cases illustrate the use of both inside and outside consultants, whereas in the third example, the status of the consultant on this dimension is unclear. The reader should consider under what circumstances consultants from outside the organization are preferable to those who are normally a part of the organization and how both types of consultants can work together to maximize consultation effectiveness (see Martin, 1978). Finally, although some type of evaluation of intervention effectiveness was attempted in each case, they vary greatly in rigor, and in no case is the evaluation as rigorous as the consultants would have liked. The reader should think about the difficulties of evaluating organizational consultation and about ways of overcoming these difficulties as preparation for the next part of this book.

Case 1

A study in which survey feedback and process consultation were used in a comprehensive O.D. intervention was reported by McElvaney and Miles (reported in Schmuck and Miles, 1971). The researcher had first asked a school district to serve as a control in an experimental research program. The district agreed to serve in this capacity, and data were collected over the course of one year. The research staff then became interested in providing data feedback to the district in a program of organization development.

As a first step, the research staff met with the administrative staff of the district as well as the psychologists serving the district to discuss how the intervention would take place. As an outgrowth of the initial meeting, a four-day meeting with the administrative staff and the psychologists was planned. When the meetings were carried out, the data discussed included: dissatisfaction people felt in relating to others with different roles, how well people felt they fit their jobs, how innovative the staff felt the district was, how important and satisfying different aspects of their jobs were, the general climate of the school district, aspects of administrative climate in each building, the ways decisions were made, principal-teacher relations in each building, teachers' perceptions of how the principal carried out his duties, relationships among the administrative staff, goals of the school, morale, relationships of the district to the community, clarity of communication between roles, and student interest in the school as seen by the teachers.

During the four days of the meeting, six different kinds of experiences were provided for those attending.

1. *Data discussion:* All the data collected were discussed on a district level or a building level, whichever seemed most appropriate.
2. *Problem-identification groups:* In small groups, participants tried to define basic problem areas brought out by the data—for example, the lack of teacher involvement in decision making.
3. *Theory sessions:* Lectures presenting the theory of group

dynamics and general organization theory were offered by the research staff.

4. *Process consultation:* During meetings devoted to other topics, the consultants would focus the group's attention on group processes taking place.

5. *Task forces:* Small groups were assigned to make recommendations on specific problems isolated by the problem-identification groups.

6. *Planning for the next steps:* The bulk of the four-day conference was spent in this activity. Decisions reached included planning for periodic meetings among administrative staff during the school year to discuss matters related to the survey feedback; having each building principal provide feedback data to their teachers and discuss the implications of the data; and designating one of the school psychologists present as a consultant to the principal during the next year regarding matters of group process.

During the following year, the appointed school psychologist served as a process consultant to the principals in their own administrative meetings and helped the principals prepare for their conferences with the teachers. His function was that of a clarifier and adviser.

After all the teachers' groups had been given feedback and the data had been discussed, task forces were formed to consider problem areas that had been identified in the teachers' meetings. These groups consisted of representatives of all school staff at all grade levels. The problem areas considered were: supervision, grouping, grading, reading, teacher load, teacher assignment, library, and curriculum. Reports were prepared and discussed at administrative staff meetings later in the year.

This intervention was systematically evaluated by the research team. Data were collected three times prior to the intervention and once six months after the first feedback of data to the principals. Within the administrative group, on thirty-six indices of organizational effectiveness only three were significantly more positive in the follow-up than in the last of the three pretests. Two measures were significantly more negative. However, teachers' ratings of principals' functioning taken from the first of the preevaluations and compared with the postevaluation showed that teachers who were most dissatisfied about principal behavior on the first test improved their opinion significantly on the postevaluation.

Interview data seemed to indicate that principals felt more active and open in their meetings and that the meetings were run better than they had been in the past. The supervising principal seemed to be more confident of his role and more accepted by the other administrators at the end of the intervention.

Another positive outcome was the feeling of the school psychologist, who felt accepted by the administrators in his new role. This acceptance was communicated formally (through questionnaire data) and informally. As an inside observer, the psychologist evaluated the changes that had taken place (subjectively) and came to the conclusion that processes had changed a good deal, but that actions to deal with specific problems had progressed little.

In summary, the objective data indicated little change as a result of this intervention; however, subjective data indicated important changes in group process if not in active problem solving.

Case 2

Parsons worked as a counselor in a parochial school in which the lay faculty had recently renegotiated a new contract. These negotiations had left some feelings of discontent and tension between members of the religious faculty and the lay teachers in the school. (Fifty percent of the staff and all administrators were religious order brothers, and the remaining fifty percent of the staff were lay teachers.)

The tension that had developed during the months of negotiation in the summer led to a "we-they" mentality, which was evident during a three-day workshop for teachers held prior to the opening of school. The purpose of the workshop was to discuss policy, programming, objectives, and so forth, and during these meetings the faculty opinions were grouped clearly according to lay-religious affiliation. The grouping was apparent even in the seating arrangement during the meetings (religious faculty on one side and lay faculty on the other side of the room), during lunch breaks (identical isolation behavior by the groups), and during recreational periods. The recreation periods were noteworthy because they had been one point of common interest and great comraderie in past years. Now they were scheduled by the staff at alternating times, so that the groups just happened to miss each other.

The conflict came to a head on the last day of the workshop, when teacher assignments were distributed and posted. Most of the lay faculty were angry, because they felt the scheduling demonstrated bias toward them. They felt that they were assigned in greater proportion the undesirable service periods (lunch proctor, study proctor, last period bus patrol), and they also believed that they were scheduled for significantly more first-period teaching, last-period teaching, and late lunches. At one faculty meeting soon after school began, these observations were aired angrily to the administration. Much negative verbal exchange between lay and religious faculty ensued, in which reference to the strike and questions regarding the ethical and moral involvement of the lay faculty were aired by the religious teachers.

In the following weeks, tension grew and the split widened. The faculty grew more belligerent, and some even attempted to involve the students by spreading rumors in their classes regarding the other faction of teachers. Consequently, Parsons (a lay teacher/counselor in the school) suggested to the principal (a member of the religious faculty) that help was needed to reestablish open lines of communication to recapture the positive educational climate that had characterized this school previously. Because of his own affiliation with the lay faculty, Parsons suggested that an outside consultant be used. The principal agreed, and the result was a weekend program, in which the consultant focused directly on the problems of class scheduling and teacher rostering.

The first day was devoted entirely to group laboratory exercises designed to increase the faculty's awareness of interpersonal and organizational processes. The general purpose of this first day was to bring the opposing subgroups into contact with each other over nonthreatening problem situations and at the same time demonstrate the importance of open, honest, effective communication in accomplishing tasks. During the second day, problem-solving skills were established to facilitate: (1) identification of problems areas through behavioral descriptions; (2) force-field analysis; (3) brain storming problem-solving strategies; and (4) developing concrete plans. In the afternoon of this second day, the groups were asked to use their new skills to develop a plan for fair teacher rostering. One subgroup (composed of both lay and religious faculty) suggested that this task would take more time than the single afternoon allowed. Instead, they proposed that the remainder of the time be spent developing a procedure for the year in which time could be allotted for working in groups on various issues, including teacher rostering. The result was a plan for a monthly afternoon session, in which school would be dismissed early and teachers would work in heterogeneous (lay/religious) groups to work on teacher rostering and other areas of concern. Parsons was asked to function as coordinator and facilitator. The program continued throughout the year, meeting eight more times. Two results were noted anecdotally: (1) The monthly meetings provided a mechanism for ventilating difficulties, tensions, and misunderstandings and deflating rumors; (2) The task groups devised an acceptable plan for teacher rostering that appeared to be fair; this plan was implemented by the administration the following year. A secondary outcome was that many of the teachers reported using the communication exercises and problem-solving techniques in their classrooms.

Case 3

An example of intervention in a crisis has been reported by Meyers and Pitt (1976). It occurred when Meyers was working as the regular psychological consultant to a parochial school (grades one through eight) located in a small-town parish near a large city. The school consisted of 14 classroom teachers, 3 supplementary teachers, a psychological consultant one day each week, and 422 students. Many students had one or more siblings attending the school. Furthermore, this particular parish had a stable population that had attended this church for years. Consequently, the members of the parish knew each other relatively well.

During school vacation, one of the sixth-grade boys died a tragic, accidental death. The school communicated its condolences to the family, but aside from this, the school had no official response to the death. The teachers were uncertain how to handle the situation, and consequently, discussion with students was generally avoided. One month later, a seventh-grade boy was injured fatally in a car accident.

In the period immediately following the deaths, several new behaviors began to be observed as problems in the school. (1) There was an increase in discipline problems in classrooms as well as on the playground. For example, there was an increase in the number of children sent to the principal by teachers for disciplinary reasons. There were specific reports of increased acting out, disruptive behavior, and lying. (2) There was a series of bomb scares at the school. There was at least some connection between the bomb scares and the deaths, since the boy responsible for one bomb scare had been a friend of one of the deceased youngsters. Projective test findings and dream material revealed an emphasis on fantasies about the friend's death. (3) Superstitious rumors began to spread through the school and community. People said that bad things occur in threes and therefore a third child would die. Since Chris and Joseph were the first two children who died, it was rumored that the third child to die would be an eighth-grader named Mary. There were two eighth-grade girls named Mary. (4) The final behavioral indication of problems was that the first- and second-grade children evidenced denial of the deaths through fantasy. One example of this process was a fantasy, in which this group of children reported seeing parts of the boys' bodies in the church basement.

During a consultation visit soon after the bomb scares, Meyers presented to the principal his observations about the effects the deaths were having on the school. It was agreed that a teacher workshop would be the most economical means to help the school cope more effectively with the crisis. Two goals were set for the workshops: to help the teachers understand the disturbing student behaviors and to help the teachers encourage students to express their feelings about death and related issues. The consultant and principal met jointly with small groups of teachers for one-hour workshop sessions, which were divided into the following four segments:

1. The general importance of allowing the children to express their feelings was emphasized. The consultant indicated that adults often want to protect children from unpleasant feelings; however, a more appropriate response is to accept and understand the child's sad feelings. Selma Fraiberg's (1959) discussion of children's right to feel was used to illustrate this point.

2. Using theoretical ideas about the process of mourning (Bowlby, 1963; Krupp, 1972), the consultant presented briefly a conceptual scheme to help the teachers understand the behaviors that had been observed recently. First, the three stages of mourning were presented. Then, the teachers were asked to indicate whether they had observed any behaviors that could be associated with these stages.

3. Because understanding one's own feelings can be important for helping others, the teachers were asked how they felt about the deaths. Many emotional feelings were expressed by the principal and by individual faculty members. Specifically, though this had not been planned, in each session the principal was one of the first staff members to share the feelings of sadness and frustration she had experienced after the deaths. This may have been important in freeing other staff members to reveal feelings. The consultant responded to the staff's grief by accepting these feelings in a nonjudgmental manner. One goal was to communicate that it was acceptable to experience and reveal these normal feelings. In addition, the consultant expressed empathy by sharing his own similar feelings of grief.

4. It was recommended that the teachers encourage students to express their feelings to facilitate the successful completion of the mourning process. In addition to providing an opportunity for students to express important feelings, the students would see that at least one adult, their teacher, accepted their feelings. Another recommendation was that the teachers should not pres-

sure students to express feelings. On the contrary, teachers were encouraged only to provide an opportunity for students to express feelings. One way to implement this recommendation was by discussing spontaneous expressions of student's feelings; a second technique was to establish a structured time during class when the students and teacher would discuss feelings related to death and personal loss. Although teachers were encouraged to help the children deal with their feelings, it was made clear that they should do so only inasmuch as they felt comfortable doing it. They were encouraged to contact the consultant or the principal for help in dealing with any related situation that might arise.

One indication of success was the teachers' open reactions when they were asked to express their personal feelings about the deaths. Their reactions included guilt, anger, and sadness. Another source of evidence tentatively indicating the success of this workshop was the subsequent reduction of teacher complaints about discipline problems. Several teachers indicated to the principal or the consultant that they had discussed feelings about death with their classes, and some teachers requested help with related situations. Apparently, communication about this topic, which had been blocked previously, became open subsequent to the consultation program.

This workshop was designed to help a school deal with a crisis that may not occur frequently or with the same intensity in most schools. However, as has been argued elsewhere, school is one important place to deal with feelings about death as well as other feelings (Krupp, 1972).

Summary

Mental health specialists working in schools have traditionally involved themselves in one-to-one interventions with students. Although it has been clear to all thoughtful practitioners that the environment in which the client functions has important effects on the client, interventions into this environment have been rare and have typically not been systematically applied. The weaknesses of such environmental interventions, particularly those directed at such caretaker organizations as the school, can be attributed in part to a lack of an encompassing theoretical rationale for such interventions and a lack of a diverse set of empirically based intervention techniques.

Organizational development has gone a long way toward providing both the rationale and techniques for systematic attempts to change organizations. The rationale is in part based on an analysis of the shortcomings of traditional bureaucracies and theories about human motivation and organizational structure that point toward alternatives to bureaucracies. The techniques include a wide variety of interventions, such as laboratory interventions, data feedback, and process consultation that are grounded in the empirical research foundations of social psychology. These techniques, refined and applied by management consultants and others working primarily in industrial organizations, proved useful in educational applications in part because they fit the traditions of this type of intervention agent. The mental health worker has a different tradition, and his interventions into the organizational life of the school must take into account this tradition. Therefore, O.D. interventions must be adapted appropriately for the skills of the mental health worker and the expectations held by the school regarding such workers. The three cases in this chapter tap the essential elements of an O.D. intervention but take a form that is consistent with professional goals and situational demands of the mental health consultant.

CHAPTER NINE

Assessing the Impact of School Consultation

⊡ ⊡ ⊡ ⊡ ⊡ ⊡ ⊡ ⊡ ⊡ ⊡ ⊡

Nathan Azrin (1977) has argued that the research methodology presently dominating psychology provides competencies that are not directly applicable to applied psychology. For example, he suggests that, in the evaluation of dissertations, grant proposals, and journal articles, the *outcome* is of secondary importance when compared with the form of presentation. In other words, he feels that the clinical importance of findings are subordinated to the testing of concepts and the demonstration of scholarship. Azrin is describing what we see as a widening gap between research and practice, and, unfortunately, this gap is evident in the study of teacher consultation. The result is that the research investigating teacher consultation has had minimal relevance to practicing consultants and thus has had very little impact on the development of teacher consultation techniques.

This gap between research and the practice of consultation is consistent with the general tendency toward specialization today in both psychology and education. Professional associations like the American Psychological Association have a burgeoning number of separate divisions representing different specialties, and universities have growing numbers of programs and departments in these areas. Although these different specialties often overlap, communication between specialties is too infrequent. It has been our experience that such a gap exists between the research specialties and applied psychology and education, and, more specifically, between consultation researchers and practitioners.

Part of the problem is that most people who obtain training in consultation are committed to practice and are not particularly concerned with research. Similarly, people trained thoroughly about research techniques are rarely exposed to the potential effects and problems associated with consultation techniques in practice. As a result, the two groups too often fail to find a common basis for communication.

There is a need for increasing collaboration between researchers and practitioners in teacher consultation, and collaboration should result in benefits for both groups. Researchers would benefit by formulating better questions and by developing research designs that have more direct applicability. Practitioners would benefit by improving their skills from the useful information that becomes available as a result of such research. By developing a base of data demonstrating the utility of consultation techniques, consultants can more effectively persuade schools to implement successful consultation approaches. The overall result should be more development of consultation techniques that are increasingly effective. To accomplish this goal, it will be important to develop research methodologies that are equally relevant and feasible to teachers and consultants as well as researchers. This will not be an easy task. Funding and time allocations for research and evaluation are generally difficult to obtain, because research efforts are inevitably low on the budget hierarchy of schools and community mental health centers; assessing characteristics of consultants' or consultees' personality or behavioral style is difficult, because this can stimulate resistance; and sampling consultants and consultees is difficult, because there are relatively few of them. In fact, one author, commenting on the difficulties of consultation research, concluded that adequate experimental research may be impossible (Stephenson, 1973).

With an acute awareness of these problems, it is nevertheless our contention that strides in such research can and must be made if consultation is to develop and improve as a viable technique in the schools.

To stimulate research with relevance for both practitioners and researchers, we will discuss in this chapter the principles for developing a relevant research model through a selected review of past research. We will also discuss one model for research in teacher consultation that can meet the needs of both researcher and practitioner through a brief review of research consistent with this model.

Basic Principles for Consultation Research

Relevance to both practitioner and researcher should be the guiding principle underlying consultation research. That is, in addition to heuristic value, research designs should be feasible enough to be implemented by large numbers of professionals with minimal financial support. In addition to this guiding principle, we feel that the relevance of consultation research can be determined by considering research questions appropriate for teacher consultation, weaknesses in past research, and threats to validity in consultation research. Each of these criteria will be discussed in some detail in the following sections.

Research Questions in Teacher Consultation. One useful way to conceptualize which questions are appropriate for consultation research is to consider the three components of consultation as input variables, process variables, and output variables. Examples of *input variables* might include the consultee's characteristics, the consultant's characteristics, the problem presented by the consultee, and the consultant's recommendations.

Process variables include those techniques used by the consultant to encourage the consultee to do something about the problem. Process refers to what actively takes place during consultation, and so any variables reflecting what happens during consultation are process variables. Warmth, congruence, the freedom to accept or reject the consultant's recommendations, and all other qualities constituting a communication style are considered relevant process variables.

Outcome variables are the changes resulting from consultation. In the school, these changes would be observable behavior or attitudes of teachers and students.

Each part of this model can be used as the focal point for developing appropriate questions and related research strategies. However, we also agree with Azrin (1977) that research should focus on outcome, and, consequently, that any research questions relating to input or process variables should only be raised in conjunction with questions of outcome. There is little utility in investigating consultation process variables unless this is done to determine the practical impact of such variables on consultation outcome. Questions with practical implications will be most relevant to the development of school consultation.

From such a research framework, the following research questions would be appropriate for consultation investigation. First, how do various process variables (for example, number of words spoken by consultant and consultee) and relationship variables (consultant empathy, genuineness, and so forth) affect the outcome of consultation? Secondly, how can these process and relationship variables be used to maximize consultation outcome? Third, what are the effects of various consultation techniques (such as theme interference reduction or indirect confrontation)? Fourth, what trait variables (cognitive style, locus of control, dogmatism) and what demographic variables (age, sex) characterize effective and ineffective consultants? Similarly, what characteristics of teachers suggest whether a teacher is likely to profit from consultation? Finally, a long-range goal should be to focus on the interactions among the relationships implied in each question.

Principles Derived from Past Research. Research regarding the processes and outcomes of the relationship between consultant and teacher is rare (Mann, 1973; Meyers, Martin, and Hyman, 1977). Furthermore, the research that has been done shows inconsistent results (Mannino and Shore, 1975).

Mannino and Shore reviewed the existing outcome investigations of mental health consultation during the period 1958–1972. An indication of the relative paucity of research in this area is that they reported only thirty-five outcome studies, and many of these were unpublished doctoral dissertations. Of the thirty-five studies cited, only fourteen were clearly investigations of mental health consultation with teachers. Seven of the fourteen investigations had positive outcomes, four reported negative outcomes, and three reported mixed results. Three of these investigations, however, supported by substantial grants, represent important beginning research efforts in consultation and have been quoted frequently. Unfortunately, all three had either mixed results or generally negative results. Our review of these studies, along with our consideration of their strengths and weaknesses, has contributed to the elaboration of the research model presented later in this section, which we feel circumvents such weaknesses in consultation research. We will review the three investigations to provide the reader with similar insight into the limitations of such consultation research designs.

The first of these three investigations to be discussed is the research of mental health consultation by Richard Cutler and Elton McNeil (1966). Their goal was to help school personnel handle classroom problems and improve the general mental hygiene of the school.

According to Mannino and Shore's (1975) report of this research, parents, children, teachers, and administrators were given questionnaires to evaluate effectiveness. There were no planned control groups. Improvement was observed in the staff's understanding of personal relationships with colleagues and in their overall effectiveness, as measured by the staff's self-report. Teachers viewed themselves as stronger and more assertive following consultation, and they were generally more satisfied than those who were not exposed to consultation. In particular, those with more intense exposure to consultation showed increased flexibility in their relationships with children and increased openness in interpersonal relationships.

In contrast to the apparent changes in teacher behavior,

student measures of change were in the appropriate direction but failed to reach significance. In other words, the three-year study showed change in teacher attitudes but failed to find corresponding changes in student attitudes.

Richard Schmuck (1968) describes the second investigation, which was a consultation project carried out in Philadelphia designed to change teachers' attitudes toward and understanding of child behavior. Also, it sought to train teachers to deal directly and more effectively with problem children in the classroom. Six schools were used, and each contained large numbers of emotionally disturbed youngsters. The six principals supported the mental health consultation program. In total, there were fifty-nine volunteer teachers from these six schools, and two of the schools were used as controls.

Each consultant met with a group of teachers in each of the four treatment schools for fifteen sessions. The consultants also had individual conferences with teachers and visited their classrooms upon request. All sessions were oriented toward problem-solving discussions about the teachers' relationships with students, other teachers, and parents.

The project evaluated change in teachers' and students' attitudes using questionnaires administered on a pre-post basis. The questionnaires administered to teachers revealed generally positive and significant changes in teacher attitudes, including teacher self-concept, perception of students, perception of mental health factors in the classroom, and their relationship to academic performance. In contrast, the questionnaires administered to students revealed no improvement in student perceptions of informal group process in the classroom, self-esteem, measures of classroom friendship patterns, or attitudes toward school and academic work. Thus, although mental health consultation showed a significant effect on teachers, no concomitant effect on students was observed.

The third of these early investigations was carried out at the University of Texas by Ira Iscoe and his colleagues (Iscoe and others, 1967; Pierce-Jones, Iscoe, and Cunningham, 1968). In this comprehensive study of school consultation, trained graduate students served as child-behavior consultants. Fourteen experimental schools and fourteen control schools participated in this program.

At least seven separate self-report measures evaluated changes in the teachers, including: (1) teachers' need for help with a variety of problems; (2) teachers' perception of the child's behavior; (3) teachers' conception of an ideal pupil; (4) teachers' attitudes regarding child behavior; (5) assessment of the degree to which the consultation program was known and the degree to which it was used; and (6) an assessment of teachers' perceptions of the interactions between school and community. Although the degree of rapport between consultant and consultee increased during the consultation program, there were no significant changes for any of the other measures.

We feel that each of these three studies are of particular value to future consultation research. Their value is an instructional one, which lies not in their somewhat ambiguous findings but in their clear failure to meet criteria essential for meaningful consultation research.

Although each of these investigations attempted to determine the outcome of consultation, each failed to consider either input variables or process variables, which may explain why the results obtained are ambiguous. Secondly, each of these investigations used large numbers of subjects, which makes it particularly difficult to control the consultation techniques used. Furthermore, there is no evidence that such control was attempted or that an effort was made to record consultation process to check whether the stated consultation techniques were implemented adequately. A third weakness common to each study is that none had a sufficiently specific and clear definition of consultation to have pragmatic value to the practitioner. In other words, a practitioner could not use the description of consultation techniques as a clear guide of how to do it. This last point is not a weakness distinctly unique to these earlier investigations, for it presently underlies most efforts to do research about consultation. Although there have been some early efforts to clearly define consultation and the specific techniques employed (see Caplan, 1970; McGehearty, 1969; Newman, 1967; Sarason and others, 1966; Schmuck, Runkel, and Langmeyer, 1969; Snyder and Berman, 1960; Winicki, 1972), there have not been a sufficient number of these efforts, and most of this research has not been clear enough to permit replication.

The best exception to the tendency toward insufficient specificity may be Caplan's (1970) description of theme interference reduction. Although this technique may be limited in its general applicability by school consultants, it serves as a model for the degree of specificity that is needed. Further efforts must specify a broader variety of consultation techniques in clear operational terms. This specificity is a necessary prerequisite to developing the experimental control that will lead to more effective research. Specification of such procedures will similarly allow a clearer interpretation of results, with more specific knowledge regarding precisely which techniques account for precisely which results.

Finally, an examination of the criteria used to assess consultation impact reveals that, although the evaluations were extensive, there was a reliance on a variety of self-report measures for both students and teachers to the exclusion of measures based on directly observable behavior. This is not to imply that the utilization of such self-reports is wrong or inappropriate. This type of criteria allows the researcher to determine the phenomenological views of the teacher and student, which are such an integral part of the helping process in consultation. These criteria are also important because they provide an economical way of obtaining objective assessments of change in teachers or students.

However, consultation research has relied on these self-report measures almost exclusively. For example, only two of the investigations described by Mannino and Shore's (1975) literature review used systematic assessment of directly observable behavior as the criterion. Although self-report measures are one appropriate type of criterion, directly observable behavior should be assessed also. By considering data that show carefully defined, observable behavior changes in teachers and students following consultation, researchers will be able to learn more about the specific effects of consultation techniques. Furthermore, Schmuck (1968) implied that attitudinal changes resulting from consultation are not necessarily associated with behavior changes. This issue can only be determined with certainty by assessing directly observable behavior as one criteria. A final reason why observable behavior changes should be assessed is that such data will be important in supporting the implementation of the consultation role; administrators concerned about accountability will want to know whether consultation results in meaningful behavior changes in students. As a result of these arguments, we feel that consultation investigations should assess both phenomenological, self-report measures as well as directly observable behavior of teachers and students. Some recent investigations have focused on measures of directly observable teacher behavior (Friedman, 1977; Meyers, Freidman, and Gaughan, 1975) and student behavior (Freidman, 1977; Meyers, 1975a).

Recent Large-N Investigations. As we noted in our review of previous investigations, a major common weakness of consultation research has been its failure to consider the process of consultation in a systematic manner. The research we described did not address the relationship between the process and the outcome of consultation. Lately, research has appeared that attempts to focus on the relationship between process and outcome using large numbers of subjects. As with all research, the studies we will review demonstrate both strengths and weaknesses.

Bergan and Tombari (1975) examined the relationship between consultation process and outcome from a behavioral viewpoint. They used eleven school psychologists from different communities across the country, and they consulted with teachers regarding 806 children. They used a wide variety of consultant measures in the categories of service efficiency, skill in applying psychological principles, and interviewing skill. Interviewing skill was determined from transcripts of audio tapes from one problem-identification interview and one problem-analysis interview of unspecified lengths of time.

Multiple Regression Analyses were performed, and it was found that the average time from referral to the initial interview, the flexibility of the consultant in applying psychological principles, and the proportion of statements designed to elicit information or action from the teacher all contributed significantly to the multiple correlation with problem identification. Furthermore, it was found that, once the consultation relationship achieved problem identification, problem solution almost invariably resulted.

This investigation must be considered as one of the most important research investigations that has been completed at this time. It is based on a large number of cases, and the findings show a relationship between certain process variables and problem iden- tification. It is significant that, in almost every case where problem identification occurred, the problem was solved. A final strength of this investigation is that the techniques which the researchers suggested to the consultants and the outcome criteria were gener- ated conceptually from a behavior modification model. Con- sequently, their research is guided by a framework emphasizing clear definitions of the stimuli and reinforcers that have an impact on consultation.

A second series of studies of the process of consultation is that presented by Marvin Fine. These are some of the first efforts to study process, and they represent an early effort at a program of research rather than a single study.

The first of these (Tyler and Fine, 1974) is an experimental investigation, which attempted to define *limited* and *intensive* case- centered consultation. The study also compared the relative effec- tiveness of these techniques in leading to teacher satisfaction. Briefly, they found the intensive approach to be superior, using teacher and psychologist self-reports as criteria. Although there were specific definitions of limited and intensive consultation, there was no attempt to define and control the quality of the in- teraction between the consultant and teacher.

A follow-up investigation attempted to address this latter issue (Schowengerdt, Fine, and Poggio, 1976). This study used a self-report by sixty-three psychologists regarding three successive case-centered (Level I) consultation problems that did not result in special class placement. The study examined the relationship be- tween a variety of input variables and some measures of process as they affected teacher satisfaction with consultation. Teachers filled out a questionnaire identifying their age, sex, college degrees, years of teaching experience, satisfaction with consultation, and perception of the psychologist's facilitative characteristics. Using step-wise Multiple Regression Procedures, they found that, based on teachers' perceptions, the psychologists who exhibited warmth, understanding, and empathy were significantly more likely to have teachers who were satisfied with consultation. Furthermore, they found that these facilitative characteristics were more important in generating teacher satisfaction than the amount of time spent in consultation.

Taking the two studies together, there is tentative evidence that a minimum amount of time may be necessary and that facilitative factors reflecting the quality of interaction between consultant and consultee are important in predicting successful outcomes of consultation.

A third report is presented by Margaret Wilcox (1977). The investigation addressed the issue of the effect of consultant style and group environment on the consultee's attitudes toward group mental health consultation and the consultant. In this study, post-doctoral psychologists trained in school-based consultation lead consultation groups for student-teachers. Approximately 150 consultees participated in one of twenty, ten-week consultation groups. Outcome was defined in terms of the self-reported consultee attitudes toward consultation and the consultant. Consultation process was identified by a twenty-seven-item style questionnaire and a ninety-item group-environment scale (see Moos, Insell, and Humphrey, 1974) completed by the consultees.

Using factor analysis and discriminative analysis techniques, the author reported that three process factors—consultant's emphasis on content, structural group order and organization, and consultant's humanistic orientation—accounted for 56 percent of the variance in consultee attitudes toward consultation and 54 percent of the variance in their attitudes toward the consultants. In addition to significantly adding to the limited data on consultation process factors, this investigation demonstrated the feasibility of examining the contribution of group process to attitudinal measures of consultation outcome.

Although the investigations we have described (Bergan and Tombari, Schowengerdt, Fine, and Poggio, and Wilcox) are not the only recent studies, they are representative of the strengths and weaknesses of what has been done. Each study was primarily descriptive and was based on relatively large numbers of subjects. Each is felt to have taken significant steps toward developing meaningful data on consultation process. However, to fully appreciate their strengths as well as their limitations, this descriptive research needs to be considered within the context of the goal of science in general and the goal of consultation research in particular.

Ultimately, no matter what the scientific discipline, the goal of science is the description, understanding, and control of its subject matter. Further, underlying every science are observation and measurement, which provide a description of events and a way of quantifying them that is essential to later attempts at manipulation and control. The three investigations reviewed have clearly added to the observation and measurement of consultation process. They have addressed strictly descriptive issues, such as "what was" happening in terms of consultation process and outcome, and correlational issues, such as "what will be" happening. They have even attempted to discover the "how" and "why" of consultation outcome. Each of these functions serves a very important first step in consultation research. However, such observations by themselves are not enough to achieve the ultimate goals of prediction and control. Research needs to move from observation and description of consultation to the search for order, consistencies, and uniformities—for functional, lawful relationships among events. To achieve these ends, techniques that will allow experimental control and manipulation of the events under investigation are needed.

This point about experimental control and manipulation represents the principal weakness of previous research. For example, although Bergan and Tombari (1975) make an important contribution to the consultation literature, this study was descriptive and made no effort to provide experimental control. Further, just as this investigation is important because of its very large number of cases, this very strength becomes a liability in the difficulty of controlling consultant behavior. Although an effort was made to be specific about consultation procedures by differentiating between problem identification and problem analysis and by defining several indices of interview skill, there was little chance to control the behavior of the consultants. The consultants were far apart geographically, and their consulting style was only checked on two tapes, which may not have been totally representative. This weakness minimizes the usefulness of their efforts to provide specific definitions of consultation process and techniques, since we do not really know the extent to which they were implemented throughout the variety of consultation relationships. In fact, it is somewhat surprising (and suggestive of the importance of the positive results obtained) that any significant relationships were obtained between consultant process measures taken from two tapes with outcome measures derived from a large number of complete consultation relationships.

Also, all the criteria involving problem identification, plan-implementation, and outcome were based on self-reports by the consultants. A more useful measure of outcome based on self-reports should also include measures of the teachers' and students' perceptions of outcome to avoid consultant bias. In addition, there should also be criteria based on directly observable behavior of the teachers and students in the classroom, although this type of assessment may simply be unrealistic in the large-N investigation.

Similarly, the study described by Tyler and Fine (1974), although attempting to specifically define limited and intensive consultation as the treatment variable, made no attempt to define or control the quality of the interaction between the consultant and teacher. Further, like Bergan and Tombari (1975), Schowengerdt, Fine and Poggio (1976), and Wilcox (1977), they relied exclusively on self-report measures as criteria.

Small-N Design for Consultation Research

It should be clear that the large-N investigations have made a contribution to the literature and are having a continuing influence on research. However, the limitations of such research designs—for example, their failure to clearly define consultation and the consultation process, their lack of experimental control, and their failure to employ directly observable measures of outcome, along with other weaknesses summarized in the previous section—have stimulated the development of an alternative research strategy using a multiple baseline design for a small number of subjects.

Multiple Baseline Design. The multiple baseline design (Baer, Wolf, and Risley, 1968; Hall and others, 1970) is well suited to study the effects of teacher consultation using observable outcome measures and small numbers of subjects. This design was originally conceived to study multiple behaviors treated one at a time in a step-wise manner. It has also been used to study the effects of one treatment administered to more than one subject in a step-wise manner, and this is how it could be used to study teacher consultation.

We will describe an application of this design to illustrate its use. Four teachers could be chosen as subjects, and the outcome measure might be the amount of teacher praise. This study would last for five weeks, and each teacher would be observed at the same time once a day for the duration of the study. The first week would consist of baseline observations for each of the four teachers before any consultation is initiated. At the beginning of week two, consultation treatment (this treatment would be described in a detailed manner) would be started with teacher 1 (each teacher being randomly assigned to treatment week), whereas teachers 2, 3, and 4 would remain in baseline conditions during week two. The experimental control provided is clear. If there is a change in behavior for teacher 1 but not for teachers 2, 3, and 4, there is evidence that the treatment provided for teacher 1 accounted for the change.

Then, at the beginning of week three, teacher 2 would receive consultation treatment, treatment would continue for teacher 1, and teachers 3 and 4 would receive no treatment; at the beginning of week four, teacher 3 would receive consultation treatment (along with teachers 1 and 2), while teacher 4 would remain in the baseline condition; and, finally, at the beginning of the fifth week, teacher 4 would receive consultation treatment. The investigation would be complete at the end of the fifth week. Hypothetical results are presented in Figure 5, which illustrates this design with four effective consultation relationships.

This design has several beneficial characteristics. First, each teacher has the opportunity to benefit from the consultation treatment rather than some being treated and others not, as in the traditional experimental control-group design. Secondly, there is an opportunity to examine both immediate effects and longer-term effects of the treatment. This occurs automatically with the multiple baseline, because, when the last teacher (teacher 4) begins treatment, teacher 1 is in his fourth week of treatment.

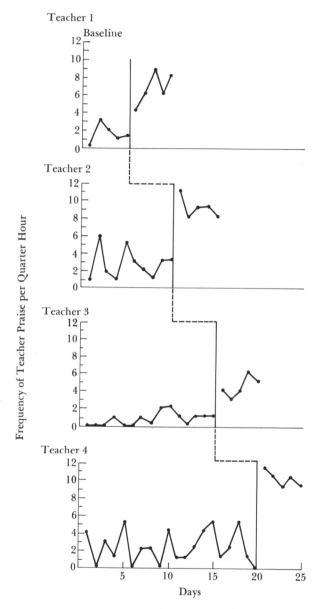

Figure 5. Multiple Baseline Design Applied to Consultation with Four Teachers

Evaluating Research Designs. Such small-N approaches to research have their critics, and the utility of small-N designs has been questioned as to their validity. Campbell and Stanley (1963) have provided one thorough approach to evaluating research designs in terms of internal and external validity. A guide of this sort is important not only for small-N paradigms but for all designs. We do not mean to imply that such standards be used as a means of trying to ensure perfect experiments, but we hope instead that a clear awareness of the weakness in a given design will stimulate the researcher to state clearly the possible weaknesses and to make appropriately conservative conclusions.

Campbell and Stanley (1963) consider two basic types of threats to the validity of experimental research—internal and external validity. Researchers should consider each type of threat in relation to the types of questions being researched as well as the general state of the research in the field.

It is not our purpose to define each separate threat to validity. The reader is encouraged to examine Campbell and Stanley's (1963) general treatment of each threat or to consider Meyers and others' (1978b) description of each threat in relation to small-N designs for consultation research. However, we would like to note the practical importance of the two types of threats to validity in developing a research design. Internal validity involves the question as to whether or not the treatment had a causal relationship to the observed effects. Internal validity is, therefore, a necessary requisite for making any kinds of causal conclusions from a research study. In other words, if we cannot conclude that our treatment rather than some other extraneous variable accounts for the observed experimental effects, then we really cannot conclude anything from a research study. Questions of generalizability or external validity are irrelevant and perhaps even misleading until the internal validity is clearly established. It is our contention that the first priority for consultation research is to show what specific techniques and designs facilitate a consistent ability to obtain such internal validity; then and only then is external validity an issue. We have found that the small-N multiple baseline design affords the researcher the needed control against threats to internal validity and thus is a research paradigm of special value.

Examples of Multiple Baseline Designs

One significant investigation using a modification of a multiple baseline design was a behavior modification consultation reported by Cossairt, Hall, and Hopkins (1973). In this study, three teachers received consultation, and they each selected four of their students with low attending behavior and low instruction-following behavior. Students' attending behaviors were observed, and the teachers' behaviors were recorded when they reinforced attending behavior, provided attention (even if negative) for nonattending behavior, or ignored the child's behavior. In addition, a specific number of post-observation consultation sessions were tape recorded, which allowed the calculation of the number of the consultant's positive comments of teacher praise.

In this investigation, a sophisticated multiple baseline design was used to try to determine the effects of the consultant's instructions, feedback, and feedback plus social praise in increasing teacher praise. Prior to the introduction of the experimental conditions, baseline recordings of (1) the percent of intervals that students attended to the teacher, (2) the number of intervals of teacher praise, and (3) the number of intervals of teacher attention to the nonattending student were made for all three teachers. Consistent with the multiple baseline design, the length of these baseline periods varied for each of the teachers. Baselines for teachers A and B ran concurrently for the first ten sessions, following which (session 11), teacher A was introduced to the first experimental condition (instruction) and teacher B continued baseline for ten more sessions. Teacher C's baseline period was ten sessions and followed the same procedures used with teachers A and B. However, unlike A and B, where the experimental treatment was introduced in succession, teacher C received a "package" experimental program, in which all three experimental conditions were introduced simultaneously.

The essence of this design and the graphic records of behaviors for teacher A and B are shown in Figure 6. Similarly, teacher C's praising behavior, the students' behavior, and the experimenter's behavior are presented in Figure 7.

A second experiment using a multiple baseline design to assess the outcome of consultation was conducted by Meyers,

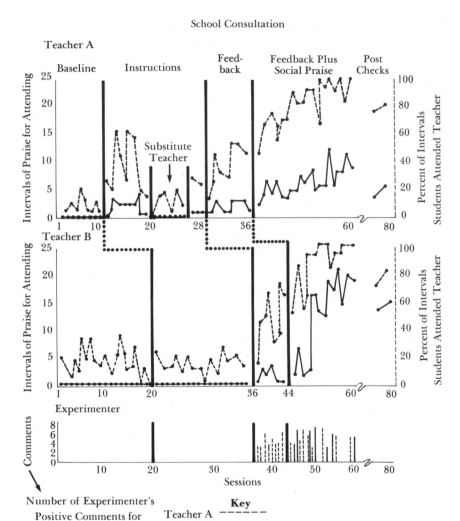

Figure 6. Praising Behavior of Teachers A and B, Percent of Students Attending Each Teacher, and Number of Experimenter's Positive Comments for Teacher Praise

Freidman, and Gaughan (1975). In this investigation, the negative verbal behavior of three teachers was observed on a daily basis in each classroom. Following a common baseline period of one week, the consultation treatment was introduced randomly to each of the three teachers, one at a time in a step-wise manner.

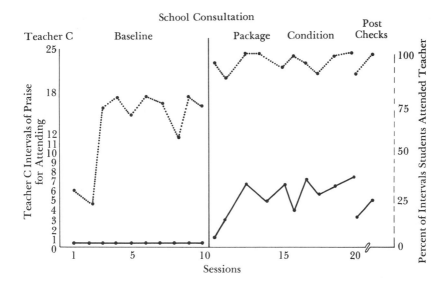

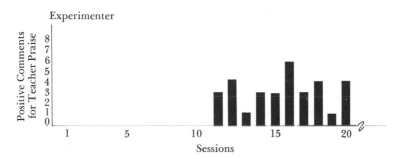

Figure 7. Praising Behavior of Teacher C, Percent of Students Attending Teacher C, and Number of Experimenter's Positive Comments for Teacher Praise

Table 2 shows that consultation began for teacher 1 during observation period 2, at which time teachers 2 and 3 remained in the baseline condition. The experimental control for teacher 1 is that the observed changes occurring for teacher 1 during observation period 2 should not be observed in the other two teachers at that time.

Table 2 shows that this experimental control worked partially for teacher 1. While teacher 1 decreased in negative behavior after consultation during observation period 2 (period 1 = 5.47

**Table 2. Mean and Standard Deviation of Percentage of
Negative Teacher Behavior During Baseline and Consultation**

		Observation Periods			
		1	2	3	4
Teacher					
1	Condition	Baseline	Consultation	Consultation	Consultation
	Mean	5.47	1.74	2.54	3.60
	SD	1.71	1.39	3.73	3.86
Teacher					
2	Condition	Baseline	Baseline	Consultation	Consultation
	Mean	8.38	7.23	3.02	2.13
	SD	7.08	4.15	2.84	2.84
Teacher					
3	Condition	Baseline	Baseline	Baseline	Consultation
	Mean	10.20	4.55	1.42	1.77
	SD	9.66	2.83	2.09	1.81

percent, period 2 = 1.74 percent), teacher 2 remained relatively stable during the same period, which was her baseline (8.38 percent to 7.23 percent). This suggests that changes in teacher 1 did result from consultation. However there was also a reduction in teacher 3's negative behavior during her baseline periods (period 1 = 10.2 percent, period 2 = 4.55 percent). This places doubt on the apparent experimental effect for teacher 1.

Table 2 also shows a clear decrease in negative behavior for teacher 2 from her baseline period to her consultation period (observation period 2 = 7.23 percent; observation period 3 = 3.02 percent). However, this occurred simultaneously with a similar decrease during the control teacher's (teacher 3) baseline periods (observation period 2 = 4.55 percent; observation period 3 = 1.42 percent). Consequently, although changes were apparent for teacher 2, it cannot be concluded definitely that these changes resulted from consultation rather than some other extraneous factor. Also, there was a small increase in negative teacher behavior during teacher 3's treatment period (observation period 4), and this indicates that the experimental conditions had no effect for this teacher. To summarize, although the experimental design suggests caution in interpreting the results, this study did demonstrate a reduction in negative teacher behavior, which may have been due to consultee-centered consultation for two teachers (teachers 1 and

2). This study was one of the first multiple baseline investigations; we have presented it because it demonstrates the design. However, although consultation techniques were defined in a manner consistent with direct service to the teacher, there was no effort to ensure that the consultants actually implemented the techniques through analysis of consultation tapes. More recent investigations of teacher consultation using a small-N multiple baseline approach (Freidman, 1977; Parsons and Meyers, 1978) have corrected this lapse. And the interested reader is referred to these additional investigations for a careful examination. In reviewing these and other small-N studies, several significant strengths of the multiple baseline design become apparent.

By an intensive examination of individual data, details about specific processes and techniques can be considered easily while determining the exact effects of these variables. Individuals' specific behavior is likely to be ignored in studies using large numbers of subjects because the researcher usually focuses on the mean and tries to avoid individual differences by conceptualizing them as random error. Averages of data for a group can conceal the important individual data.

A second strength of small-N studies is their experimental control of clearly defined consultation procedures, which is crucial to obtaining internal validity. A small-N approach can foster such control, because the focus is on only a few consultants. Although such control over consultant behavior should theoretically be possible with large-N designs, it is a particularly difficult task to achieve.

Third, since consultation research only began in the past twenty years, conclusive findings have not yet appeared; therefore, it is important to emphasize internal validity rather than external validity at this time. Small-N investigations have an advantage in promoting internal validity. (Of course, it is virtually impossible to control against all possible threats to internal validity.) As part of the task of providing experimental control minimizing the likelihood that competing hypotheses account for the observed effect, the researcher must explicitly identify those alternative hypotheses that exist. Small-N designs such as those we have discussed provide adequate experimental control and encourage the consideration of alternative hypotheses by examining individual cases at length.

It has been our position throughout this chapter that consultation research should focus on outcome. In addition, we noted that outcome should be examined in relation to techniques, process variables, or characteristics of consultant, consultee, or setting. We feel that a fourth major strength to small-N designs is their encouragement of such an approach by the intensive consideration of few cases.

Finally, we suggest that researchers use phenomenological assessments as well as measures of the observable behavior of the consultee and the client. Tape recording of consultation sessions may be useful to assess process variables and to monitor consultant behavior. These procedures, which were used in the small-N studies we discussed, are difficult to implement on a large scale, and they become prohibitively expensive for unfunded researchers if large numbers of subjects are used. We have presented consultation as an extremely complex phenomenon in which it is difficult to draw out those factors that account for certain outcomes. Precisely for this reason, we have emphasized the individualistic approach to examining consultation in detail. Small-N designs offer the opportunity for control of experimental variables, they can be implemented widely, and they can potentially produce data that would be useful to both researchers and practitioners.

Summary

In this chapter, we presented several basic principles that should influence consultation research: (1) Consultation research investigations should have relevance for all professionals interested in consultation. (2) Research designs should be feasible for implementation by large numbers of professionals with minimal financial support. (3) Research questions should focus on some combination of input and/or process variables along with outcome variables. (4) Consultation investigations should attempt to determine the specific impact of various aspects of consultation, which are carefully defined by the researcher. (5) Research needs to demonstrate explicit relationships between attitude changes occurring during consultation and behavioral outcomes. (6) There should be clear connections between consultation techniques and the consultee and client behavior that is assessed. (7) Consultation investigations should measure directly observable behavior of teachers, students, and consultants as well as phenomenological measures. (8) Finally, research designs in this new area should focus primarily on obtaining adequate control of the threats to internal validity.

These principles have guided the development of the small-N design for consultation that we presented. This paradigm should provide a useful tool for future research.

CHAPTER TEN

Trends in Practice, Orientation, and Training

▣ ▣ ▣ ▣ ▣ ▣ ▣ ▣ ▣ ▣ ▣

We began our discussion of school consultation techniques in Chapter Two with a brief historical perspective. To complete this picture of consultation approaches within a broad historical framework, it may be helpful to consider some current trends and potential future trends in school consultation. Specifically, we will discuss the present trends and postulated future increases in: (1) the practice of consultation in the schools; (2) consultation at the organizational level; (3) a systems approach to consultation in the schools; (4) the focus of consultation research on the process of consultation; (5) the consultant as advocate; and (6) development of consultation training programs.

192

Increased Consultation in the Schools

One apparent trend is the growing focus on consultation in the schools. This trend has been evident in a number of different ways. During the past two decades, there has been an increase in written accounts of relevant approaches, the formal teaching of consultation techniques in university programs, and empirical research in consultation. There is no direct evidence indicating a concomitant increase in the application of consultation in the schools. However, the other trends we mentioned suggest that this probably is happening and that the application of consultation techniques in the schools will continue to increase in the future. In particular, as research literature demonstrating the effectiveness of consultation techniques grows, there will be a firmer basis from which to advocate consultation in the schools.

The increased application of consultation in the schools will not occur easily, however, since a number of factors can interfere with this trend, including expectations for individual casework and recent legislation.

Expectations for Individual Casework. Counselors and school psychologists are expected to provide direct service to children without working through teachers. Teachers often hold this expectation, and, as a result, attempts to consult with teachers are often met with comments like, "If only he could receive the help he needs in a special education class" or "Perhaps she would improve if you spend some time counseling her." School administrators also seem to expect individual casework, and, as a result, case loads are often so great that there is no time to see teachers. For example, in one urban school system the school psychologists are expected to evaluate ten children per week, which obviously leaves little time for consulting.

This time restriction also interferes with the teachers' utilization of the consultant. Teachers often do not have enough time to meet with the consultant. If consultation approaches are to be applied increasingly in the schools, it will be necessary for time to be structured in the role descriptions of consultees. Further, it must be recognized that time spent consulting will necessarily reduce the number of individual cases the consultant sees. Since one common way that school psychologists and counselors are evaluated is based on the number of individual evaluations or sessions, those who attempt to shift their role toward consultation may be evaluated negatively. This criterion for evaluation can hinder the mental health specialist's attempt to implement a consultation model.

A related expectation that can interfere with the implementation of a consultation model is the attitudes of other professionals working in the school system to the application of a nontraditional service delivery approach. Initially, many teachers and many non-consulting counselors and psychologists are resentful of school consultants, who appear to have an easy job. To combat this resistance to the consultation role, consultation research must focus on practical applications. Such research would provide standards for evaluation based on effectiveness rather than the number of cases processed. In contrast to Caplan's view that the consultee is totally responsible for outcome, the model we are advocating implies some degree of consultant responsibility for outcome. This model is consistent with the growing emphasis on accountability in education, and, in the long run, this data-based approach to evaluation should contribute to an improvement in mental health services in the schools.

Legislation Affecting the Consultation Role. Recent legislative trends regarding the education of special children have culminated in the *Education for all Handicapped Children Act of 1975 (PL 94-142)*, which specifies the right to education in the least restrictive environment for all handicapped children. This legislation has conflicting implications for consultation. On the one hand, the right to education in the "least restrictive environment" will put pressure on the educational system to place increasing numbers of handicapped children in regular programs. As special children are placed in regular education programs, all teachers will have a greater need for consulting services to help deal with children whom they feel ill prepared to teach.

Unfortunately, no such consulting role has been written clearly into the legislation, although currently, Division 16 of the American Psychological Association is working on developing such legislation. This results in a serious problem, because the competing impact of this legislative trend is to place greater emphasis on individual psychoeducational diagnostic procedures for school psychologists. The potential effects of such legislation are exemplified by the case of Pennsylvania, where the decision by the Pennsylvania Association of Retarded Children has been in effect since 1972. Official procedures were developed, whereby parents could challenge the placement and educational programming decisions made for their children. The positive effect could be more thorough diagnostic work, followed by detailed consultation with teachers to set up adequate programming. However, because of the fear of legal challenges and the inadequate number of psychologists available, the result frequently has been an increased focus on diagnosis and neglect of consultation follow-up.

To clarify the impact of this legislation, consider that, not only have administrators and psychologists had to defend their diagnostic and programming decisions, but in addition, private psychologists have been hired by parents and have presented data conflicting with the school psychologist's diagnosis. As a result, school psychologists have focused on the establishment of a defensible diagnostic procedure. This concern with defensibility requires that an excessive amount of time be spent on each case, which, when combined with the small number of personnel, helps to explain why the psychologist in the school has little time to devote to other tasks besides diagnosis. The result is that consultation services are the first to be dropped. This is most unfortunate, because if psychoeducational diagnosis were done within a consultive framework (Level I), classroom behavior observations as well as teacher conferences would be stressed. Such observational data would complement the diagnosis, resulting in more defensible decisions. It is essential that administrators, psychologists, and legislators see the potential advantages of emphasizing the consultive aspects of the diagnostic process.

The fear of lawsuits, hearings, and official challenges to psychologists' professional judgment is very real at this time, and this fear affects their approach to service delivery. Rather than try to implement new roles creatively, it is more likely that these mental health specialists will try to be protective of their traditional roles. Consultation, however, is a service model that does not force the mental health specialist to abandon old roles, but instead offers a redefinition of those roles, which satisfies the traditionalist while allowing for a potentially broader preventive impact.

A related legislative trend that is interfering with the possible implementation of consultation procedures within the schools is evident in Pennsylvania, where it is now mandatory that exceptional children be reevaluated once every two years. This increased demand for reevaluation further reduces the time available for consultation. For example, in many private schools, two or three reevaluations per day are required of the psychologists.

Our purpose is not to suggest that there is anything inherently wrong with the goals of the legislation we have discussed. Generally, the aim is to help ensure the best possible service for each individual child. The problem is that such legislation seems to be implemented without careful regard for the system as a whole, and there is a strong possibility that the practical results of this legislation will be to interfere with important indirect services such as consultation.

To support and maintain preventive and consultive services, legislative changes may be necessary. It can be expected that, in the coming years, school mental health specialists will attempt to influence legislation in an effort to stimulate and mandate more preventive approaches, including consultation, in the schools. And, although the picture presented so far appears somewhat bleak, the legislative trend can be summarized optimistically by considering such legislation in relation to placement in historical context. Beginning in 1905 with Alfred Binet in France, psychologists were asked to determine whether children should be included or excluded from the educational system. Although the types of children educated within American educational systems has increased over the years, the psychologist's role has remained basically the same—to determine whether the child can be educated within the public system. However, the recent legislation has indicated that *everyone* has a right to education, even those with serious problems. Perhaps the next legislative trend in education will be to suggest that, not only are all children entitled to an education, but all children have a right to an environment that is likely to prevent or reduce future problems. If such is the case, then consultation may very well emerge as the technique of choice.

Consultation at the Organizational Level (Level IV)

Our discussion about trends in legislation makes clear that, despite the frequent and eloquent pleas for a preventive orientation, this orientation is difficult to implement in practice. Professional educators, counselors, psychologists, legislators, and the public still think of problems in terms of a medical model, where the focus of the problem is perceived as existing within the child. Our approach throughout this book has been to focus on extrapersonal, environmental factors. Unfortunately, we live in a reactive world. An active stance may be advocated, but implementing preventive approaches will always be difficult as long as present crises need to be confronted.

In this book we discussed four distinct approaches to consultation: direct service to the child, indirect service to the child, direct service to the teacher, and direct service to the organization. Our discussion of recent legislation indicates that the approach to consultation with the most immediate opportunity for growth is Level I, direct service to the child. Also, there may be some opportunity for increased service consistent with Level II, indirect service to the child. When teacher consultation has been implemented in the past, it has primarily been via these first two levels. Level III (direct service to the teacher) and Level IV (direct service to the organization) have been much less frequent, and one reason is that both of these functions are more clearly tied to a preventive approach to mental health consultation. As preventive functions come to be viewed as increasingly important, there will be a trend toward more consultation focusing on direct service to the teacher and the organization. We expect the trend to be for increased consultation services at all levels; however, there will be even greater increases in the implementation of the more preventive consultation services.

We project that the increased utilization of a consultation model in the schools and the acquisition of data supporting its effectiveness will be a major impetus for administrators and consultants to increase consultation at the organizational level. To illustrate this point, one needs to consider the cost-efficiency of consultation versus traditional direct service.

Traditional direct service delivery involves costly and time-consuming one-on-one interaction, with little consideration of extrapersonal, environmental forces affecting the referred child. This approach is neither efficient nor economical. A shift to Level I and II service delivery will not only increase the population served, but will also serve a preventive function and thus be more cost-efficient. That is, Level I and II consultation afford the consultant the opportunity to effect environmental changes, which affect the referred child and the other children in the classroom as well. Often, the recommendations intended for a specific child will have a preventive applicability to other high-risk children in the same environment.

As the cost-efficiency of these approaches becomes clearer to administrators, we expect their use to increase. If such is the case, then we further foresee the increased involvement of the consultant at the organizational level as a potential trend for the future, since at this level the consultant's recommendations would have the widest impact and the greatest preventive function. One specific type of organizational involvement that is presently in evidence and will likely increase is teacher training.

Parallel Systems: Teacher Training. The concept of teacher training as a role for school consultants is an idea that has appeared frequently in the professional literature and in practice. One example is McDaniel and Ahr's (1965) position that the school psychologist's role should include providing inservice training to teachers. Similarly, Hyman (1972a) presents the consultant in the role of teacher trainer, but with a somewhat different perspective.

Hyman has indicated that recent changes in the politics and philosophy of education may affect school consultation. These changes include demands for accountability in education, evaluations in terms of behavioral objectives, and performance criteria for certifying teachers, with a concurrent reduction in the need for new teachers. He projects that these forces will create a demand for increased inservice training and staff development. If this projection is accurate, and we feel that it is, then it provides a unique opportunity for consultants to involve themselves at the organizational level as potential agents of change.

To take advantage of the increasing need for inservice training, Hyman (1971, 1972a) has proposed a parallel systems model for the consultant. In this model, the consultant sets up an inservice training program to promote new teaching methods. A parallel system is defined as an organizational structure that functions along with one already in existence. The parallel system is autonomous in crucial decision-making areas, so that it can perpetuate itself until it becomes the major system. Such an approach is probably most likely to be effective if the participants receive official recognition, such as prestige or credits toward salary increases.

The consultant's goal would be to improve the learning climate in all classrooms in the school. The consultant would use the empirical data that is available regarding teacher-pupil interaction (Flanders, 1970; Good and Brophy, 1973); the role of flexible, cooperative, kind, democratic, and humane attitudes (Hamacheck, 1968; Hyman, 1964); the impact of questioning strategies by the teacher (R. Hyman, 1968; Rosenshine, 1970; Venduin, 1967); the effects of teacher expectations (Brophy and Good, 1974; Rist, 1970; Rosenthal and Jacobson, 1968; Thorndike, 1968); the effects of student self-image and ego strengths (Ahammer and Schare, 1970); the effects of pupil anxiety level (Martin and Meyers, 1974; Phillips, Martin, and Meyers, 1972; Turner, 1970); and the effects of aptitude by treatment interactions in education (Cronbach and Snow, 1977).

Finally, inservice training appears to be one area for increased consultation at the organizational level, which we, like Hyman, feel will continue to grow in relevance in the future.

Focus on the System

Whether or not consultants within the school increase their involvement at the organizational level as projected, it is apparent that they must continue to increase their knowledge of the school as a system if they hope to be effective in consultation.

A variety of issues relating to the entire school organization affect whether consultation is implemented and how effective consultation can be. This is true, of course, not only with consultation but with the implementation of any new technique in the schools. For example, several writers have noted that reasons for failure to implement school innovations include lack of consideration of the teacher as a person in this process, lack of detailed understanding of the total school environment, and lack of understanding of the meaning of the innovation for the particular school or school system making the implementation.

Organizational Factors and Behavioral Consultation. As it is no longer sufficient (or efficient) for the consultant to focus solely on the child, it appears that a future trend will be the increased acceptance of a systems approach to mental health service in the school. The result will be increased consideration of the interdependent nature of the individual units that comprise the system (student, teacher, administrator, contracts, rules, and so forth).

One clear example of the value of a systems orientation can be found in behavioral consultation. While process skills (such as the use of positive reinforcement by the consultant) provide one way to help ensure the consultee's effective implementation of behavior modification (Cossairt, Hall, and Hopkins, 1973; Meyers, Martin, and Hyman, 1977; Parsons, 1976b), it is equally important for the behavioral consultant to consider carefully the organizational structure, climate, and values (Abidin, 1972; Tharp and Wetzel, 1969; Winett, 1976).

Recommendations from a behavioral orientation often conflict with the school's value system. For example, one frequent behavioral recommendation is for the teacher to reinforce positive behavior and ignore negative behavior. A considerable body of empirical data support this recommendation, and yet, as any behavioral consultant knows, it does not work all the time. One reason for this failure is the consultant's lack of attention to the values of the system. It is important for the consultant to understand that teachers are not supposed to allow disruptive student behavior, and students are supposed to show their respect by acting appropriately. Consequently, many teachers feel that they are expected to suppress negative student behavior. Also, teachers have no generally accepted vehicle for expressing their angry feelings about children who show their disrespect by acting inappropriately. Of course, some teachers will complain during lunch or over coffee. Aside from such complaining, one of the few additional vehicles for expressing such feelings is by attending to the negative behavior with various forms of punishment. When the consultant's behavioral recommendation removes this outlet, the consultant must recommend alternative ways for the teacher to express these feelings appropriately. Without this understanding of the school as a system, many behavioral recommendations will be less effective.

An example will demonstrate further how organizational values can interfere with the use of behavioral approaches in the classroom. Meyers was asked to conduct a two-day inservice workshop for teachers on behavior modification techniques. Before the workshop took place, a lengthy interview was held with the school principal to determine specific goals, motivations, and organizational factors that might affect the workshop. Despite this interview, Meyers was not informed of a conflict between teachers and administrators in that district. The principal did not state that the superintendent had begun the year with an authoritarian communication to all teachers indicating that behavior modification techniques were to be widely implemented. The implication of this communication was that teachers did not have adequate control of their classes.

Meyers began this inservice workshop by attempting to understand the teachers' general resistance to behavior modification. Since he had no knowledge of the background, it was difficult for him to understand the teachers' highly vocal, adamant, almost complete rejection of behavioral principles. The teachers never mentioned the underlying issues, and, during the first day, the consultant was unable to move beyond the feelings of resistance to a productive examination of behavior modification. After the first day ended, the consultant finally learned the important political background. The next day, these issues were opened for discussion, and the teachers' resistant feelings were discussed more thoroughly and more openly. Following these discussions, some of the teachers began to accept the behavioral approach. In this instance, an understanding of organizational factors was a necessary step for the consultant effectively to promote the behavior modification intervention.

The clear implication of this example is that behavioral consultants need to have knowledge not only of operant principles, schedules of reinforcement, and principles of classroom management, but also a broader understanding of schools as systems.

Organizational Factors Affecting School Consultation. Organizational factors must be considered by any consultant delivering service to the school, and behavior modification is only one approach where this is apparent. Some authors have begun to conceptualize the school as a system and to determine those factors that may affect consultation. One example of such an approach is Gallessich's (1973) discussion of the external forces, internal forces, the school's trajectory, and the staff's perception of the consultant's role. She describes these four organizational factors and their implications for the consultant.

External forces are defined to include any organizations outside the school's immediate environment that exert influence on a school. External organizations can include the central administration, other schools in the district, local action groups, neighborhood problem areas, state educational agencies, state and federal laws and programs, accrediting changes, teacher unions, and nearby universities. The school consultant must recognize these external sources of influence and must discuss these influences with the staff.

Internal forces are the organizational features of the school itself. For example, the consultant needs to understand leadership roles and functions, the formal and informal methods of communication across various internal boundaries, and the patterns of decision making in the school. Specifically, the consultant must understand the roles of personnel and must learn the school norms. For intervention to have a realistic probability of success, the consultant must harness the knowledge, motivation, and creative energies of the entire school staff.

The *school's trajectory* is Gallessich's conceptualization of the movement of the school over time. It may be important to know the school's history, its present functioning, and its future directions and goals. For example, the consultant will attempt to understand relevant trends regarding the status of the school, faculty morale, educational orientation, community real estate values, and so forth. This type of understanding should help the consultant to determine the implications of various intervention strategies for the school as part of a constant process of change.

The final organizational factor discussed by Gallessich is the *staff's perceptions of the consultant's role.* Is the consultant expected to affect a miraculous change of some school problem? Is the consultant expected to respond to crises rather than work preventively? Is the consultant needed as a scapegoat to share the blame for an impending disaster? Is the consultant expected to influence the school staff to accept a program predesigned by the administration? One implication of this factor is that, just as the consultant helps the school to clarify its expectations, the consultant should make his own expectations about the consultation role clear. Some examples may help to clarify the potential importance of these four organizational factors in consultation.

The first example describes a school with a conflict between the administration and the teachers. This was a small private school for handicapped children. There were about twelve teachers, ten aides, a physical therapist, an occupational therapist, a speech therapist, and a psychologist. The psychologist functioned as a school consultant in addition to performing psychodiagnostic evaluations. Until the time of the incidents described here, an optimistic trend (trajectory of the school) had been apparent in the school. It seemed to be in the process of changing from a school that did little more than baby sit to a school with an exciting, positive outlook on educational programming. This new outlook had occurred as a result of a change in power on the board of directors of the clinic, which was ultimately in control of the school (external factor).

At the beginning of the following year, the president of the board suggested that the teachers disband their union. In view of the optimistic atmosphere, the teachers agreed to this request. Then, at the end of the year, four of the twelve teachers were fired. Some of the teachers who were fired had openly expressed differences with the administration. Most of these teachers were thought to be highly competent by the professional staff. Naturally, the school atmosphere changed dramatically. Teachers were afraid to communicate with each other; they tried to avoid contact with anyone associated with the administration; they rigidly adhered to innocuous rules; and they became reluctant to seek consultation (internal forces). In fact, the psychologist's role was changed to more testing and less consultation, and, as a result, the psychologist was perceived increasingly as a tester rather than a consultant (perceptions of the consultant role).

  This entire sequence of events had a devastating impact on consultation in several ways. First, there was a sharp reduction in the number of teachers seeking consultation. In fact, only new teachers who had not been part of the school during these incidents, sought a sustained consultation relationship. Only one teachers, who had not been part of the school during these incioccasions during the year. Second, in one consultation relationship, inevitably the teacher would divert the conversation from the consultation problem to her general frustration with the political situation, which she felt was stifling. Although some progress was made early during consultation, this progress became seriously limited, as the teacher's energies were turned toward complaining. A third effect was that the consultation relationship with another teacher was sporadic. Although this was a new teacher who did want help with a difficult class, the lack of a clearly defined sanction for consultation made it difficult to arrive at meeting times that were long enough to be fruitful, even though this had never been a problem in the past. Generally, few changes in children could be attributed to consultation. Any recommendation for increased contact with other staff members was doomed to failure. The teacher would agree, and then it was often a matter of months before such contact was initiated. Even when one student did show improvement, remediation was not carried over to other learning settings, other problem situations, or other students. Problems were considered in isolation, and there was little opportunity for general improvement in the mental health atmosphere. The consultation goals related to preventive mental health were not obtainable, even in those few instances where small strides were made with individual children.

  This consultation program was ineffective because of the devastating organizational changes that took place. Although this is a dramatic and extreme example used to demonstrate a point, these same principles always exert some influence on consultation. In this example, the consultant's mistake was the failure to understand the impact of the observed organizational factors on consultation. For example, the consultant underestimated the widespread effect of this situation in inhibiting communication between staff members, and he was naive about the stifling effect the administration could have on his role and the school as a whole. The error in consultation procedure is that the consultant did not use the knowledge of these organizational issues in formulating consultation strategies. Had this been done, the consultant might have confronted his role definition directly with both administration and teachers; he would have focused on the serious communication gap between the administration and the teaching staff; and he would have attempted to improve communication and increase cooperative problem solving within the school.

In another example of the impact of organizational factors, a school district was in the process of changing from traditional, self-contained special education classes to mainstreaming (the trajectory of the school). Special education needs were met by sending children to a resource room in each school for a short period of the day, and the regular classroom teachers had to contend with a significant increase in the number of disruptive students (as well as g.:eater ranges of academic ability). The regular classroom teachers were angry with the administration of the district, which had implemented this program despite their vigorous protests (external force). Also, the teachers were angry at the special service personnel, who were seen as supporting mainstreaming and the resource room concept (internal force). Furthermore, they were resentful of the many disruptive students who populated their classes, and they wanted these students returned to self-contained special education classes (internal force).

As a result, any efforts by the special services team met with teacher resistance. On some occasions, teachers agreed to try recommendations, which later did not work; on other occasions, there were overt refusals to cooperate. The teachers did not want to respond to recommendations for controlling the behavior of children they felt did not belong in their classes. If the children's disruptive behavior were to continue, there would be more opportunity to apply pressure to reinstate special classes. In this sense, the members of the special services team were not perceived as consultants but were perceived as antagonists in a political struggle (perceptions of the consultant role). For effective consultation in this setting, the issues relating to school climate, communication between various subgroups, leadership, and the decision-making process needed to be clarified. In addition, there was a need to clarify goals of the various subgroups involved in the conflict.

One of the most comprehensive statements underscoring organizational factors as a key in successful school consultation has been made by Richard Schmuck and Patricia Schmuck (1974). They reviewed a variety of approaches relating to the therapeutic, behaviorist, mental health, and group-process approaches. They indicated the strengths of each approach; however, they concluded that each has failed to provide systematic and planned attempts to humanize the climates of our schools. They feel that each approach by itself is too specific, focusing on too narrow a range of school personnel. In summary, these approaches are each limited because of the lack of focus on organizational factors. Schmuck and Schmuck make a plea for a broad-ranged, humanistic focus on the organizational factors of the school, which they describe as including the following six factors: (1) student influence on the learning group; (2) teacher influence on the learning group; (3) the principal's influence on the school organization; (4) the impact of learning groups on their individual members; (5) the impact of school organization; and (6) the impact of the school's social environment. They argue that, as consultants focus on these issues in a systematic fashion, and as they develop and maintain a humanistic outlook, they can have a meaningful impact on the prevention of mental health problems in the future.

The Consultant as Advocate

The Child Advocate. There has been an emerging focus on the school consultant as child advocate (Hyman and Schreiber, 1975). This view of consultation differs from most approaches, in that the consultant is not responsible to the school administration or the classroom teacher. Instead, the consultant is responsible to the child. It is common for a school consultant to be caught in a conflict, where a recommendation in the best interest of the school as a whole might conflict with the recommendation that would be in the best interest of the child. If the consultant is in the role of child advocate, then he must attempt to implement the recommendation that is in the best interest of the child rather than the system. Students are not accustomed to being recognized as a legitimate group that can and should make inputs into the decision-making process in the schools, and thus they are in need of a supportive advocate. The mental health consultant may in the future concern himself with functioning as a student advocate in such matters as making students aware of their legal rights in cases of suspension, special class placement, expulsion, and so forth; fostering organizational change to allow for student input into areas of decision making, including the school board; and functioning as the advocate for the student in matters of grievance and redress between student and teacher or student and administration.

Advocacy and the Use of Conflict. Another approach to consultation involving advocacy has been presented by Chesler, Bryant, and Crowfoot (1976). They provide a much broader framework, which focuses on conflict and the need for social change rather than on child advocacy in particular. They view schools as a reflection of society, each containing multiple and conflicting partisan groups. Some of these groups are stratified on the basis of race, sex, social class, and age. The school's organizational procedures (tracking, curriculum decisions, rules for behavior, disciplinary strategies, teaching techniques, and so forth) work to the advantage of some groups and the disadvantage of others. At the heart of most traditional school policy is the principle that there is consensus among groups as to educational goals and priorities, and, as a result, conflict is viewed by most school people as fearful and distasteful. Consequently, conflict between groups is repressed in the schools.

The consulting role suggested by Chesler, Bryant, and Crowfoot is based on the notion that such conflict between groups should not be repressed. They feel that the consultant should stimulate the open discussion of such conflict, which should lead to productive change. Furthermore, they propose that the consultant cannot function in the detached, neutral, nonpartisan manner that is traditionally espoused in the consultation literature. Instead, when there is conflict, the consultant must make a value judgment and then act in an appropriate partisan manner. (The implication is that the consultant will act in a partisan manner anyway, without knowing it.) Thus, the consultant takes a partisan role in school conflicts with the aim of effecting positive change in the school, which may have a similar positive impact on society. Chesler and his colleagues feel that consultants will have to make hidden injustices visible, so that these issues can be dealt with both in school and society, and thus they feel that the school consultant must act as an advocate for the many oppressed groups in our schools and in society rather than providing partisan consultation on the side of established power. These views are inconsistent with more traditional approaches to school consultation, and they provide a fresh framework for considering school consultation roles. There is not yet sufficient detail about precisely how such consultants would function, and there needs to be a careful consideration of the realistic problems inherent in implementing such roles. However, these ideas are provocative and should be considered carefully by school consultants and educators.

An Advocate for the Teacher. One logical extension of the ideas presented by Chesler, Bryant, and Crowfoot (1976) would be for the consultant to function as an advocate for the teacher. Although it may not be readily apparent, teachers are often in the position of an oppressed group.

Very often, decisions regarding class size, teacher load, school calendars, teacher evaluation, and promotion procedures are made without forethought to the educational or mental health implications for the student and teacher. Under such conditions, the mental health consultant in the school, with expertise in psychological principles of motivation, development, learning, and group functioning, may serve as a valuable advocate for promoting optimal working conditions for teachers. The consultant may use his skills to offer the theoretical and empirical support for the necessity of reduced class size or the need for teacher time to be used as a catharsis or the legitimacy of a mental health day. Further, such an advocate may assist in the development of teacher-evaluation tools and strategies to ensure the validity and reliability of such procedures. Although at best far from practical implementation, the idea of the consultant as advocate for the teacher appears to be part of the future of consultation in the schools.

Training for School Consultation

One final trend in consultation that we project for the future, which follows as a natural result of the projected increased use of consultation services, is the development and elaboration of training models for school consultation.

Training in school consultation has received very little systematic attention. Didactic and practicum courses devoted solely to school consultation have been a very recent occurrence in graduate programs on counseling and school psychology. Also, this topic has been skirted in the professional literature. For example, we have found only one article in the *Journal of School Psychology* devoted primarily to the training of school consultants (Gallessich, 1974).

Gallessich (1974) presents an adequate rationale for training in consultation, and she presents a comprehensive description of various topics she would cover during training. However, like most other writers on consultation, she does not provide sufficiently detailed descriptions of the training techniques, and this will have to be a goal for future work.

At present, the only sources regarding relatively specific training techniques derive from reports of research grants (for example, Barclay, 1967; Bergan, 1977) and some dissertations (for example, Freidman, 1977; Parsons, 1976a). However, each of these approaches is fairly narrow in its focus. As examples, Bergan focused on a behavioristic model, and Parsons focused on a Transactional Analysis model. None of them have focused in a sufficiently broad and detailed manner.

Thus, one goal for consultation in the future will be to extend the work of Gallessich to describe detailed training procedures for the broadly focused approach to school consultation presented throughout this book.

Summary

Consultation has been defined as the model affording the mental health specialist in the school the most efficient and economical approach to the delivery of mental health services. We have attempted to present the "what" and "why" for consultation as well as the "how." In this final chapter, we reiterated our orientation and discussed possible trends in consultation for the future. This analysis suggests that, not only will the practice and training of consultation increase in the future, but the types of consultation procedures will change from those used today. We hypothesize that in the future the consultant will use a systems approach to deliver service to the organization as a whole and will focus on such issues as student and teacher advocacy, inservice training, and perhaps parallel-system development. If this description of trends is accurate, we can expect many new developments in the promotion of research and the practice of consultation in the schools.

Annotated
Bibliography

◩ ◩ ◩ ◩ ◩ ◩ ◩ ◩ ◩ ◩ ◩

Beisser, A. (with R. Green). *Mental Health Consultation and Education.* Palo Alto, Calif.: National Press Books, 1972.

Beisser's view of mental health consultation derives largely from Gerald Caplan's work, although it is also based on experience gained from consulting in industry. This book considers the application of mental health consultation techniques to any appropriate community organization—such as groups of ministers, health departments, probation departments, rehabilitation agencies, schools, and welfare agencies—and stresses the social context of mental health consultation. Further, its process orientation underscores those aspects of the interaction between consultant and consultee, which the authors assume are necessary for effective consultation. One chapter is devoted specifically to mental health consultation with groups.

The book was written to meet requests received by the authors for education in mental health consultation. Consequently,

211

the book is a primer that attempts to avoid a single theoretical framework. It is organized as a dialogue of questions and answers between a student and teacher. Following each lesson is a group of exercises designed to demonstrate the lesson. While this text provides a concise statement of some consultation principles useful to beginners, it does not provide the in-depth analysis necessary for advanced students.

Blake, R. R., and Mouton, J. S. *Consultation*. Reading, Mass.: Addison-Wesley, 1976.

Blake and Moulton present the entire scope of the consulting field in a systematic manner. Throughout, the authors emphasize the dynamics of the interaction between consultant and client. For each approach presented, the consultation techniques are described so that the reader can learn something about the approach and its how-to-do-it aspects, and concrete examples taken from the literature help demonstrate the approach. Perhaps the most significant contribution of this book is the orienting framework based on three dimensions of consultation: kinds of issues, the units of change, and the focal issues. These three dimensions are presented as a cube of 100 cells designed to conceptualize all approaches to consultation.

      The conceptualization of consultation presented is so broad as to include individual counseling as a form of consultation. And although this broad conceptualization is valuable, it does prevent in-depth analysis of consultation in a particular setting.

Caplan, G. *The Theory and Practice of Mental Health Consultation*. New York: Basic Books, 1970.

Caplan's career in community psychiatry and mental health consultation spans twenty-five years in a wide variety of settings, and this book is a clearly written, comprehensive presentation of the important ideas forged in that experience. The focus is on the four types of consultation defined by Caplan in an earlier publication (1963): client-centered case consultation, consultee-centered case consultation, program-centered administrative consultation, and consultee-centered administrative consultation. This classification is based on two dimensions: whether the consultation is directed toward the care-giver who is experiencing difficulty with a client or toward a problem in administration that involves institutional programs and policies; and whether the goal of consultation is to help a consultee solve one particular problem or to improve the general problem-solving capacity of the consultee. Consultee-centered case consultation is generic in Caplan's theorizing, and the chapter devoted to this type of consultation is now considered somewhat of a classic.

Another of Caplan's major contributions to the field of consultation is the technique of "theme interference reduction," to which he devotes a chapter in this book. Although the technique is a creative one, it is applicable only to a specific set of circumstances and does not have much general utility.

Some of the most useful information contained in the book is presented in three chapters that describe methods of establishing mental health programs and methods of building relationships with consultee organizations and individual consultees. In these chapters Caplan analyzes the social forces that operate within care-t..ker organizations and the communities in which they are located as they affect mental health consultation programs.

The generalizations in this book, presented in an ego-psychology framework, are based on Caplan's experience. The viewpoints of other theoretical frameworks are not presented, nor is the reader supplied with empirical documentation for Caplan's generalizations. Nevertheless, the book is a classic in that it has set the stage for much current thinking about consultation.

Carlson, J., Splete, H., and Kern, R. (Eds.). *The Consulting Process.* Washington, D.C.: American Personnel and Guidance Association, 1975.

This book of readings contains forty-eight articles taken exclusively from the *Elementary School Guidance and Counseling Journal,* the *Personnel and Guidance Journal,* and the *School Counselor.* All articles were originally published between 1967 and 1973. While the articles reflect a bias toward "humanistic" and Adlerian conceptualizations of the consultation process, a variety range from position statements to empirical pieces. It is an excellent sampling of thought from the counselor's viewpoint during those years when ideas about consultation were in their formative stages.

Dinkmeyer, D., and Carlson. J. *Consultation.* Columbus, Ohio: Merrill, 1973.

Written by two of the most prolific contributors to the consultation literature, this text discusses Adlerian and humanistic perspectives and how these conceptual and philosophical positions relate to the consultation process. Chapters on the problems and procedures of consulting with individual teachers, groups, parents, and families—as well as chapters on promoting client mental health and on learning in the classroom—form the backbone of the text. The remainder of the book argues for the humanistic position, and the preponderance of pages spent on this topic is the primary weakness of the book. However, there is a good deal of useful information, and the book is clearly the most comprehensive discussion of consultation from the Adlerian and humanistic perspectives.

Meyers, J., Martin, R., and Hyman, I. (Eds.). *School Consultation: Readings About Preventive Techniques for Pupil Personnel Workers.* Springfield, Ill.: Thomas, 1977.

School Consultation includes many classic articles to present a variety of school consultation techniques available to pupil personnel workers. The editors offer a broad-based definition of consultation that describes the consultant as relating directly with the consultee but not the client and that extends this traditional paradigm to include situations wherein the consultant relates with the child's teacher following individual diagnosis or treatment of the client.

After elaborating on this model and reviewing the historical development of school consultation, the editors present four content approaches that they feel should be available to pupil personnel workers. The first content section focuses on psychoeducational diagnosis and looks at the validity of the psychodiagnostic model, the importance of precision of diagnostic procedures, the value of behavioral data in psychoeducational assessment, and the usefulness of consultation as a tool for improving communication of meaningful recommendations. The second section discusses the use of behavioral principles not only to help the teacher cope with a student's behavior but also to investigate and facilitate the consultation process. The third section on mental health consultation discusses using consultation techniques to provide direct service to the teacher. The final section of the text focuses on the consultation model as one that effectively stimulates organizational change and looks at both the theory and application of organizational development consultation.

Newman, R. G. *Psychological Consultation in the Schools: A Catalyst for Learning.* New York: Basic Books, 1967.

Anecdotal case reports drawn from consultants' narrative logs form the basis of this informative, descriptive text on the application of consultation in a variety of settings. Five consultants, trained in a psychodynamic orientation, describe their individual experiences in five settings—elementary schools, junior high schools, high schools, nursery schools, and a residential treatment center. Each narrative report focuses on the relationship of consultant to staff members, of staff members to the children they service, and of staff members to the school or center which employs them. Each consultant attempts to identify what the teachers needed and the pitfalls of trying to implement a consultation model, and each provides clear examples of the flexibility required of the successful consultant.

     Newman notes that the consultant's role must be flexible— varying from passive, nondirective to expert; from utilizing testing and research to giving advice and oblique conversation, all of which depends on the unique circumstances in which the consultant is working.

     A major contribution of this classic work to the literature on school consultation is that Newman presents consultation as a model not limited to crisis situations but one that should be implemented on a continuous and regular basis. Further, Newman analyzes consultation as a method for in-service teacher training and discusses the qualifications most useful for this type of work.

     The book offers readers an excellent descriptive analysis of

consultation in a variety of settings and is therefore highly recommended for the serious student of consultation. It should be noted,
however, that with its psychodynamic orientation the work often
fails to present some of the techniques currently used by consultants in the schools, such as task analysis and behavior modification.

Rogers, E. M., and Shoemaker, F. F. *Communication of Innovations.*
(2nd ed.) New York: Macmillan, 1971.

This major work is not devoted to consultation in the sense that the
term is normally used. It is rather one of the cornerstones of the
literature on diffusion, that area in sociology and social psychology
that focuses on how new technology gets communicated and
adopted. Diffusion research looks at such problems as how doctors
learn about and begin to use new medications, why some farmers
adopt improved strains of seeds more readily than others, and what
types of communication (for example, mass media versus person-
to-person) are most successful in convincing homemakers to use
new products in the home.

   This book is organized around a number of generalizations
or hypotheses for which the authors provide substantial empirical
support. Most of these generalizations have major implications for
the techniques of mental health consultation. The diffusion viewpoint forces the mental health professional, if just for a moment, to
look at the consultative enterprise as one in which the consultant
serves as a salesman of new ideas, ideas derived from basic research
in child development, psychopathology, mental hygiene, and so on.
This frame of reference offers refreshing insights to the consultation process, insights not easily derived from the helping relationship view typically held by mental health consultants.

Sarason, S. B. *The Culture of the School and the Problem of Change.*
Boston: Allyn & Bacon, 1971.

Sarason looks at the school as a community—an organized, structured set of roles and expectations that control, to a greater or
lesser extent, the behavior of those who work there. Proceeding
from this premise, he devotes much of the book to clarifying what
the culture of the school is and does so by examining the roles and

typical behaviors of students, teachers, principals, and others in the school community. A secondary theme of this book, closely tied to the first, is the idea that the organization must be the focus of change in order to bring about change in schools. This point has, of course, been made by many others, most notably by the practitioners of organization development. However, Sarason's analysis contains original ideas about specific aspects of school culture that make change difficult, points covered only in a generic way by others.

Sarason, S. B., Levine, M., Goldenberg, I. I., Cherlin, D. L., and Bennet, E. M. *Psychology in Community Settings.* New York: Wiley, 1966.

This is one of the classic books about mental health consultation. Basically, it presents an account of the psychoeducational clinic developed by Sarason at Yale University. A key principle guiding this clinic was the deemphasis on diagnostic and treatment work done *in the clinic*. Instead, the focus was on the natural setting—for example, the school. Although the book describes the consultation model implemented in schools, it also considers a variety of community agencies that received services from the clinic. The description of this program is sufficiently detailed to permit understanding of how one mental health consultation program worked. The book is particularly useful, for example, in its discussion of entry problems and techniques for gaining entry to the system. This volume represents the initial view of consultation provided by one of the leaders in the field.

Schein, E. H. *Process Consultation: Its Role in Organization Development.* Reading, Mass.: Addison-Wesley, 1969.

Schein is a social psychologist by training who turned to the analysis of organizational behavior and later to the processes used by consultants who work in large organizations. He is one of the primary theorists in the consultation movement that has come to be known as "organization development." Although Schein has done most of his work in industrial organizations, the book does contain helpful material for readers interested in educational settings or community service organizations.

This book focuses on process consultation, an organization development technique—specifically, an intervention in which the consultant primarily concentrates on involving clients in the diagnosis and solution of their own problems. The consultant's expertise on a specific organizational problem is less relevant than his expertise in creating conditions under which clients are able to solve their own problems. This involves making the clients aware of interpersonal processes that affect their work in the organization. These processes include: communication, member roles and functions in groups, group problem solving and decision making, group norms and group growth, leadership and authority, and intergroup cooperation and competition. A chapter is devoted to each of these processes; likewise, separate chapters deal with the five steps involved in such an intervention—establishing contact with the organization, selecting a setting, gathering data, intervening, and evaluating results.

This book should be required reading for students of the consultation process; it remains one of the most influential in the field.

Schmuck, R. A., and Miles, M. B. (Eds.). *Organization Development in Schools.* Palo Alto, Calif.: National Press Books, 1971.

Perhaps the most useful book in print on organization development in the schools, this volume contains a clear overview of, and introduction to, the history of this type of intervention. It contains an edited selection of articles on school applications—not only from a variety of professional journals but also previously unpublished papers. Unfortunately, since the book was published in 1971, it does not cover recent material on organization development.

Schmuck, R. A., and Schmuck, P. A. *A Humanistic Psychology of Education: Making the School Everybody's House.* Palo Alto, Calif.: National Press Books, 1974.

Schmuck and Schmuck provide an overview of four models of consultation, including the behavioral approach, the mental health approach, the group dynamics approach, and the organization development approach. They review available research in each area to determine what impact each approach has had in terms of humanizing the schools. They conclude that although each has strengths and weaknesses, an organizational framework is necessary if consultation is to be significantly effective.

Walton, R. E. *Interpersonal Peacemaking: Confrontations and Third-Party Consultation.* Reading, Mass.: Addison-Wesley, 1969.

Another volume in the Addison-Wesley series on organization development relevant and useful to the school consultant is Walton's book on consultation as an intervention in conflict situations. Walton's thesis is that most confrontations in organizations (between organizational units or individuals) are ineffective in that neither group or party is satisfied with the outcomes. Further, since these confrontations are ineffective, they tend to escalate into long-term standoffs that waste organizational energy and impede productive organizational behavior. Walton proposes that the behavioral consultant has a place as a conflict manager—to help the conflicting parties clarify their problems and manage their differences in such a way that long-term organizational disabilities do not result. The techniques suggested are based on group dynamics notions (for example, open and honest expression of feelings), and thus these techniques can be thought of as a type of process consultation. Group and individual conflict is a major problem in schools, and mental health consultants have seldom played an influential role in helping to resolve these problems more appropriately. Walton provides some useful generalizations for the consultant considering this type of intervention.

References

Abidin, R. A. "A Psychosocial Look at Consultation and Behavior Modification." *Psychology in the Schools,* 1972, *9,* 358–364.

Ahammer, I. M., and Schare, K. W. "Age Differences in the Relationship Between Personality Questionnaire Factors and School Achievement." *Journal of Educational Research,* 1970, *61,* 193–197.

Albee, G. W. *Mental Health Manpower Trends.* New York: Basic Books, 1959.

Albee, G. W. "The Relation of Conceptual Models to Manpower Needs." In E. L. Cowen, E. A. Gardner, and M. Zax (Eds.), *Emergent Approaches to Mental Health Problems.* New York: Appleton-Century-Crofts, 1967.

Alderson, J. J. "Models of Schools' Social Work Practice." In R. Sarri and F. F. Maple (Eds.), *The School in the Community.* Washington, D.C.: National Association of Social Workers, 1972.

Allen, G. J., and others. *Community Psychology and the Schools.* New York: Halsted Press, 1976.

Alpert, J. L. "Some Guidelines for School Consultation." *Journal of School Psychology,* 1977, *15,* 308–319.

Amidon, E. J., and Simon, A. "Teacher-Pupil Interaction." *Review of Education Research,* 1965, *25,* 130–140.

Anderson, R. G., and Faust, G. W. *Educational Psychology.* New York: Dodd, Mead, 1973.

Argyris, C. *Intervention Theory and Method.* Reading, Mass.: Addison-Wesley, 1970.

Aronson, E., Willerman, B., and Floyd, J. "The Effects of a Pratfall on Increasing Interpersonal Attraction." *Psychonomic Science,* 1966, *4,* 227–228.

Aubrey, R. F. "Application of Therapy Models to School Counseling." *Personnel and Guidance Journal,* 1969, *48,* 273–278.

Axelrod, S. *Behavior Modification for the Classroom Teacher.* New York: McGraw-Hill, 1977.

Azrin, N. H. "A Strategy for Applied Research: Learning Based but Outcome Oriented." *American Psychologist,* 1977, *32,* 140–149.

Baer, D. M., Wolf, M. M., and Risley, T. R. "Some Current Dimensions of Applied Behavioral Analysis." *Journal of Applied Behavioral Analysis,* 1968, *1,* 91–97.

Bales, R. F. *Interaction Process Analysis: A Method for the Study of Small Groups.* Reading, Mass.: Addison-Wesley, 1959.

Barbanel, L., and Hoffenberg-Rutman, J. "Attitudes Toward Job Responsibilities and Training Satisfaction of School Psychologists: A Comparative Study." *Psychology in the Schools,* 1974, *11,* 425–429.

Barclay, J. R. *Changing the Behavior of School Psychology: A Training Rationale and Method.* Haywood, Calif.: California State University, 1967.

Bardon, J. (Ed.). "Problems and Issues in School Psychology —1964." *Journal of School Psychology, 1964, 3,* 1–57.

Beckhard, R. *Organization Development: Strategies and Models.* Reading, Mass.: Addison-Wesley, 1969.

Bennis, W. G. *Organizational Development: Its Nature, Origins, and Prospects.* Reading, Mass.: Addison-Wesley, 1969.

Bergan, J. R. *Behavioral Consultation.* Columbus, Ohio: Merrill, 1977.

Bergan, J. R., and Caldwell, T. "Operant Techniques in School Psychology." *Psychology in the Schools,* 1967, *4,* 136–141.

Bergan, J. R., and Tombari, M. L. "The Analysis of Verbal Interaction Occurring During Consultation. *Journal of School Psychology,* 1975, *13,* 209–226.

Bergin, A. E., and Strupp, H. H. *Changing Frontiers in the Science of Psychotherapy.* Chicago: Aldine, 1972.

Berlin, I. N. "Some Learning Experiences as a Psychiatric Consultant in the Schools." *Mental Hygiene,* 1956, *40,* 215–236.

Berlin, I. N. "Mental Health Consultation in Schools as a Means of Communicating Mental Health Principles." *Journal of the American Academy of Child Psychiatry,* 1962, *1,* 671–679.

Bernard, H., and Fullmer, D. *The School Counselor-Consultant.* Boston: Houghton Mifflin, 1972.

Berne, E. *Games People Play: The Psychology of Human Relationships.* New York: Grove Press, 1964.

Bersoff, D., and Grieger, R. Interview Model for the Psychosituational Assessment of Children's Behavior." *American Journal of Orthopsychiatry,* 1971, *41,* 483–493.

Blake, R. R., and Mouton, J. S. *Consultation.* Reading, Mass.: Addison-Wesley, 1976.

Blanco, R. *Prescriptions for Children with Learning and Adjustment Problems.* Springfield, Ill.: Thomas, 1972.

Bloom, B. L. *Community Mental Health: A Historical and Critical Analysis.* Morristown, N. J.: General Learning Press, 1973.

Bloom, B. L. *Community Mental Health: A General Introduction.* Monterey, Calif.: Brooks/Cole, 1977.

Bloom B. S. (Ed.). *Taxonomy of Educational Objectives.* Vol. 1: *Cognitive Domain.* New York: McKay, 1956.

Bower, E. M. *Early Identification of Emotionally Handicapped Children in School.* (2nd ed.) Springfield, Ill.: Thomas, 1969.

Bowlby, J. "Pathological Mourning and Childhood Mourning." *Journal of the American Psychoanalytic Association,* 1963, *11,* 500–541.

Brophy, J. E., and Good, T. L. *Teacher-Child Dyadic Interaction: A Manual for Coding Classroom Behavior. Report Series, 27.* Austin, Tex. Research and Development Center for Teacher Education, 1969.

Brophy, J. E., and Good, T. L. "Teacher's Communication of Differential Expectations for Children's Classroom Performance." *Journal of Educational Psychology,* 1970, *61,* 365–374.

Brophy, J. E., and Good. T. L. *Teacher-Student Relationships: Causes and Consequences.* New York: Holt, Rinehart and Winston, 1974.

Buktenica, N. A. "Interpretation of Clinical Data by the School Psychologist. *Psychology in the Schools,* 1964, *1,* 267–272.

Campbell, D. T., and Stanley, J. C. *Experimental and Quasiexperimental Designs for Research.* Chicago: Rand McNally, 1963.

Caplan, G. "A Public Health Approach to Child Psychiatry." *Mental Hygiene,* 1951, *35,* 235–249.

Caplan, G. (Ed.). *Emotional Problems of Early Childhood.* New York: Basic Books, 1955.

Caplan, G. (Ed.). *Prevention of Mental Disorders in Children.* New York: Basic Books, 1961.

Caplan, G. "Types of Mental Health Consultation." *American Journal of Orthopsychiatry,* 1963, *3,* 470–481.

Caplan, G. *Principles of Preventive Psychiatry.* New York: Basic Books, 1964.

Caplan, G. *The Theory and Practice of Mental Health Consultation.* New York: Basic Books, 1970.

Caplan, G. *Support Systems and Community Mental Health.* New York: Behavioral Publications, 1974.

Carkhuff, R. R. *Helping and Human Relations: A Primer for Lay and Professional Helpers.* Vol. 1: *Selection and Training.* New York: Holt, Rinehart and Winston, 1969a.

Carkhuff, R. R. *Helping and Human Relations.* Vol. 2: *Practice and Research.* New York: Holt, Rinehart and Winston, 1969b.

Carkhuff, R. R., and Berenson, B. *Beyond Counseling and Therapy.* New York: Holt, Rinehart and Winston, 1967.

Carlson, J. "Consulting: Facilitating School Change." *Elementary School Guidance and Counseling,* 1972, *7,* 83–88.

Chesler, M. A., Bryant, B. I., and Crowfoot, J. E. "Consultation in Schools: Inevitable Conflict, Partisanship, and Advocacy." *Professional Psychology,* 1976, *7,* 637–645.

Ciavarella, M. A. "The Counselor as a Mental Health Consultant." *The School Counselor,* 1970, *18,* 121–125.

Cook, V. J., and Patterson, J. G. "Psychologists in the Schools of Nebraska: Professional Functions." *Psychology in the Schools,* 1977, *14,* 371–376.

Cooke, R. *America.* New York: Knopf, 1973.

Cooper, M. L., Thomson, C. L., and Baer, D. M. "The Experimental Modification of Teacher Attending Behavior." *Journal of Applied Behavior Analysis,* 1970, *3,* 153–157.

Cossairt, A., Hall, R. V., and Hopkins, B. L. "The Effects of Experimenter's Instruction Feedback and Praise on Teacher Praise and Student Attending Behavior." *Journal of Applied Behavior Analysis,* 1973, *6,* 89–100.

Costin, L. B. "School Social Work." In *Encyclopedia of Social Work.* New York: National Association of Social Workers, 1971.

Costin, L. B. "Social Work Contribution to Education in Transition." In R. Sarri and F. F. Maple (Ed.), *The School in the Community.* Washington, D.C.: National Association of Social Workers, 1972.

Cowen, E. L., Gardner, E. A., and Zax, M. (Eds.). *Emergent Approaches to Mental Health Problems.* New York: Appleton-Century-Crofts, 1967.

Cremin, L. A. *The Transformation of the School.* New York: Random House, 1961.

Cronbach, L. J., and Snow, R. E. *Aptitudes and Instructional Methods.* New York: Wiley, 1977.

Cutler, R. L., and McNeil, E. B. *Mental Health Consultation in the Schools: A Research Analysis.* Ann Arbor: Department of Psychology, University of Michigan, 1966.

Davis, O. L., and Hunkins, F. P. "Textbook Questions: What Thinking Processes do They Foster?" *Peabody Journal of Education,* 1966, *43,* 285–292.

Dinkmeyer, D. "The Counselor as Consultant: Rationale and Procedures." *Elementary School Guidance and Counseling,* 1968, *2,* 187–194.

Dinkmeyer, D., and Carlson, J. *Consultation.* New York: Wiley, 1973.

Dusay, J. M., and Steiner, C. "Transactional Analysis in Groups." In H. I. Kaplan and B. J. Sadock (Eds.), *New Models for Group Therapy.* New York: Aronson, 1972.

Dustin, R., and Burden, C. "The Counselor as a Behavior Consultant." *Elementary School Guidance and Counseling,* 1972, *7,* 14–19.

Dworkin, A. L., and Dworkin, E. P. "A Conceptual Overview of Selected Consultation Models." *American Journal of Community Psychology,* 1975, *3,* 151–160.

Eckerson, L. O., "The White House Conference: Tips or Taps for Counselors?" *Personnel and Guidance Journal,* 1971, *50,* 167–174.

Edwards, N., and Richey, H. G. *The School in the American Social Order.* (2nd ed.) Boston: Houghton Mifflin, 1963.

Egan, G. *The Skilled Helper.* Monterey, Calif.: Brooks/Cole, 1975.

Ellis, A. *Reason and Emotion in Psychotherapy.* New York: Stuart, 1963.

Engelmann, S. "Relationship Between Psychological Theories and the Act of Teaching." *Journal of School Psychology,* 1967, *5,* 93–100.

Eysenck, H. "The Effects of Psychotherapy: An Education." *Journal of Consulting Psychology,* 1952, *16,* 319–324.

Faust, V. "The Counselor as a Consultant to Teachers." *Elementary School Guidance and Counseling,* 1967, *1,* 112–117.

Fein, L. G. *The Changing School Scene: Challenge to Psychology.* New York: Wiley, 1974.

Fine, M., and Tyler, M. "Concerns and Directions in Teacher Consultation." *Journal of School Psychology,* 1971, *9,* 436–444.

Flanders, N. A. *Analyzing Teacher Behavior.* Reading, Mass.: Addison-Wesley, 1970.

Forness, S. R. "Educational Prescription for the School Psychologist." *Journal of School Psychology,* 1970, *8,* 96–98.

Fraiberg, S. H. *The Magic Years.* New York: Scribner's, 1959.

Freidman, M. "Mental Health Consultation with Teachers: An Analysis of Process Variables." Unpublished doctoral dissertation, Temple University, 1977.

French, J. R., Jr., and Raven, B. "The Basis of Social Power." In D. Cartwright (Ed.), *Studies in Social Power.* Ann Arbor: Institute of Social Research, University of Michigan, 1959.

French, W. L., and Bell, C. H., Jr. *Organization Development.* Englewood Cliffs, N.J.: Prentice-Hall, 1973.

Gallessich, J. "A Systems Model of Mental Health Consultation." *Psychology in the Schools,* 1972, *9,* 8–12.

Gallessich, J. "Organizational Factors Influencing Consultation in Schools." *Journal of School Psychology,* 1973, *11,* 57–65.

Gallessich, J. "Training the School Psychologist for Consultation." *Journal of School Psychology,* 1974, *12,* 138–149.

Gazda, G. M., and others. *Human Relations Development: A Manual for Educators.* Boston: Allyn & Bacon, 1973.

Giebink, J. W., and Ringness, T. A. "On the Relevancy of Training in School Psychology." *Journal of School Psychology,* 1970, *3,* 43–47.

Gilmore, G., and Chandy, J. "Educators Describe the School Psychologist." *Psychology in the Schools,* 1973, *10,* 397–403.

Ginott, H. G. *Teacher and Child.* New York: Macmillan, 1972.

Glidewell, J. C., and Swallow, C. S. *The Prevalence of Maladjustment in Elementary Schools: A Report for the Joint Commission of the Mental Health of Children.* Chicago: University of Chicago Press, 1969.

Goldstein, A. P., Heller, K., and Sechrest, L. B. *Psychotherapy and the Psychology of Behavior Change.* New York: Wiley, 1966.

Good, T. L., and Brophy, J. E. "Teacher-Child Dyadic Interactions: A New Method of Classroom Observation. *Journal of School Psychology,* 1970, *8,* 131–138.

Good, T. L., and Brophy, J. E. *Looking in Classrooms.* New York: Harper & Row, 1973.

Goodman, P. *Compulsory Mis-Education.* New York: Vintage Books, 1964.

Goodwin, D. L., Garvey, W. P., and Barclay, J. R. "Microconsultation and Behavioral Analysis: A Method of Training Psychologists as Behavioral Consultants." *Journal of Consulting and Clinical Psychology,* 1971, *37,* 355–363.

Gordon, J. W. "The Psychologist as a Consultant in an Inservice Program of Children and Youth." *Journal of School Psychology,* 1969, *6,* 18–21.

Gordon, J. W. *My Country School Diary.* New York: Dell, 1970.

Gordon, T. *Teacher Effectiveness Training.* New York: Wyden, 1974.

Grieger, R. M. "Teacher Attitudes as a Variable in Behavior Modification Consultation." *Journal of School Psychology,* 1972, *10,* 279–287.

Gross, S. J. "A Basis for Direct Methods in Consultee-Centered Consultation." Unpublished manuscript, Indiana State University, 1978.

Grossman, L., and Clark, D. "Sensitivity Training for Teachers: A

Small Group Approach." *Psychology in the Schools,* 1967, *4,* 267–271.

Gutkin, T. B., Singer, J., and Brown, R. "Empirical Analyses of Teacher Reactions to School Consultation Services." Paper presented at the 86th annual meeting of the American Psychological Association, Toronto, 1978.

Hall, L. "Comments." *Journal of School Psychology,* 1971, *9,* 269–270.

Hall, R. V., Lund, D., and Jackson, D. "Effects of Teacher Attention on Studying Behavior. *Journal of Applied Behavior Analysis,* 1968, *1,* 1–12.

Hall, R. V., and others. "Teacher and Parents as Researchers Using Multiple Baseline Designs." *Journal of Applied Behavioral Analysis,* 1970, *3,* 247–255.

Hamacheck, D. E. "What Research Tells Us About the Characteristics of Good and Bad Teachers." In D. E. Hamacheck (Ed.), *Human Dynamics in Psychology and Education.* Boston: Allyn & Bacon, 1968.

Hammill, D. D., and Bartel, N. R. *Teaching Children with Learning and Behavior Problems.* Boston: Allyn & Bacon, 1975.

Hawkins, P. R., and others. "Behavior in the Home: A Problem of Amelioration of Problem Parent-Child Relations with the Parent in a Therapeutic Role." *Journal of Experimental Child Psychology,* 1966, *4,* 99–107.

Heinicke, C. M. "Research on Psychotherapy with Children: a Review and Suggestions for Further Study." *American Journal of Orthopsychiatry,* 1960, *30,* 483–493.

Heisey, M. "A Review of Literature as a Service to Teachers." *Elementary School Guidance and Counseling,* 1967, *2,* 50–53.

Henry, J. *Culture Against Man.* New York: Random House, 1965.

Human Relations Media Center. *Adolescence: Challenges to Growth.* Pleasantville, N.Y.: Human Relations Media Center, 1977.

Huse, E. F. *Organization Development and Change.* St. Paul: West, 1975.

Hyde, E. M. "School Psychological Referrals in an Inner City School." *Psychology in the Schools,* 1975, *12,* 412–420.

Hyman, I. A. "Some Effects of Teaching Style on Pupil Behavior." Unpublished doctoral dissertation, Department of Educational Psychology, Rutgers University, 1964.

Hyman, I. A. "Sensitivity Training as a Component of a Parallel

System to Initiate Educational Change." Paper presented at the 79th annual meeting of the American Psychological Association, Washington, D.C., 1971.

Hyman, I. A. "Change Through Consultation and Staff Development." Unpublished manuscript, Temple University, 1972a.

Hyman, I. A. "Consultation in Classroom Management Based on Empirical Research." Paper presented at the 80th annual meeting of the American Psychological Association, Honolulu, 1972b.

Hyman, I.A. "An Overview of Problems in Consultation." Paper presented at the 82nd annual meeting of the American Psychological Association, New Orleans, 1974.

Hyman, I. A., and Schreiber, K. "Selected Concepts and Practices of Child Advocacy in School Psychology." *Psychology in the Schools,* 1975, *12,* 50–58.

Hyman, R. (Ed.). *Teaching: Vantage Points for Study.* Philadelphia: Lippincott, 1968.

Iscoe, I., and others. "Some Strategies in Mental Health Consultation: A Brief Description of a Project and Some Preliminary Results." In E. L. Cowen, E. A. Gardner, and M. Zax (Eds.), *Emergent Approaches to Mental Health Problems.* New York: Appleton-Century-Crofts, 1967.

Ivey, A. E. *Microcounseling: Innovations in Interviewing Training.* Springfield, Ill.: Thomas, 1971.

Jackson, P. W. *Life in Classrooms.* New York: Holt, Rinehart and Winston, 1968.

James, W. *Talks to Teachers on Psychology and to Students on Some of Life's Ideals.* New York: Dover, 1962. (Originally published 1899.)

Jongeward, D., and James, M. *Winning with People: Group Exercises in Transactional Analysis.* Reading, Mass.: Addison-Wesley, 1973.

Kaplan, M. S., Clancy, B., and Chrin, M. "Priority Roles for School Psychologists as Seen by Superintendents." *Journal of School Psychology,* 1977, *1,* 75–80.

Kazdin, A. E. *Behavior Modification in Applied Settings.* Homewood, Ill.: Dorsey Press, 1975.

Kennedy, D. A. "A Practical Approach to School Psychology." *Journal of School Psychology,* 1971, *9,* 484–489.

Kicklighter, R. H. "School Psychology in the U.S.: A Quantitative Study." *Journal of School Psychology,* 1976, *14,* 151–156.

Kounin, J. S. *Discipline and Group Management in Classrooms.* New York: Holt, Rinehart and Winston, 1970.

Kozol, J. *Death at an Early Age.* New York: Houghton Mifflin, 1967.

Kraft, A. "New Directions for the School Psychologist." *Education Forum,* 1970, *34,* 551–557.

Krasner, L., and Ullman, L. (Eds.). *Research in Behavior Modification.* New York: Holt, Rinehart and Winston, 1965.

Krupp, G. "Maladaptive Reactions to the Death of a Family Member." *Social Casework,* 1972, *53,* 425–434.

Kuhn, T. S. *The Structure of Scientific Revolutions.* Chicago: University of Chicago Press, 1962.

Kuriloff, P. J. "The Counselor as Psychoecologist." *Personnel and Guidance Journal,* 1973, *51,* 321–327.

Lambert, N. M. "A School Based Consultation Model." *Professional Psychology,* 1974, *5,* 267–276.

Lawrence, P. R., and Lorsch, J. W. *Developing Organizations: Diagnosis and Action.* Reading, Mass.: Addison-Wesley, 1969.

Lesiak, W. J., and Lounsbury, E. "Views of School Psychological Services: A Comparative Study." *Psychology in the Schools,* 1977, *14,* 185–188.

Levine, M., and Levine, A. *A Social History of Helping Services.* New York: Appleton-Century-Crofts, 1970.

Levitt, E. E. "The Results of Psychotherapy with Children: An Evaluation." *Journal of Consulting Psychology,* 1957, *21,* 189–196.

Levitt, E. E. "Psychotherapy with Children: A Further Evaluation." *Behavior Research and Therapy,* 1963, *1,* 45–51.

Lewis, J. A., and Lewis, M. D. *Community Counseling,* New York: Wiley, 1977.

Liberman, R. "Personal Influence in the Use of Mental Health Resources." *Human Organization,* 1965, *24,* 231–235.

Lighthall, F. F. "A Social Psychologist for School Systems." *Psychology in the Schools,* 1969, *6,* 3–12.

Lippitt, G. L. "A Study of the Consultation Process." *Journal of Social Issues,* 1959, *15,* 43–50.

Lippitt, R., Watson, J., and Westley, B. *The Dynamics of Planned Change.* New York: Harcourt Brace Jovanovich, 1958.

Lubove, R. *The Professional Altruist: The Emergence of Social Work as a Career, 1880–1930.* Boston: Harvard University Press, 1965.

Lundquist, G., and Chamley, J. "Counselor-Consultant: A Move Toward Effectiveness." *The School Counselor,* 1971, *18,* 362–366.

McDaniel, L., and Ahr, E., "The School Psychologist as a Resource Person Initiating and Conducting Inservice Teacher Education." *Psychology in the Schools,* 1965, *2,* 220–224.

McElvaney, C. T., and Miles, M. B. "Using Survey Feedback and Consultation." In R. A. Schmuck and M. B. Miles (Eds.), *Organization Development in Schools.* Palo Alto, Calif.: National Press Books, 1971.

McGehearty, L. "Case Analysis: Consultation and Counseling." *Elementary School Guidance and Counseling,* 1969, *4,* 54–58.

McGregor, D. *The Human Side of Enterprise.* New York: McGraw-Hill, 1960.

McGuire, W. J. "The Nature of Attitudes and Attitude Change." In G. Lindzy and E. Aronson (Eds.), *The Handbook of Social Psychology,* Vol. 3 (2nd ed.) Reading, Mass.: Addison-Wesley, 1969.

McNamara, J. E. "Teacher and Students as Sources of Behavior Modification in the Classroom." *Behavior Therapy,* 1971, *2,* 205–213.

Magary, J. F. "Emerging Viewpoints in School Psychological Services." In J. F. Magary (Ed.), *School Psychological Services.* Englewood Cliffs, N.J.: Prentice-Hall, 1967.

Mann, P. A. "Student Consultants: Evaluations by Consultees. *American Journal of Community Psychology,* 1973, *1,* 182–193.

Mannino, F., and Shore, M. Consultation Research. *Public Health Monograph,* No. 79, 1971.

Mannino, F., and Shore, M. "The Effects of Consultation: A Review of Empirical Studies." *American Journal of Community Psychology,* 1975, *3,* 1–21.

Marino, M. F. "The Effectiveness of Teacher-Centered Versus Case-Centered Consultation in the Reduction of Classroom Management Errors and Negative Classroom Behavior of Students." Unpublished doctoral dissertation, Temple University, 1975.

Martin, R. "Increasing Teacher Awareness Through Systematic Classroom Observation: A Neglected Model of Psychological Consultation." Unpublished paper, Temple University, 1974.

Martin, R. "A Critique of Two Major Assumptions of Caplan's Approach to Mental Health Consultation." Unpublished paper, Temple University, 1977.

Martin, R. "Expert and Referent Power: A Framework for Understanding and Maximizing Consultation Effectiveness." *Journal of School Psychology,* 1978, *16,* 49–55.

Martin, R., and Keller, B. "Teacher Awareness of Classroom Dyadic Interactions." *Journal of School Psychology,* 1976, *14,* 47–55.

Martin, R., and Meyers, J. "Effects of Anxiety on Quantity of Examination Preparation." *Psychology in the Schools,* 1974, *11,* 217–221.

Meyers, J. "The Process of Training Consultants in an Alternative Educational Setting." Paper presented at the 81st annual meeting of the American Psychological Association, Montreal, 1973a.

Meyers, J. "A Consultation Model for School Psychological Services." *Journal of School Psychology,* 1973b, *11,* 5–15.

Meyers, J. "Consultee-Centered Consultation as a Technique in Classroom Management." *American Journal of Community Psychology,* 1975a, *3,* 111–121.

Meyers, J. "Mental Health Consultation." Paper presented at the annual meeting of the National Association of School Psychologists, Atlanta, 1975b.

Meyers, J., Freidman, M. P., and Gaughan, E. J. "The Effects of Consultee-Centered Consultation on Teacher Behavior." *Psychology in the Schools,* 1975, *12,* 288–295.

Meyers, J., Martin, R., and Hyman, I. (Eds.). *School Consultation.* Springfield, Ill.: Thomas, 1977.

Meyers, J., and Pitt, N. "A Consultation Approach to Help a School Cope with the Bereavement Process." *Professional Psychology,* 1976, *7,* 559–564.

Meyers, J., and others. "An Approach to Investigate Anxiety and Hostility in Consultee-Centered Consultation." *Psychology in the Schools,* 1978a, *15,* 292–296.

Meyers, J., and others. "A Research Model for Consultation with Teachers." *Journal of School Psychology,* 1978b, *16,* 137–145.

Miller, F. W. *Guidance: Principles and Services.* Columbus, Ohio: Merrill, 1961.

Moorish, I. *Aspects of Educational Change.* New York: Wiley, 1976.

Moos, R. H., Insell, P. M., and Humphrey, B. *Preliminary Manual for Family Environment Scale, Work Environment Scale, Group Environment Scale.* Palo Alto, Calif.: Consulting Psychologists Press, 1974.

Morice, H. "The School Psychologist as Behavioral Consultant: A Project in Behavior Modification in a Public School Setting." *Psychology in the Schools,* 1968, *5,* 253–261.

Mullen, F. A. "The Role of the School Psychologist in the Urban School System." In J. F. Magary (Ed.), *School Psychological Services in Theory and Practice, a Handbook.* Englewood Cliffs, N.J.: Prentice-Hall, 1967.

Neisworth, J., Deno, S., and Jenkins, J. *Student Motivation and Classroom Management: A Behavioristic Approach.* Lemont, Pa.: Behavior-Technics, 1969.

Newman, R. G. *Psychological Consultation in the Schools.* New York: Basic Books, 1967.

Newman, R. G., and others. "Psychoeducational Consultation." In N. Long, W. Morse, and R. Newman (Eds.), *Conflict in the Classroom.* Belmont, Calif.: Wadsworth, 1971.

Nieberl, H. R. "Breaking out of the Bind in School Social Work Practice." In R. Sarri and F. F. Maple (Ed.), *The School in the Community.* Washington, D.C.: National Association of Social Workers, 1972.

Oakland, T. Diagnostic Help 5$^{\text{¢}}$: Examiner Is In. *Psychology in the Schools,* 1969, *6,* 359–367.

O'Leary, K.D., and O'Leary, S. G. (Eds.). *Classroom Management: the Successful Use of Behavior Modification.* Elmsford, N.Y.: Pergamon Press, 1972.

Palmo, A., and Kuznian, J. "Modification of Behavior Through Group Counseling and Consultation." *Elementary School Guidance and Counseling,* 1972, *6,* 258–262.

Parker, B. "Some Observation on Psychiatric Consultation with Nursery School Teachers." *Mental Hygiene,* 1962, *46,* 559–566.

Parsons, R. D., "Transactional Analysis: A Model for the Identification of, and Training in, Variables Which Facilitate the Consultative Process." Unpublished doctoral dissertation, Temple University, 1976a.

Parsons, R. D. "Overcoming Teacher Resistance to Behavior Modification." *The Guidance Clinic,* 1976b, April, 12–14.

Parsons, R. D. "The Investigation of Consultation Process: A Small-N Approach." Paper presented at the 85th annual meeting of the American Psychological Association, San Francisco, 1977.

Parsons, R. D. "The Counselor's Secretary: A Behavior Modification Programmer." *The Guidance Clinic,* 1978, April, 5–9.

Parsons, R. D., and Meyers, J. "The Training and Analysis of Consultation Process Using Transactional Analysis. *Psychology in the Schools,* 1978, *15,* 545–552.

Parsons, R. D., Stone, S. S., and Feuerstein, P. "Teacher-In-Service Training: A Tool for Maximizing Counselor Effectiveness." *The Guidance Clinic,* 1977, March, 13–16.

Phillips, B. N., Martin, R., and Meyers, J. "Interventions in Relation to Anxiety in School." In C. D. Spielberger (Ed.), *Anxiety: Current Trends in Theory and Research,* Vol 2. New York: Academic Press, 1972.

Pierce-Jones, J., Iscoe, I., and Cunningham, G. *Child Behavior in Elementary Schools: A Demonstration and Research Program.* Austin: University of Texas Press, 1968.

Piper, T. *Classroom Management and Behavioral Objectives.* Belmont, Calif.: Fearon, 1974.

Powell, J., Martindale, A., and Kulp, S. "An Evaluation of Time-Sample Measures of Behavior." *Journal of Applied Behavior Analysis,* 1975, *8,* 463–470.

Randolph, D. L. "Behavior Consultation as a Means of Improving the Quality of a Counseling Program." *School Counselor,* 1972, *20,* 30–35.

Reger, R. "Mixed Reactions to Barclay." *American Psychologist,* 1971, *26,* 937–938.

Reschly, D. J. "School Psychology Consultation: 'Frenzied, Faddish, or Fundamental?'" *Journal of School Psychology,* 1976, *14,* 105–113.

Rist, R. "Student Social Class and Teacher Expectation: The Self-Fulfilling Prophesy in Ghetto Education." *Harvard Educational Review,* 1970, *40,* 411–451.

Roberts, R. "Perceptions of Actual and Desired Role Function of School Psychologists and Teachers." *Psychology in the Schools,* 1970, *7,* 1–25.

Rogers, C. R. *Client-Centered Therapy.* Boston: Houghton Mifflin, 1951.

Rogers, C. R. "The Necessary and Sufficient Conditions of Therapeutic Change." *Journal of Consulting Psychology,* 1957, *21,* 95–103.

Rogers, C. R. "A Tentative Scale for the Measurement of Process in Psychotherapy." In E. A. Rubinstein and M. B. Perloff (Eds.), *Research in Psychotherapy.* Washington, D.C.: American Psychological Association, 1959.

Rogers, C. R. *On Becoming a Person.* Boston: Houghton Mifflin, 1961.

Rogers, C. R. *The Therapeutic Relationship and Its Impact.* Madison: University of Wisconsin Press, 1967.

Rogers, C. R. *Freedom to Learn.* Columbus, Ohio: Merrill, 1969.

Rogers, E. M., and Shoemaker, F. F. *Communication of Innovations.* New York: Free Press, 1971.

Rosenshine, B. "Evaluation of Instruction." *Review of Educational Research,* 1970, *40,* 279–300.

Rosenshine, B., and Furst, N. "Research on Teaching Performance Criteria." In B. O. Smith (Ed.), *Research in Teacher Education.* Englewood Cliffs, N.J. Prentice-Hall, 1971.

Rosenthal, R., and Jacobson, L. *Pygmalion in the Classroom: Teacher Expectation and Pupils' Intellectual Development.* New York: Holt, Rinehart and Winston, 1968.

Rosenzweig, S. "A Transvaluation of Psychotherapy—A Reply to Hans Eysenck." *Journal of Abnormal and Social Psychology,* 1954, *49,* 298–304.

Sanders, N. M. *Classroom Questions.* New York: Harper & Row, 1966.

Sarason, S. B. *The Culture of the School and the Problem of Change.* Boston: Allyn & Bacon, 1971.

Sarason, S. B., and others. *Psychology in Community Settings.* New York: Wiley, 1966.

Scheff, T. S. *Being Mentally Ill: A Sociological Theory.* New York: Aldine, 1966.

Schein, E. H. *Process Consultation.* Reading, Mass.: Addison-Wesley, 1969.

Schmuck, R. A. "Helping Teachers Improve Classroom Group Processes." *Journal of Applied Behavioral Science,* 1968, *4,* 401–436.

Schmuck, R. A., and Miles, M. B. (Eds.). *Organization Development in the Schools.* Palo Alto, Calif.: National Press Books, 1971.

Schmuck, R. A., Runkel, P. J., and Langmeyer, P. "Improving Organizational Problem Solving in a School Faculty. *Journal of Applied Behavioral Science,* 1969, *5,* 455–482.

Schmuck, R. A., and Schmuck, P. *Group Processes in the Classroom.* Dubuque, Iowa: Brown, 1971.

Schmuck, R. A., and Schmuck, P. *A Humanistic Psychology of Education: Making the School Everybody's House.* Palo Alto, Calif.: National Press Books, 1974.

Schmuck, R. A., and others. *Handbook of Organization Development in Schools.* Palo Alto, Calif.: National Press Books, 1972.

Schowengerdt, R. V., Fine, M. J., and Poggio, J. P. "An Examination of Some Bases of Teacher Satisfaction with School Psychological Services." *Psychology in the Schools,* 1976, *13,* 269–275.

Simon, A., and Boyer, E. G. *Mirrors for Behavior: An Anthology of Observation Instruments.* Philadelphia: Research for Better Schools, 1967, 1970, and 1970 supplement.

Singer, D., Whiton, M., and Fried, M. "An Alternative to Traditional Mental Health Services and Consultation in the Schools: A Social Systems and Group Process Approach." *Journal of School Psychology,* 1970, *8,* 172–179.

Smith, H., and Eckerson, L. *Guidance Services in Elementary Schools: A National Survey.* Washington, D.C.: U.S. Government Printing Office, 1966.

Snyder, B., and Berman, L. "The Use of Psychoanalytic Group Approach with Teachers in a Junior High School." *American Journal of Orthopsychiatry,* 1960, *30,* 767–779.

Spaulding, R. L. *An Introduction to the Use of the Coping Analysis Schedule for Educational Settings (CASES).* Durham, N.C.: Education Improvement Program, Duke University, 1967.

Stephens, T. M. "Psychological Consultation to Teachers of Learning and Behavior Handicapped Children Using a Behavioral Model." *Journal of School Psychology*, 1970, *8*, 13–18.

Stephenson, P. S. "Judging the Effectiveness of a Consultation Program to a Community Agency." *Community Mental Health Journal*, 1973, *9*, 253–259.

Sulzer-Azaroff, B., McKinley, J., and Ford, L. *Field Activities for Educational Psychology: Carrying Concepts into Action*. Santa Monica, Calif.: Goodyear, 1977.

Surratt, P. R., Ulrich, R. E., and Hawkins, R. P. "An Elementary Student as a Behavioral Engineer." *Journal of Applied Behavior Analysis*, 1969, *2*, 85–92.

Szasz, T. S. *The Myth of Mental Illness*. New York: Hoeber, 1961.

Tharp, R., and Wetzel, R. *Behavior Modification in the Natural Environment*. New York: Academic Press, 1969.

Thomas, D. R., Becker, W. C., and Armstrong, M. "Production and Elimination of Disruptive Classroom Behavior by Systematically Changing Teachers' Behavior." *Journal of Applied Behavior Analysis*, 1968, *1*, 35–45.

Thorndike, E. *Educational Psychology*. New York: Lemcke & Beuchner, 1903.

Thorndike, R. L. "Review of R. Rosenthal and L. Jacobson, *Pygmalion in the Classroom*." *American Educational Research Journal*, 1968, *5*, 708–711.

Tindall, R. H. "Trends in Development of Psychological Services in the School." *Journal of School Psychology*, 1964, *3*, 1–12.

Tobiessen, J., and Shai, A. "A Comparison of Individual and Group Mental Health Consultation with Teachers." *Community Mental Health Journal*, 1971, *7*, 218–226.

Truax, C. B., and Carkhuff, R. R. "Significant Developments in Psychotherapy Research." In L. E. Abt and B. F. Riess (Eds.), *Progress in Clinical Psychology*. New York: Grune & Stratton, 1964.

Turner, R. L. "Good Teaching and Its Contexts." *Phi Delta Kappan*, 1970, *52*, 155–158.

Tyler, M. M., and Fine, M. J. "The Effects of Limited and Intensive School Psychologist-Teacher Consultation." *Journal of School Psychology*, 1974, *12*, 8–16.

Ullman, L. P. and Krasner, L. *A Psychological Approach to Abnormal Behavior*. Englewood Cliffs, N.J.: Prentice-Hall, 1969.

Valett, R. E. "The Evaluation and Programming of Basic Learning Abilities." *Journal of School Psychology,* 1968, *6,* 227–236.

Venduin, J., Jr. *Conceptual Models in Teacher Education.* Washington, D.C.: American Association of Colleges of Teacher Education, 1967.

Wallin, J. E. W., and Ferguson, G. "The Development of School Psychological Services." In J. F. Magary (Ed.), *School Psychological Services in Theory and Practice, a Handbook.* Englewood Cliffs, N.J.: Prentice-Hall, 1967.

Walton, R. E. *Interpersonal Peacemaking: Confrontations and Third-Party Consultation.* Reading, Mass.: Addison-Wesley, 1969.

Waters, L. G. "School Psychology as Perceived by School Personnel: Support for a Consultation Model." *Journal of School Psychology,* 1973, *11,* 40–45.

Webster's New Collegiate Dictionary. (8th ed.) Springfield, Mass.: Merriam, 1977.

Wilcox, M. R. "Variables Affecting Group Mental Health Consultation for Teachers." Paper presented at the 85th annual meeting of the American Psychological Association, San Francisco, 1977.

Winett, R. A. "Environmental Design: An Expanded Behavioral Research Framework for School Consultation and Educational Innovation." *Professional Psychology,* 1976, *7,* 631–636.

Winicki, S. "Case Conference as a Consultation Strategy." *Psychology in the Schools,* 1972, *9,* 21–24.

Wolfensberger, W. "Diagnosis Diagnosed." *The Journal of Mental Subnormality,* 1965, *11,* 62–70.

Wolpe, J. *Psychotherapy by Reciprocal Inhibition.* Stanford, Calif.: Stanford University Press, 1958.

Woody, R. "Forms of Mental Health Consultation." *Journal of Community Psychology,* 1974, *2,* 283–285.

Yalom, I. D. *The Theory and Practice of Group Psychotherapy.* (2nd ed.) New York: Basic Books, 1975.

Zajonc, R. B. "The Attitudinal Effects of Mere Exposure." *Journal of Personality and Social Psychology,* 1968, *8,* 21–27.

Zax, M., and Spector, G. A. *An Introduction to Community Psychology.* New York: Wiley, 1974.

Index

Abidin, R. A., 200, 220
Abnormality, concept of, 11
Accurate empathy, concept of, 56, 57–58, 59
Adler, A., 38
Affective factors, observing, 124–125
Ahammer, I. M., 199, 220
Ahr, E., 198, 230
Albee, G. W., 13, 14, 220
Alderson, J. J., 16, 220
Allen, G. J., 12, 220
Alpert, J. L., 89, 221
American Personnel and Guidance Association, 25
American Psychological Association (APA), 21–22, 170, 194
Amidon, E. J., 122, 124, 221
Anderson, R. G., 107, 221
Argyris, C., 145, 146, 221
Armstrong, M., 109, 236
Aronson, E., 49, 221
Assessment of consultation impact, 78, 81, 84, 86, 169–191

Attitude change, principles of, in consultation, 45–51
Aubrey, R. F., 13, 221
Axelrod, S., 110, 221
Azrin, N. H., 169, 172, 221

Baer, D. M., 110, 181, 221, 224
Bales, R. F., 32, 221
Barbanel, L., 17, 221
Barclay, J. R., 110, 209, 221, 226
Bardon, J., 16, 221
Bartel, N. R., 95, 227
Becker, W. C., 109, 236
Beckhard, R., 147, 149, 221
Behavior modification: and consultation, 109–116, 123; research on, 185; and school consultation, 26
Beisser, A., 211–212
Bell, C. H., Jr., 149, 225
Bennett, E. M., ix, 14, 34, 69, 175, 217, 234
Bennis, W. G., 145, 149, 221
Berenson, B., 55, 57, 58, 223

238